Human Rights and Radical Social Transformation

Against the recent backdrop of sociopolitical crisis, radical thinking and activism to challenge the oppressive operation of power has increased. Such thinkers and activists have aimed for radical social transformation in the sense of challenging dominant ways of viewing the world, including the neoliberal illusion of improving the welfare of all while advancing the interests of only some. However, a question mark has remained over the utility of human rights in this activity and the capability of rights to challenge, as opposed to reinforce, discourses such as liberalism, capitalism, internationalism and statism. It is at this point that the present work aims to intervene. Drawing upon critical legal theory, radical democratic thinking and feminist perspectives, *Human Rights and Radical Social Transformation* seeks to reassess the radical possibilities for human rights and explore how rights may be re-engaged as a tool to facilitate radical social change via the concept of 'human rights to come'. This idea proposes a reconceptualisation of human rights in theory and practice which foregrounds human rights as inherently futural and capable of sustaining a critical relation to power and alterity in radical politics.

Kathryn McNeilly is a lecturer in law at Queen's University Belfast.

Human Rights and Radical Social Transformation

Futurity, Alterity, Power

Kathryn McNeilly

a GlassHouse book

First published 2018
by Routledge
2 Park Square, Milton Park, Abingdon, Oxon OX14 4RN

and by Routledge
711 Third Avenue, New York, NY 10017

a GlassHouse Book

Routledge is an imprint of the Taylor & Francis Group, an informa business

© 2018 Kathryn McNeilly

The right of Kathryn McNeilly to be identified as author of this work has been asserted by her in accordance with sections 77 and 78 of the Copyright, Designs and Patents Act 1988.

All rights reserved. No part of this book may be reprinted or reproduced or utilised in any form or by any electronic, mechanical, or other means, now known or hereafter invented, including photocopying and recording, or in any information storage or retrieval system, without permission in writing from the publishers.

Trademark notice: Product or corporate names may be trademarks or registered trademarks, and are used only for identification and explanation without intent to infringe.

British Library Cataloguing in Publication Data
A catalogue record for this book is available from the British Library

Library of Congress Cataloging in Publication Data
Names: McNeilly, Kathryn, author.
Title: Human rights and radical social transformation : futurity, alterity, power / Kathryn McNeilly.
Description: New York, NY : Routledge, 2017. | Includes bibliographical references and index.
Identifiers: LCCN 2017010619| ISBN 9781138690219 (hardback) | ISBN 9781134990597 (adobe reader) | ISBN 9781134990665 (epub) | ISBN 9781134990733 (mobipocket)
Subjects: LCSH: Human rights. | Social change. | Law--Philosophy. | Sociological jurisprudence.
Classification: LCC K3240 .M3883 2017 | DDC 323--dc23
LC record available at https://lccn.loc.gov/2017010619

ISBN: 978-1-138-69021-9 (hbk)
ISBN: 978-1-315-53710-8 (ebk)

Typeset in Galliard
by Taylor & Francis Books

Printed and bound in Great Britain by
TJ International Ltd, Padstow, Cornwall

Contents

Acknowledgements viii

1 **Introduction** 1
   Notes 11

2 **The excesses of human rights: beginning to think of a futural future for human rights** 15
   Introduction 15
   Mainstream history of human rights: liberalism, capitalism, internationalism and statism 16
   Human rights as existing in excess: parallel histories 20
   Human rights as driven by excess and a futural future: human rights to come 23
   Conclusion: the future of the history of human rights 28
   Notes 29

3 **(Re)Doing rights: the performativity of human rights to come** 34
   Introduction 34
   From rights as objects to rights as a performative doing 35
   The performativity of human rights to come: a 'doing in futurity' 39
       The present and the future in the performative 40
       Futurity, performativity and rights 41
   Human rights to come as redoing human rights 44
       Performative reiteration 45
       Reiterating rights 46
   Conclusion 50
   Notes 51

4 Universality as universalisation: the universality of human rights to come 55
Introduction 55
Engagements with the universality of human rights 56
For a futural conception of the universal: universality as universalisation 60
Universalisation and the radical: the universal content and subject of human rights 64
   The universal content of human rights 65
   The universal subject of human rights 68
Conclusion 71
Notes 72

5 Beyond consensus: the agonism of human rights to come 76
Introduction 76
Consensus and the politics of human rights 77
From consensus to agonism: human rights to come as an agonistic politics of rights 82
Human rights to come as towards agonistic democracy to come 89
Conclusion 91
Notes 92

6 Rethinking paradoxical sovereignty: the ontology of human rights to come 96
Introduction 96
The paradoxical sovereign subject of human rights 97
Rethinking ontology: vulnerability as a source of critical engagement with alterity and power 101
Reapproaching paradoxical sovereignty: vulnerability as a source for resistant action 107
Conclusion 111
Notes 113

7 On translation: the practice of human rights to come 116
Introduction 116
The practice of human rights and translation 117
Cultural translation and a disruptive and futural practice of human rights to come 122
For a holistic practice of human rights to come: the role of the translator 127

Conclusion 132
Notes 133

8 **Rereading feminist engagements with rights via human rights to come**   135
Introduction 135
Rereading the history of feminist engagements with human rights 136
    Stage one: formal equality (1948–1970s) 137
    Stages two and three: deconstruction of law (1980s–1990s); reconstruction, reconceptualisation and reinterpretation (1990s–present) 138
    Stage four: reflection, re-evaluation and reassessment (2000s–present) 141
A new future for feminist engagements with human rights: human rights to come and the right to gender flourishing 144
    Stage five? Feminist engagements and human rights to come 144
    A contemporary competing universal: the right to gender flourishing 145
Conclusion 151
Notes 151

9 **Conclusion as non-conclusion**   156
The possibilities of non-conclusion 158
The challenges of non-conclusion 160
A future in the futural 161
Notes 162

Index   163

Acknowledgements

This work has been shaped in many ways by a variety of people. Thanks must go to those who kindly read and commented on various chapters and drafts of the work, including Keith Breen, Natasa Mavronicola, Sara Ramshaw, Alex Schwartz and Bal Sokhi-Bulley. More broadly, sincere thanks are due to Sara as the generous supervisor of the DEL-funded PhD project which constituted the early foundations of this work, and to this project's examiners, Bal and Elena Loizidou. Over the past two years or so the ideas contained in the pages to follow have been critically engaged with, and enriched, by many others. Sections and themes of this work were presented at the University of Belgrade in November 2015 as part of a conference entitled 'How to Act Together: From Collective Engagement to Protest', at the Critical Legal Conference hosted by the University of Kent in September 2016, and as part of the 'Human Rights Theory and Practice' workshop organised by Chris McCrudden at the University of Michigan in November 2016. Sections of Chapter 4 were initially thought through as an article entitled 'Reclaiming the Radical in Universal Human Rights: Universality as Universalisation' published in 2015 in the *International Human Rights Law Review*. Many thanks must also go to the Institute for Feminist Legal Studies at Osgoode Hall Law School, York University, Toronto, in particular to Sonia Lawrence, who offered me space to work on final drafts of the book in September 2016. I am additionally indebted to Aaron Kirkland who engaged in careful and painstaking proof reviewing of the manuscript. Finally, and always, to W.B.

Chapter 1

Introduction

> What does and does not count as a universal, as the universal reach of human obligation and right? That is a question that is constantly on the table.
> Judith Butler (Butler, Olson and Worsham 2000: 756)

> Human rights are the projection of the 'not yet' into the 'always there', a necessary but impossible promise.
> Costas Douzinas (2000: 318)

> [T]he very idea of a radical social transformation may appear as an impossible dream – yet the term 'impossible' should make us stop and think.
> Slavoj Žižek (2010)

It is something of an understatement to say that human rights have emerged as a vibrant area of study and debate over the past number of decades. Throughout this time, both academic and non-academic commentary on, and engagement with, human rights has proliferated and demonstrated the discourse to be provocative, challenging, emboldening and frustrating often in equal measure. It has become something of a truism to assert that we now live in an 'age of human rights' where rights discourse enjoys strong global currency,[1] as Ben Golder notes, 'if not in the sense of a universal observance of and commitment to its norms, then surely in the political and discursive sense of diverse groups articulating claims for justice or opposition to oppression in its terms' (2015: 158). This position solidified throughout the twentieth century, as human rights and rights politics advanced in earnest across local social movements and activism, international relations and law, and a critical mass of national legal systems around the world. However, at the same time as the apparently ever-increasing dominance of rights language, claiming and thought, a collection of probing questions was directed towards human rights, their role, usages and conceptualisations from the late twentieth century onwards. These included questions such as: who can be said to be the subject of human rights? What is the relation between human rights and regimes of power? Can human rights still be considered an emancipatory discourse? Indeed, were they ever a truly emancipatory discourse? Such questions, asked in varying degrees of forcefulness by a multiplicity of voices speaking from a range of perspectives, provoked much pause for thought, and contributed to the forging of new directions for rights scholarship and practice.

The opening years of the twenty-first century have brought with them a changing social, political and economic context with the crisis of capitalism, global threats of terror, challenges to neoliberalism, crises of borders and migration, increasing instances of riots, revolts and uprisings and the related rise of highly polarised politics which has accompanied these trends.[2] Against this contemporary backdrop of crisis, radical thinking and activism aiming to challenge the restrictive and oppressive operation of power, and its impact on those on the margins, has increased (Douzinas and Žižek 2010: viii).[3] Such activism, in diverse ways, has aimed for radical social transformation in the sense of staging a fundamental challenge to dominant ways of viewing the world, including the neoliberal illusion of improving the welfare of all while advancing the interests of only some (Harvey 2007: 175–182), rupturing them to refocus on social solidarity, to achieve meaningful realisation of the ideals of liberty and equality and to facilitate new ways of living and being together.[4] In this context the questions previously raised about human rights continue to be of relevance, but, importantly, new questions also arise. In a period where demands for such radical social change have taken on momentum, what role does the discourse and practice of human rights have to play? While human rights have been critiqued as appropriated in ways that cohere with neoliberal principles and interests over the past two decades, for example as a 'sword of empire' in military interventions progressing under the guise of freedom and rights for all (Harvey 2007: 178),[5] can they offer possibilities for contemporary radical politics? In other words, what is the relationship between human rights and radical social transformation today? Can human rights be utilised to meaningfully challenge, as opposed to reinforce, restrictive regimes of power, and so provide an additional vehicle for radical politics in the current context?

These are questions which have emerged as fiercely contested among radical and critical thinkers, activists and groups. Indeed, the relationship between human rights and radical politics has proved to be a complex one. A definite trend towards what Costas Douzinas terms a 'rights revisionism' can be observed in radical thinking from the 1970s onwards (2010: 81). In this category of rights revisionists, we may include post-Marxist thinkers such as Claude Lefort (1986: 239–272) and Jacques Rancière (2004) who have engaged in a rethinking of the political possibilities for rights, as well as a plethora of other critical thinkers including Étienne Balibar (2013), Wendy Brown (2000; 2004) and Judith Butler (2004: 31–39). This work has done much to excavate the language and discourse of rights from its dominant understandings, and to consider alternative usages and potential for rights which advance more radical aims. Evidence of ongoing use of the ideas and language of human rights can also be observed in contemporary radical activism including the Occupy movement, Black Lives Matter activism and struggles for the Arab Spring (Manfredi 2013: 3–4). Thus, as Zachary Manfredi comments, 'on the one hand, human rights are the object of critique as they are deployed as part of Western state power and military intervention. On the other hand, however, they form an essential part of the basic normative language for expressing condemnation of injustice' and have been re-engaged in radical work on this basis (2013: 6). Accordingly, while thinkers and activists interested in advancing the ends of radical social transformation and displacing oppressive power relations may have rejected mainstream interpretations and usages of human rights[6] as not radical enough, an enduring (re)use of human rights in recent radical politics and thought is undeniable.

However, this is not all there is to the relationship between human rights and radical politics, and it is by no means possible to state that radical work has engaged in a widespread embrace of human rights as a discourse or site for a productive speaking back to power in recent times. For example, it is important to note that following his statement cited above, Manfredi goes on in his analysis to comment that despite the utility of the discourse of human rights to challenge the kind of injustices radical politics engages, 'on the left, those willing to offer even a limited apology for human rights are few' (2013: 6). This is an assertion that is indeed substantiated by a survey of recent writings as a disinclination towards the language and discourse of human rights has gained force in the post-2001 period of crisis. Evidence to this effect can be found in the work of David Kennedy, who, reflecting on the purchase that the claims of his earlier work may be thought to have in the contemporary period, reaffirmed that human rights can no longer be conceived as the way forward for critical and radical politics (2012: 34). In his consideration of radical writings on rights, Douzinas also advances that at the beginning of the twenty-first century 'the rejection of the earlier rights revisionism is almost complete' (2010: 81). Douzinas is by no means the only thinker to make this claim. Others taking up this assertion include Daniel McLoughlin who states that 'the critique of human rights indicates that the project of mobilising them for radical democratic purposes now faces some very serious limits and pressures thrown up by their recent history', namely, the 'very definite series of counter-revolutionary inscriptions of the term' (2016: 318). While acknowledging that the possibilities which human rights offer for radical politics depend on the contingent time and context when rights are being engaged, McLoughlin ultimately concludes that in the contemporary conjucture human rights are of limited utility (2016: 319).

Thus, it appears that there is an ongoing struggle with, or at the very least a question mark over, the relationship between human rights and work aiming towards radical social transformation. Radical thinking and politics has demonstrated a somewhat ambivalent approach to human rights, and in the current context of crisis where human rights have often fallen victim to appropriation by dominant power regimes, there may be, we are led to believe, ever fewer reasons to revisit rights as a site of radical possibility. It is at this point that the present work seeks to intervene, to reassess the political possibilities for human rights and add to thinking on how human rights may be conceived of as a vehicle of use in radical politics seeking to challenge restrictive relations of power in the contemporary period. In doing so, discussion picks up on David Harvey's assertion that 'it proves impossible to wean society away from some dominant social processes (such as that of capital accumulation through market exchange) to another (such as political democracy and collective action) without simultaneously shifting allegiance from one dominant conception of rights and justice to another' (2007: 180). I advance that an alternative conception of rights compatible with the promotion of different regimes of class, gendered, racial, ablest and heteronormative power and meaningful social equality is made possible through the concept of 'human rights to come'. This concept is articulated throughout the chapters to follow as a means of rethinking the relationship between radical politics and human rights in both theory and practice to offer a potential role for rights and their politics in contemporary work for radical social change.

Before turning to introduce this concept in more detail, it is necessary to ask at the outset why, given widespread scepticism regarding the radical possibilities of human rights, it is asserted that activity to re-engage human rights is productive. In light of recent developments and the use of rights in global politics over past decades, surely, it might be said, radical politics may more productively draw on differing tools which are less tied up with the very discourses and regimes of power that such politics seeks to challenge. Three main reasons may be identified as underpinning this work's assertion that it is possible to advance productive re-engagements with human rights today. The first of these is well rehearsed. It relates to the significance that the discourse of human rights, and the practice of articulating claims in the language of rights, holds. Human rights as a language, in law and politics, has global purchase and symbolic value. It is a language recognised and utilised on a daily basis globally in a wide range of locations from grassroots politics to the halls and boardrooms of national governments, court chambers and powerful institutions such as the United Nations. Human rights, therefore, constitute a vehicle which offers a viable means to present wrongs or injustices taking a variety of forms, translating them into a format that is widely recognisable and comprehensible. In this sense, as has been recognised by many,[7] the discourse and practice of human rights continue to hold a strategic importance for radical politics. However, it is asserted that strategic usage of human rights in such politics need not remain within the confines of rights discourse as understood in its currently dominant or mainstream form. Human rights, as a malleable politico-legal language with widespread purchase, stand to be engaged in a modified way which makes claims of injustice understandable yet simultaneously serves to challenge, as opposed to work within, what the dominant presents as given or known. Radical thinkers and activists may seek to engage with the language and practice of human rights in a new way, aiming to subvert the discourse from the inside in order to make its values more concrete. This assertion and approach of immanent critique is not new. However, the contemporary context where dominant discourses of power are in disarray and alternatives are being demanded potentially offers a useful moment to engage in the reworking of symbolic ideas such as human rights, returning to liberal democracy's key tenets, its recognisable concepts, in a different way that aims to facilitate radical social transformation. This possibility to draw upon the symbolic importance and purchase of the language and practice of human rights in an alternative manner is one which threads through discussion in the subsequent chapters.

The second reason driving this work's assertion that re-engagements with human rights may offer productive possibilities for radical politics in the contemporary context relates to the fact that human rights are, and always have been, an inherently political discourse through which diverse struggles play out within contexts of power. This link may be returned to and potentially capitalised on. Here it is useful to draw upon the distinction engaged by Claude Lefort (1988), Jean-Luc Nancy (1991), Chantal Mouffe (2005), Jacques Rancière (1999) and others between politics, a formal domain, and the political, the space within which power can be contested. While human rights have throughout their history fallen into and been utilised within both categories, at its core the language and politics of human rights is rooted in the political; challenging the oppressive use of power and facilitating debate on what is required to live a viable life within current contexts of power generally (Douzinas 2007: 12–13). This relation between human rights and the political is an essential reason why those deemed 'rights revisionists' have considered there to be possibilities for human rights to advance the aims of radical social transformation. In particular, the language of the 'human' is central to the radical political potential of human rights, offering a space to contest what it means to be human, how the human is constructed within discourses of power and what politico-social obligations flow from recognising another as human. In the contemporary period, human rights have, as Rancière identifies, undergone a significant degree of depoliticisation which leaves them leaning more towards politics than the political (2004: 307). It is, nevertheless, advanced that the political dimension of human rights remains and may be productively tapped into by radical politics seeking to open up debate on relations of living and being within present conditions of power. Increasing codification of human rights in international law and usages of rights in ways that further as opposed to challenge neoliberalism and the interests of the political elite in the contemporary period are no doubt problematic, but they do not indicate that the political nature of human rights has been fully eradicated. While it is by no means a certainty that the link between the political and human rights may be successfully reignited, this longstanding link indicates that the discourse and practice of human rights may offer particular opportunities to reinvigorate the political in contemporary politics. In the current circumstance where radical politics is running out of tools to meaningfully challenge hegemonic regimes of power, this appears to be an avenue that may be usefully pursued. This is what the idea of human rights to come seeks to work towards.

The final reason driving the present work's assertion that it is possible to advance productive radical re-engagements with human rights today relates to the connection that may be made between human rights and crisis. In the contemporary context of crisis, which has posed many challenges for human rights and their potential place in radical politics, instead of turning away from human rights as too flawed or too connected with problematic power regimes to advance the aims of radical social transformation, interesting possibilities emerge when it is noted that international human rights themselves may be conceived as a 'discourse of crisis'.[8] The idea of crisis has had multiple functions in the development of human rights, not least in their emergence in international law in the wake of the Second World War. Human rights in their dominant form today came into being as a response to the horrors of the Holocaust and the global landscape of the 1940s. Benjamin Authers and Hilary Charlesworth comment that 'this sense that the foundations of human rights law were a reaction to crisis has continued to shape the discipline' (2013: 20). Crisis is so central to human rights that 'the crises of the (now generalised) past are seen to be part of the framework of rights themselves' (Authers and Charlesworth 2013: 27). In this way, the discourse of human rights may be viewed as intimately caught up with crisis, legitimised by it and as representing a utopian collective future which exists beyond the calamity of the past/present (Authers and Charlesworth 2013: 28). Rather than undermined and weakened by contexts of crisis, human rights gain their meaning and possibilities from such.

Accordingly, while there have been instances of problematic appropriation of human rights in the post-2001 period of crisis, this does not mean that any recourse to human rights, in particular any radical recourse, must be abandoned. On the contrary, human rights by their very nature hold possibilities to be used to gesture towards a future that is better than the present and the current oppressive use of power within it. This future may be imagined as one compatible with the aims and aspirations of radical politics. In this respect, in contexts of crisis, human rights may be a vehicle for envisaging and working towards new forms of sociopolitical relations that challenge instead of reinforce those presently dominant and for facilitating radical social change. Here it may be useful to draw from the comments of Dianne Otto who asks whether it is possible to 'turn the momentum of a crisis to more progressive ends', asserting that 'a crisis, whether real or imagined, always creates opportunities that did not exist before … Although these opportunities seem particularly amenable to capture by neoliberal forces, there surely is also the possibility of turning them to progressive ends' (2015: 130). The opportunities created by recent crises may involve a possibility to return to the discourse of human rights, using the promise it offers to transcend what is wrong with the present, in a new, more radical way by reflecting on the manner in which human rights gain meaning from crisis and (re)appropriating this for the aims of radical politics.

Following from this, human rights appear as a discourse that may be productively re-engaged in contemporary radical politics, a site where the radical may be reclaimed.[9] As noted above, the way in which this is advanced as possible is through a rethinking of human rights via the idea of human rights to come. While the contours of this concept will be more fully outlined in the chapters to follow, it is pertinent to gesture towards what understanding human rights as human rights to come involves in a general sense. This idea seeks to propose a holistic way to reconceptualise human rights and engage in a more radical politics of rights which is of use to both scholars and activists, movements or groups. It begins with the assertion that human rights always exist in excess of their current articulation, capable of alternative usages and conceptualisations, and, more than this, asserts that human rights can be understood as in fact driven by excess in the sense of involving an ongoing process of articulation and rearticulation to meet the ineradicable limits of any dominant rights concept. This process of articulation and rearticulation may be approached in a radical or more critical way by foregrounding the inherent limitations of human rights as related to alterity within current relations of power. Through foregrounding the fact that rights will always be exclusive in some way, reflecting wider conditions of alterity within dominant power regimes, human rights and their politics emerge as permanently unsettled and unfinished, always striving towards a fully formed conception of themselves, and of relations of living and being together more generally, which eradicates alterity. In this view, human rights remain inherently 'to come' and may be conceived as a site to strive towards a futural conception of living and being that is free from alterity. Rather than leading to inertia, this futural nature of human rights should spur radical politics on, facilitating an ongoing working and reworking of dominant human rights ideas which sustains the critical in human rights politics and allows human rights to emerge as a productive site to advance a critical approach to relations of power and the ends of radical social transformation. From this understanding it is necessary to reapproach the theoretical underpinnings and practice of human rights in a way that foregrounds the futural. It is not enough to import a futural sense of human rights into their current form. In contrast, to advance a radical practice of human rights to come the underpinnings of rights themselves must be reconsidered and restaged. Significantly, re-engagement of human rights in this way is not restricted to one particular group. The idea of human rights to come may be utilised in diverse ways in radical politics; by feminists, lesbian, gay, bisexual, transgender and intersex activists, those engaging in critique of economy and capital, race activists, a variety of groups, thinkers and activists interested in the aims of radical social transformation and the reworking of restrictive discourses of power.

In order to explore what it might mean for radical thinkers and activists to reapproach human rights as human rights to come, a number of differing theoretical resources are drawn upon, including critical legal theory, radical democratic thinking and feminist perspectives. In particular, the thought of Judith Butler threads through much analysis in this work. As noted above, Butler has been categorised as a contemporary critical 'rights revisionist'. Moving from scepticism regarding the language and politics of universal human rights, especially as a legal discourse, in her earlier work,[10] in more recent years Butler has engaged in exploration of alternative, critical possibilities for the practice of human rights (2004: 17–39). However, while the more recently hospitable relationship between Butler's thinking and human rights provides a background for discussion to follow, this in itself is not the reason for engaging Butlerian resources in the present work. Rather, the reason for doing so lies in the fact that in beginning to imagine a conception of human rights that foregrounds the radical and, specifically, the futural, a number of supporting resources can be located in Butler's thought. At the core of Butler's corpus is an aim to radically transform existing relations of living and being, to engage in politics that challenge the hegemony of restrictive power regimes so that greater possibilities for life may be brought into being. Alongside this drive for radical social transformation, Butler stresses the value of democratic practices and, in various ways, considers themes of futurity and alterity.[11] Butler's thinking on these issues may be woven together with critical thinking on rights to help articulate the idea of human rights to come and, in this respect, offers a fruitful starting point to begin to imagine what this idea's reworking of the theory and practice of human rights might look like. It is also important to note, however, that while the concept of human rights to come may be described as having Butlerian origins it does not always remain committed to use of Butler's thinking in a way that coheres with her own work and, also being shaped by other radical and critical resources, cannot be described as an exclusively Butlerian concept.

From this overview, it may be stated that the present work aims to explore the possibilities for human rights and radical politics and to spur on the (diverse) project to utilise human rights as a tool to work towards radical social transformation. It links into the uncertainty regarding the future which has in many ways characterised the contemporary period and seeks to redeploy this in a new, more hopeful, and critical, way. The uncertainty, and often apparent impossibility, of the future and of human rights can be positioned as a driving force for radical politics, directing towards a futural horizon of a form of sociopolitical relations of living and being which transcends current restrictions and inequalities. The present work is, at its heart, an invitation to consider a radical future for human rights in the futural, and to investigate how this may be done in a way that interlinks the theoretical underpinnings and the everyday practice of human rights.

To provide a guide to how this exploration will proceed: in Chapter 2 human rights are considered as a concept that has been tied to problematic discourses and relations of power in their dominant or mainstream history, but also an inherently excessive concept which cannot be contained by such discourses and relations. The radical possibilities of this excess are brought into view and explored. In doing so, this chapter will introduce more fully the idea of the futural in human rights and how it may be foregrounded to direct the new re-engagement with the theory and practice of rights which human rights to come advances. Following on from this, Chapters 3–6 then proceed to explore the way in which key theoretical foundations of human rights may be re-engaged to foreground the futural and render human rights more amenable to use towards the ends of radical social transformation.

Chapter 3 begins this analysis by considering how the approach of human rights to come must involve a reappraisal of rights as a politico-legal activity, of what is involved in the everyday use of human rights. Drawing upon the performative tradition found in the work of J. L. Austin and its development by Butler, as well as its extension to the practice of rights claiming by Karen Zivi, this chapter asserts that understanding and embracing the performativity of human rights is central to the concept of human rights to come. However, more than this, it is advanced that the performativity of human rights to come involves something more than provided in accounts such as that of Zivi. First, it is necessary to understand the activity of human rights to come as not just a performative doing but a performative doing in *futurity*, foregrounding and capitalising on the futural in the performative. Second, it is asserted that the performative doing involved in human rights to come also must be thought of as a kind of performative *re*doing, stressing the possibilities, and indeed the need, to rearticulate the discourse of rights in new ways beyond their current mainstream iterations. Both these performative (re)understandings are of crucial importance in beginning work to re-engage human rights in contemporary radical politics.

In Chapter 4 attention turns to the universality of human rights as the second theoretical underpinning to be brought into consideration and thought anew. This chapter starts with the assertion that understanding human rights as human rights to come, as fluid concepts continually articulated and rearticulated without end, requires moving beyond traditional ideas of universality as a static characteristic of rights to be endorsed or rejected. Discussion in this chapter explores how human rights to come does not, however, involve a rejection of universality or a conception of universal human rights altogether, but encourages a reapproaching of universality. Instead of a static attribute or characteristic of rights, informed by Butler's work on universality, human rights to come frames universality as an ongoing process of universalisation that radical politics must engage in as a perpetual and futural striving towards a final perfect conception of the universal, and one which must never be closed off. As a result, universality becomes a site where the 'to come' of human rights is sustained. This is explored in relation to the universal content and subject of human rights.

Chapter 5 considers the ideas of consensus and conflict within the politics of human rights. While mainstream conceptions of human rights have foregrounded consensus and consensus-forging as at the heart of rights and their politics, the idea of human rights to come requires an active embrace of conflict in human rights. This embrace of conflict is explored as necessary to sustain a futural conception of rights and an ongoing critical relation to alterity and power in their politics. In exploring this assertion further, discussion engages Chantal Mouffe's concept of agonism and how it is of use in thinking through the central element of conflict in human rights to come. It is asserted that the latter, involving ongoing conflict on the limits and inadequacies of current human rights concepts and relations of power, is a fundamentally agonistic approach to rights and, moreover, allows human rights to become a site to sustain the agonistic in democratic politics. In this sense, the practice of human rights to come is advanced as holding potential to feed into a wider vision of agonistic democracy which also remains to come.

Following from this, Chapter 6 moves to engage with the ontological dimensions of human rights. Discussion explores the way in which the sovereign subject traditionally central to human rights is problematic but, in addition, is also defined by a paradox; this subject possesses rights as a sovereign individual only to the extent that s/he is in fact vulnerable to being injured by external forces acting upon her/him. This paradox is explored as a starting point for an alternative ontological approach to human rights which does not flee from vulnerability to advance an illusion of sovereignty, but embraces the complex and nuanced relationship between these two concepts. Drawing from the work of Martha Albertson Fineman and Butler, what is asserted is that vulnerability can be brought into view in the concept of human rights to come as offering both a source of ongoing critical engagement with alterity and power and a source for resistant action in a radical politics of human rights. Resultantly, those who approach human rights as human rights to come are practising a different ontological understanding of our lives generally and of what rights are capable of offering or doing in relation to our ontological condition. This draws attention to differential experiences of vulnerability within contexts of power and facilitates responses to such. This alternative conception of vulnerability must not be perceived as disempowering or preventing agentic action. Rather, the political activity of human rights to come is made possible not by sovereign action, but by the subject's vulnerability to injury and harm.

While there is of course a natural link between the theoretical aspects explored in Chapters 3–6 and the everyday practice of human rights, Chapter 7 moves to consider more fully, or explicitly, what it would mean to practise human rights as human rights to come in radical politics. Important in making this idea useful for those involved in the everyday practice of rights, and eschewing a purely theoretical re-engagement with human rights, discussion in this chapter seeks to tie together the theory and practice of human rights to come in a tangible way. To do so, it advances looking to resources already available in the practice of human rights and using them in a slightly different manner. To this end, the concept of translation is brought into view as possible of reiteration beyond understandings which focus on top-down translation or the power of the dominant to integrate the subordinate to foreground a specifically disruptive and futural practice of translation. In this discussion, Butler's model of cultural translation is explored as offering radical activists and groups the tools to facilitate such an approach and to thereby put into motion the more radical possibilities for human rights towards which human rights to come seeks to signal. However, this chapter also asserts that it is necessary to move beyond Butler alone in this task. Drawing from wider work on cultural translation, such as that of Homi Bhabha and Gayatri Spivak, the chapter also considers the role of the 'translator' as offering the possibility to envisage a holistic practice of human rights to come involving a collection of actors, places and locations which moves beyond an exclusive focus on the activist and grassroots politics.

Chapter 8, the final substantive chapter of the work, is where discussion in the preceding chapters on re-engagements with the theoretical underpinnings and practice of human rights is thought through in relation to existing human rights work and activism. Retaining focus on human rights to come as a tangible concept, this chapter considers feminist engagements with human rights and what it might mean to engage human rights as human rights to come in contemporary feminist work. This chapter rereads the history of feminist engagements with human rights, identifying the radical and not so radical elements of this history from the perspective of analysis in previous chapters, and uses this analysis to advance human rights to come as of use in facilitating a new stage of feminist engagement with rights in the contemporary period. It asserts that this new stage would involve repositioning how rights and their underpinnings are understood, in the sense outlined in Chapters 3–6, and also repositioning the practice of rights to engage in a futural and disruptive practice of translation, drawing from analysis in Chapter 7. The idea of a 'right to gender flourishing' is presented as a means by which feminist work in the current period may embrace the key elements of human rights to come and allow for new, productive engagements with human rights and their relationship to gender to emerge. While the analysis of this chapter is specific to feminist thought and activism, it is of use in gesturing towards, in a concrete way, the kind of utility that human rights to come may have for radical politics, thinkers and groups more generally.

In the comments that conclude the book, thought turns to what follows from the analysis put forward in this work, in particular considering some of the possibilities and challenges re-engaging human rights as human rights to come offers or poses radical thinkers and activists. These comments highlight how in many ways the only conclusion that can be drawn from this study for such thinkers, activists, movements and groups is one of non-conclusion. A futural conception of human rights cannot, by definition, bring certainty or final solutions for radical politics and, indeed, the real work of human rights to come must be viewed as taking place in the everyday practice of rights. Accordingly, the end of this book is only the beginning and cannot provide a precise roadmap for the journey to follow. While this may bring its own anxiety and difficulty, the non-conclusion and open, unfixed sense of human rights and rights politics which follows from an understanding of human rights to come is central and is where radical possibility, it is asserted, truly lies.

Notes

1 See Henkin (1990); Bobbio (1996).
2 As Costas Douzinas and Slavoj Žižek state in response to Francis Fukuyama's declaration of the victory of liberalism and the end of history (Fukuyama 1989), 'If 1989 was the inaugural year of the new world order, 2001 announced its decline, and the collapse of the banking system in 2008 marked the beginning of a return to full-blown history' (2010: vii–viii). For further discussion on this point, see Duménil and Lévy (2011); Feldner, Vighi and Žižek (2014); Kotz (2015).
3 In this work radical politics can be defined as incorporating a variety of leftist, post-Marxist and poststructuralist thinkers, activists, movements and groups. This diverse work aims to challenge regimes of capitalist, gendered and racial power, their restrictive effects and invisibilisation in everyday life.

4 Throughout this work the term 'radical social transformation' can be read in this sense. This activity can be thought to be of interest to a number of radical activists or groups including feminists and those interested in challenges to gendered relations, race activists, socialists and others interested in challenging existing class structures and relations of power.
5 For discussion and analysis, see Odysseos (2010); Wilson (2005); Denike (2008); Butler (2006b: 50–100); Otto (2011); O'Connell (2007). For a critical overview of scholarship thinking on the relationship between human rights and neoliberalism, see Moyn (2014).
6 In the chapters to follow the idea of a 'mainstream' conception of human rights is considered as the dominant perception of what human rights look like and can be capable of doing and saying as defined via discourses such as liberalism, capitalism, internationalism (as international human rights) and statism. The role of these ideas in shaping mainstream conceptions of human rights in a way that is not immediately compatible with the aims of radical politics is explored further in Chapter 2.
7 On this point see, for example, Manfredi (2013: 7); Douzinas (2007: 12–13); Butler (2006a: xviii–xix).
8 This phrase is drawn from Charlesworth (2002).
9 For further discussion on the idea of reclaiming a radical element within human rights, see Wall (2014).
10 These include Butler's comments in work such as *Gender Trouble* (2006a) and *Excitable Speech* (1997).
11 See, for example, Butler's contributions to the 2000 work *Contingency, Hegemony, Universality* (Butler, Laclau and Žižek 2000).

References

Authers, B. and Charlesworth, H. (2013) 'The Crisis and the Quotidian in International Human Rights Law', *Netherlands Yearbook of International Law*, 44: 19–39.
Balibar, É. (2013) 'On the Politics of Human Rights', *Constellations*, 20(1): 18–26.
Bobbio, N. (1996) *The Age of Rights*, Cambridge: Polity.
Brown, W. (2000) 'Suffering Rights as Paradoxes', *Constellations*, 7(2): 230–241.
Brown, W. (2004) '"The Most We Can Hope for …": Human Rights and the Politics of Fatalism', *South Atlantic Quarterly*, 103(2–3): 451–463.
Butler, J. (1997) *Excitable Speech: A Politics of the Performative*, New York; London: Routledge.
Butler, J. (2004) *Undoing Gender*, New York; London: Routledge.
Butler, J. (2006a) *Gender Trouble: Feminism and the Subversion of Identity*, 2nd edn, New York; London: Routledge.
Butler, J. (2006b) *Precarious Life: The Powers of Mourning and Violence*, 2nd edn, London: Verso.
Butler, J., Laclau, E. and Žižek, S. (2000) *Contingency, Hegemony, Universality: Contemporary Dialogues on the Left*, London: Verso.
Butler, J., Olson, G. and Worsham, L. (2000) 'Changing the Subject: Judith Butler's Politics of Radical Resignification', *JAC*, 20(4): 727–765.
Charlesworth, H. (2002) 'International Law: A Discipline of Crisis', *Modern Law Review*, 65(3): 377–392.
Denike, M. (2008) 'The Human Rights of Others: Sovereignty, Legitimacy, and "Just Causes" for the "War in Terror"', *Hypatia*, 23(2): 95–121.

Douzinas, C. (2000) *The End of Human Rights: Critical Legal Thought at the Turn of the Century*, Oxford: Hart.
Douzinas, C. (2007) *Human Rights and Empire: The Political Philosophy of Cosmopolitanism*, New York; London: Routledge.
Douzinas, C. (2010) 'Adikia: On Communism and Rights', in C. Douzinas and S. Žižek (eds), *The Idea of Communism*, London: Verso, 81–100.
Douzinas, C. and Žižek, S. (2010) 'Introduction: The Idea of Communism', in C. Douzinas and S. Žižek (eds), *The Idea of Communism*, London: Verso, vii–x.
Duménil, G. and Lévy, D. (2011) *The Crisis of Neoliberalism*, Cambridge, MA: Harvard University Press.
Feldner, H., Vighi, F. and Žižek, S. (eds) (2014) *States of Crisis and Post-Capitalist Scenarios*, Farnham: Ashgate.
Fukuyama, F. (1989) 'The End of History?', *National Interest*, 16: 3–18.
Golder, B. (2015) *Foucault and the Politics of Rights*, Stanford: Stanford University Press.
Harvey, D. (2007) *A Brief History of Neoliberalism*, Oxford: Oxford University Press.
Henkin, L. (1990) *The Age of Rights*, New York: Columbia University Press.
Kennedy, D. (2012) 'The International Human Rights Regime: Still Part of the Problem?', in R. Dickinson, E. Katselli, C. Murray and O. Pedersen (eds), *Examining Critical Perspectives on Human Rights*, Cambridge: Cambridge University Press, 19–34.
Kotz, D. (2015) *The Rise and Fall of Neoliberal Capitalism*, Cambridge, MA: Harvard University Press.
Lefort, C. (1986) *The Political Forms of Modern Society*, Cambridge, MA: MIT Press.
Lefort, C. (1988) *Democracy and Political Theory*, trans. D. Macey, Cambridge: Polity.
McLoughlin, D. (2016) 'Post-Marxism and the Politics of Human Rights: Lefort, Badiou, Agamben, Rancière', *Law and Critique*, 27(3): 303–321.
Manfredi, Z. (2013) 'Recent Histories and Uncertain Futures: Contemporary Critiques of International Human Rights and Humanitarianism', *Qui Parle*, 22(1): 3–32.
Mouffe, C. (2005) *On the Political*, London: Routledge.
Moyn, S. (2014) 'A Powerless Companion: Human Rights in the Age of Neoliberalism', *Law and Contemporary Problems*, 77(4): 147–169.
Nancy, J. L. (1991) *The Inoperative Community*, trans. P. Connor, L. Garbus, M. Holland and S. Sawhney, Minneapolis: University of Minnesota Press.
O'Connell, P. (2007) 'On Reconciling Irreconcilables: Neoliberal Globalisation and Human Rights', *Human Rights Law Review*, 7(3): 483–509.
Odysseos, L. (2010) 'Human Rights, Liberal Ontogenesis and Freedom: Producing a Subject for Neoliberalism?', *Millennium: Journal of International Studies*, 38(3): 747–772.
Otto, D. (2011) 'Remapping Crisis through a Feminist Lens', in S. Kouvo and Z. Pearson (eds), *Feminist Perspectives on Contemporary International Law: Between Resistance and Compliance*, Oxford: Hart, 75–95.
Otto, D. (2015) 'Decoding Crisis in International Law: A Queer Feminist Perspective', in B. Stark (ed.), *International Law and its Discontents: Confronting Crises*, Cambridge: Cambridge University Press, 115–136.
Rancière, J. (1999) *Disagreement: Politics and Philosophy*, trans J. Rose, Minneapolis: University of Minnesota Press.
Rancière, J. (2004) 'Who Is the Subject of the Rights of Man?', *South Atlantic Quarterly*, 103(2–3): 297–310.

Wall, I. (2014) 'On a Radical Politics for Human Rights', in C. Douzinas and C. Gearty (eds), *The Meanings of Rights: The Philosophy and Social Theory of Human Rights*, Cambridge: Cambridge University Press, 106–120.

Wilson, R. A. (ed.) (2005) *Human Rights in the 'War on Terror'*, Cambridge: Cambridge University Press.

Žižek, S. (2010) 'A Permanent Economic Emergency', *New Left Review*, 64: n.p.

Chapter 2

The excesses of human rights

Beginning to think of a futural future for human rights

Introduction

Throughout their history human rights have become closely tied to particular discourses; liberalism, free market capitalism, internationalism and statism have largely come to dominate how rights are understood, and rights in turn have become a tool in supporting and reinforcing such regimes.[1] This history has served to narrate human rights in certain ways, leading in particular to perceptions of human rights as a discourse which is severely limited in what it can offer political groups and activists interested in working towards meaningful challenge to restrictive regimes of power (Wall 2012: 10). In beginning to think through the links between human rights and more radical possibilities, this chapter recalls some of the historical foundations of human rights which explain why rights have been considered limited in radical utility, but also returns to other less dominant histories of rights which demonstrate that human rights are not *necessarily* tied to the above discourses. These alternative histories existing in parallel to the mainstream have been advanced as indicating that human rights always exist in excess of their dominant articulation and are characterised by a capacity to be rethought in more radical ways. Alternative approaches to human rights have always been spectrally present alongside the mainstream, challenging their articulation in ways which cohere with liberalism, capitalism, internationalism and statism, and associated power relations. These parallel histories have been central to much thinking on possibilities to radicalise rights and, therefore, pose a starting point indicating that a new future for human rights compatible with meaningful challenge to power can be brought into being.

With this context in mind, the chapter moves to introduce an important, and longstanding, question which drives and provides the central focus of the present work: what might this future look like? In beginning to envisage a useful and holistic contemporary radical re-engagement with human rights, I propose that it is possible to productively stay with the notion of excess. This involves considering the idea that human rights do not only always exist in excess of their mainstream or hegemonic form, as demonstrated through their parallel histories, but can be thought of as *driven by* excess. Currently dominant articulations of human rights may be understood as always open to interpretation, expansion and debate on what they may mean anew. The politics of human rights accordingly can be characterised as ongoing activity to rework the meanings of rights based upon that which currently lies outside them, in other words, their excess. Human rights are constantly articulated and rearticulated in attempts to respond to such excesses and cannot exist outside of this process. While this process of articulation and rearticulation has largely remained within a conservative frame in mainstream understandings of rights, it holds radical potential when it is combined with a critical approach to power and the excess of human rights is viewed as linked to alterity in line with wider social relations of power. It is asserted that this potential can be added to by foregrounding the fact that human rights will *never* be free from alterity to highlight human rights and their politics as permanently unsettled and unfinished, always striving towards a fully formed conception of themselves – and of our relations of living and being together more generally – which eradicates alterity. This leads to a futural view of human rights which sustains a critical relation to alterity in the process of articulation and rearticulation, and directs human rights towards a futural horizon which is self-refuting. Combining this futural view with critical re-engagement with the underpinnings of human rights a new approach to rights and their practice emerges which is more amenable to use in radical politics interested in advancing the position of the marginalised and challenging dominant power regimes. This is the approach articulated by the concept of 'human rights to come'.

Mainstream history of human rights: liberalism, capitalism, internationalism and statism

The history of human rights is long and diverse, stemming as far back as ancient thought and finding resources in a variety of locations from religious to secular sources, natural law to contemporary international relations (Lauren 2011: 5–42). Discussion here does not seek to comprehensively encapsulate or plot such history; work towards such ends can be found elsewhere.[2] What it does seek to do, however, is to draw attention to key points in the history of rights which demonstrate why human rights in their dominant, mainstream form have developed as a discourse which is difficult for contemporary radical politics to appropriate before exploring some of the alternative histories of human rights existing alongside this mainstream history which indicate an excess characterising human rights. Considering the historico-theoretical development of rights, it is clear how discourses of liberalism, capitalism, internationalism and statism have come to define dominant understandings of human rights today and have rendered the discourse a not immediately obvious tool of use in radical thought and activism. Three broad stages in the history of human rights help illustrate how this is so, and these are overviewed below: the classical liberal origins of human rights; modern conceptions in the twentieth century; and the contemporary development of human rights in the twenty-first century.

First, it can be noted that human rights have been perceived as a fundamentally liberal discourse.[3] The early origins of human rights are often traced to the work of seventeenth-century classical liberal and natural law theorists such as Hobbes and Locke (Shapiro 1989: 80–150). This appears a natural beginning for understanding how human rights developed to bolster and reflect the liberal tradition and its focus on individualism, the protection of property and contract-driven social relations. Informed by conceptions of natural rights and the changing relationship between the individual and state outlined in the work of Hobbes and Locke, the development of human rights is ingrained with the 'possessive individualism' Crawford MacPherson identified as defining classical liberal thought generally (1962: 2). As MacPherson elaborated, this possessiveness is found in the classical liberal conception of the individual as 'essentially the proprietor of his own person or capacities, owing nothing to society for them' (1962: 3). These possessive assumptions of classical liberal thinking, for MacPherson, correspond to the actual relations of a market economy (1962: 4). From this problem of possessiveness characterising the liberal subject, a desire to possess property was produced as an imperative and natural part of human personhood in classical liberal theory and wider liberal democracy, foregrounding the atomised individual and the wider capitalist system in which they are located.

Such possessive individualism is abundantly clear in Locke's *Second Treatise*, considered a key document in the early origins of rights (Neier 2012: 30–32). While on first blush this appears a text offering revolutionary potential and crucial in driving the French and American Revolutions, as Illan Wall outlines, Locke's conception of the right to revolt is 'fundamentally preconfigured by the question of property', and 'by placing property above revolution' Wall suggests it is clear to see 'why revolution falls away from subsequent human rights discourse' (2012: 30). This focus on property in Locke's thinking and conception of natural rights was significant in the development of the discourse of rights such as the French Declaration of the Rights of Man and of the Citizen, and appears from the outset as facilitating the link between what we now understand as human rights and capitalist regimes.[4] The possessive individualism of classical liberal-informed rights has underpinned human rights as a discourse serving to conserve property from undue interference, protecting the bounded individual's possessions and this individual *as* possession as opposed to facilitating engagements with the interdependency and fundamental *dis*possession interdependent life necessarily entails.[5] Accordingly, the historic development of human rights stemming from classical liberalism makes it difficult to render human rights an instrument of dispossession, something unsettling to hegemonic relations and conceptions of living and being together in liberal, capitalist societies. As David Chandler states, 'far from challenging the individual isolation and passivity of our atomised societies, human rights regulation can only institutionalise these divisions' (2006: 230), thereby marginalising social solidarity and reinforcing a decontextualised, disembodied property owner as the ultimate subject of rights.[6]

The development of human rights in a manner which is generally incompatible with political aims to trouble current regimes of power in a radical way continued in the modern period, which marks the second stage of development to note in the mainstream history of human rights. The term 'modern period' here refers to the period from 1945 until the turn of the century when human rights came to emerge in their modern form as 'international human rights'.[7] In addition to further solidifying a conception of human rights based upon the possessive individual, and the relationship of rights to Western, liberal capitalist regimes and associated values,[8] the modern development of human rights is noteworthy for solidifying two additional trends which have come to shape such rights, namely internationalism and statism. In terms of the former, the liberal content of human rights – negative protection against arbitrary deprivation of life, protection of liberty, security of property, etc. – was positivised in international law in a way that generated a geographical and symbolic reach of such conceptions of rights previously impossible. In the post-Second World War period international human rights became a galvanising force for a new world order, for a common conception of humanity which centred upon liberal understandings of human flourishing and harm (Cheah 2006: 145–146). This proliferation of liberal-informed human rights on a global scale and the accompanying establishment of a plethora of international and regional mechanisms, forums and means of adjudicating on human rights was significant in marginalising alternative understandings of rights and has led to an alliance between human rights and global institutions of power which radical thinkers and activists are understandably uneasy with.

This alliance is linked to the trend of statism which the modern period of international human rights has also foregrounded. Throughout this period the state can clearly be seen as forming 'the very horizon of meaning of human rights' (Wall 2012: 34). In contrast to the earlier popular impetus behind the Declaration of the Rights of Man, for example, in the modern era the state has become the central actor in human rights discourse, despite the operation of international human rights to monitor and limit state action (Kennedy 2002: 113). The mechanisms to adjudicate on human rights, the conception of how rights protections are measured, and the predominant vertical conception of human rights protections are all directed towards the state as the central focus and driving force of modern human rights (Beitz 2009: 13). This move has served to make it very difficult to utilise human rights to visibilise and meaningfully challenge state power, to foreground problematic relations of power beyond the subject–state relation, and for grassroots activists to displace the state as the central actor, so legitimising political engagements with human rights beyond formal politico-legal forums. The state has been designated in the modern era as the gatekeeper of human rights, defining who has rights and in what way, and what rights and the suffering they seek to protect against mean (Baxi 1998: 132).

The third stage significant in the development of human rights in ways that have generally prohibited more radical usages or engagements occurred in what may be called the contemporary period, from 2001 until the present. The 2001 attacks on the Pentagon and World Trade Center and the subsequent 'War on Terror' which has dominated the international agenda initiated significant implications for human rights discourse which further reified limitation of the radical potential of rights.[9] The power and legitimacy of predominantly Western states to maintain hegemonic control over law and politics at both the international and national level has been bolstered in this context, meaning that law, human rights law in particular, has often become a tool of sovereign governmentality (Butler 2006: 50–100). Human rights have been suspended, denied to certain populations, even utilised to justify violent military action in the interests of political, economic and class power.[10] In this era grassroots and bottom-up engagements with rights have also been dramatically marginalised following a reinforcement of top-down power (Reilly 2009: 17). Moreover, particular groups, such as women and lesbian, gay, bisexual, transgender and intersex activists, have come up against tension in utilising human rights given the enhanced focus on religious fundamentalism and masculinist scripts of defence and security (Reilly 2009: 17, 140–159). The result is that in this period human rights have been further tied to Western elite political agendas as opposed to protecting the most marginalised, a trend which has continued into the crisis of capitalism unfolding since 2008.[11] Accordingly, and unsurprisingly, the chasm between the discourse of human rights and radical politics has widened given the elite, state-driven use of human rights, which developments in the post-2001 period have only served to reinforce.

The insights above mapping the shaping of human rights in line with discourses of liberalism, capitalism, internationalism and statism form the basis of many critical engagements with rights.[12] These engagements, drawing from a range of resources including Marxism, post-Marxist thought, psychoanalysis and poststructuralism, have done much to demonstrate that the history framing and narrating human rights is often one that is not readily amenable to the aims of radical politics. Some have also simultaneously engaged in a 'critical redemption' of rights (Golder 2014) or, to return to the comments of Douzinas highlighted previously, a 'rights revisionism' (2010: 81), which seeks to reconceptualise or recover some political usages for rights despite their less than radical development and conceptualisation in line with problematic discourses. Following on from these latter writings, the present work asserts that human rights may be productively re-engaged in contemporary times in order to challenge, instead of merely reinforcing, the restrictive regimes of power that shape our living and being. What it advances is required in doing so is a holistic reapproach to human rights which radicalises both their underpinning theoretical foundations and their practice in an accessible way that speaks to and builds upon already existing radical work and what is known about human rights. The particular roots of this assertion, and the form such reapproaching can productively be thought to take, are located in an understanding that liberal, capitalist, internationalised and statist approaches to human rights may be hegemonic, may considerably shape what we can see, hear and conceive of as possible in relation to human rights, but they do not exhaust the possibilities for human rights discourse. Human rights can be productively thought of as *always existing in excess of their dominant or mainstream articulation*, an unfixed discourse (Douzinas 2007: 55–56; 2000a: 253–261). This excess can be capitalised on to begin to conceive of alternative approaches to human rights which are more amenable to the aims of radical politics in the sense of challenging and reworking dominant regimes of power towards less exclusive and restrictive possibilities for our lives together.

In visibilising such it is useful to consider the way in which understandings and usages of human rights have not always remained within the boundaries outlined above. Human rights are not necessarily a discourse which can only serve to address injustices within the parameters of current regimes of power. For example, as has been well established, international law's shaping of human rights in the modern period overlooks historic usages of rights as tools of sedition.[13] Parallel histories of human rights can be detected existing alongside the dominant where rights have been used and thought of as capable of challenging hegemonic discourses and regimes such as liberalism, capitalism, internationalism and statism. In the section to follow a number of instances across the history of rights where the idea and language of human rights has been conceived of in such an alternative way are explored to lay foundations for the thinking of human rights to come as a re-engagement with the fundamentally excessive discourse of rights which may usefully reclaim rights for the aims of contemporary radical social transformation.

Human rights as existing in excess: parallel histories

It is often easy for the mainstream history of human rights to dominate how such rights and the possibilities they offer are perceived. The above history tying human rights with liberal, capitalist, internationalist and statist discourses does after all have the backing of international law and powerful global institutions such as the United Nations. While radical activists may feel it is unfruitful to attempt to engage with human rights in alternative ways in such a context, that space for resistance is almost non-existent, the historical development of human rights also clearly reveals that resistant interpretations of rights have been present throughout their history. Three moments in the history of rights are considered below where the discourse has been thought or used in ways to resist, as opposed to reinforce, dominant regimes of power. It is important to note that these examples are not presented here as new revelations; such histories will no doubt be familiar to those working within leftist and critical scholarship. Human rights have long been considered an essentially contested concept which is open to appropriation,[14] and alternative readings of the histories of rights have been advanced as gesturing towards some form of radicalism in human rights.[15] Rather, the aim in recalling these parallel histories is to encourage a revisitation of these moments specifically as moments of excess and to consider excess as defining the very idea of human rights. From this it may be possible to utilise an appreciation of the excess which inherently characterises human rights as a point of rupture to begin to think a contemporary alternative future for human rights proposed via the idea of human rights to come.

The first example which can be engaged in signalling towards the excess characterising human rights relates to early possibilities for thinking rights beyond possessive individualism, property and its tie to free market capitalism. While, as outlined above, the Hobbesian and Lockean underpinnings of modern human rights did centre upon a possessive individual and the protection of this individual's property, some thinking in the seventeenth century put forward alternative conceptions of rights and property. One instance Wall points to in his consideration of the early origins of rights is the writings of Gerrard Winstanley. A Digger, or 'True Leveller', thinker, Winstanley opposed ownership and in his writings 'instead of the demand that the subject of politics is the propertied gentleman, we find the radical levelling assertion of equality of even the basest of the world' (Wall 2012: 30).[16] Winstanley and other Diggers squatted on land of wealthy property owners in the mid 1600s, challenging the property rights claims of such owners through a form of primitive communism focused on the right of the poor to use land to survive. Here, as Wall states, 'the concept of the commons returns to rupture the naturalization of the conceptions of property that we find in this era' (2012: 30). In this view, espoused at around the same period as Hobbes and Locke, the relationship between rights and property is rethought. Early ideas of rights, equality and freedom were not exclusively tied to possessive individualism, and a conception of rights was practised based on alternative, more communal conceptions of property and being together.[17] From this it is possible to begin to detect how, even from the theoretical origins of the seventeenth century, human rights could have been developed otherwise, how rights and their underpinnings were from the beginning in excess of their classical liberal articulation as per Hobbes and Locke, and how possibilities beyond possessive individualism and free market capitalism have always been present in the history of rights.

A second example can be found in early feminist activism such as that of Olympe de Gouges in the late eighteenth century. Frustrated by the limited role which the Declaration of the Rights of Man and of the Citizen was playing in relation to women in revolutionary France, de Gouges penned the Declaration of the Rights of Women and the Female Citizen in 1791. This document, drawing from, and in places parodying, the original Declaration of the Rights of Man and of the Citizen sought to reveal, and contest, the relationship between rights and gender. In doing so, de Gouges challenged dominant conceptions of equality and the subject of rights, stemming from classical liberal and natural law thinking among others, that came to inform rights discourse. She observed that while women could lose their life following public judgement at the guillotine, they were not permitted access to political life; they were not truly considered equal citizens. De Gouges's act of writing the 1791 Declaration sought to rearticulate rights, to boldly use rights in an alternative way to challenge dominant ideas of rights which were exclusive, to speak to invisibilised power regimes and make audible the experience of those on the margins. At the time while rights were being put to an ostensibly radical use in the French Revolution they were still tied to understandings of equality and citizenship which reflected the individual as man. The work of de Gouges demonstrated that rights could be imagined in a way that went beyond these dominant understandings, that they could be used to initiate a more radical challenge to the established order of things than was hitherto the case.[18]

A third, and more recent, example of action revealing human rights as in excess of their historical tying to discourses of statism in particular can be found in activism surrounding migrant rights from the 1990s onwards. While modern human rights concepts such as the right to equality, the right to work and right to be free from torture and inhumane and degrading treatment appear relevant protections for migrants, these concepts have been traditionally interpreted in a way that coheres with the agendas of Western states, state sovereignty and liberal capitalist economy which benefit from the suppression of migrant rights, especially socio-economic rights. In the late twentieth century migrants and their advocates began to utilise the state-centric language of human rights in a manner that worked against the interests of states and couched their claims increasingly as rights claims.[19] In this way the 'counter-hegemonic discourse of migrants' rights provide[d] the language to the excluded groups of migrants ... to claim rights from which these migrants are excluded' (Basok 2009: 190). Work using the language of human rights to advance the interests of migrant communities has remained important in the post-2001 context which has effected heightened precarity for those who lack citizenship within Western nation states. Thus, in this period, when migrants have couched their claims in the language of rights they have often been engaging an interpretation of rights which is in excess of the highly nationalised, state-centric approach dominant in the contemporary era. Such action demonstrates that the discourse of human rights can be utilised to work towards more inclusive, less violent ways of living and being together, detaching rights from the agendas of Western nation states.

These are just three examples where the theoretical underpinnings and usages of human rights have demonstrated themselves in excess through thinkings of rights that depart from hegemonic regimes and discourses such as liberalism, capitalism, internationalism and statism and related power relations. In returning to such parallel histories often invisibilised or whitewashed within mainstream rights discourse it is possible to see how the discourse and practice of human rights can be thought anew, specifically in more radical ways. Human rights are not ineradicably tied to any particular discourse or regime; while the currently hegemonic discourse of international human rights may be problematic and restrictive in terms of advancing radical political aims, this is not all there is to human rights. As Douzinas states, 'the concept of rights is flexible rather than stable, fragmented rather than unitary and fuzzy rather than determinant' (2000a: 254). In other words, human rights is a discourse that exists in excess of attempts to contain it. This is not to say that alternative approaches to human rights will be, or have always been, successful or are capable of completely debunking the dominant, but it is to say that the discourse of human rights can be returned to in ways that go beyond the traditional boundaries of what rights can do, say and achieve.

Therefore, given the excess characterising the history of human rights rendering such capable of alternative, more radical usages and conceptualisations, the task is to find a way of alternatively approaching human rights in the contemporary period which allows rights to emerge as potential tools of radicalisation, a site to challenge as opposed to merely reinforce dominant discourses of power. Various suggestions have been put forward as to how this may be achieved.[20] Building on, although at times taking a different direction from, such previous work I assert that a convincing alternative way of approaching human rights can be facilitated through the idea of human rights to come, a means of radically re-engaging human rights which is holistic, in the sense of offering an interrelated reapproach to both the theoretical underpinnings and the practice of rights that is thus accessible for radical thinkers as well as activists, movements and groups. However, how may we begin to engage further with this concept and the approach to human rights it advances? Characterising the parallel histories of human rights as visibilising moments of excess is important because it not only helps re-narrate the past of human rights, but it can also help in beginning to understand the more radical future for human rights that human rights to come proposes. The particular contours of this future start to come into focus by staying with the idea of excess, conceiving the discourse of human rights as not only developed and used throughout its history in excess of liberalism, capitalism, internationalism and statism, but also by conceiving human rights and their politics as *driven by* excess.

Human rights as driven by excess and a futural future: human rights to come

If understanding human rights as driven by excess is important in grounding the more radical conception and usage of rights which the concept of human rights to come advances, the first question we must ask is what does this understanding mean? Human rights emerge as driven by excess when we consider that currently dominant articulations of rights are open to interpretation and expansion, and debate over the particular inadequacies or limitations constituting these articulations or the possibilities of what they could mean forms the basis of human rights politics. The politics of human rights can be thought of as an ongoing activity to rework the meanings of rights based upon their excess. Human rights are constantly articulated and rearticulated in attempts to respond to such excess and cannot exist outside of this process. Any human rights concept – equality, liberty, life, etc. – has demonstrated itself as open to shifting and modulation throughout the history of rights. In order to meet the demands of a particular time, context or circumstance rights concepts have been rearticulated to varying degrees and political engagement surrounding rights has centred on such. In mainstream approaches to human rights, particularly as international human rights, this ongoing articulation and rearticulation stemming from the excessive character of rights has been recognised and embraced, but has largely remained within a conservative frame; modifying the surface reach, remit or understanding of rights concepts while not disrupting their underpinnings at a deeper level. However, the fact that human rights and their politics may be understood as driven by excess holds potential to be exploited in a more radical way. This is possible when the excess characterising human rights is brought into view as linked to *alterity* in line with a critical approach to restrictive regimes of power more generally and processes of articulation and rearticulation are undertaken on this basis.

Indeed, it may be possible to return to the three examples gesturing towards the parallel histories of human rights outlined above to demonstrate where such has taken place and has allowed radical politics to exploit the fact that human rights are driven by excess. Winstanley's alternative approach to the idea of rights and property was based on an observation that rights to property did not have to be conceived of in terms of the possessive individual of classical liberalism; the relationship between rights and property was viewed as lying in excess of this. The excessiveness of this relationship for Winstanley and the Diggers was thought through alongside everyday experiences of alterity – those of the poor – and rearticulation of the relationship between rights and property to express a communal as opposed to possessive individual was undertaken on this basis. Similarly, Olympe de Gouges's demonstration that rights could be used to render a fundamental shift in contemporary discourses of gender and citizenship began by exposing the excess haunting dominant conceptions of the subject of rights as linked to alterity. Women appeared in excess of the subject of rights, lying outside what rights at the time were considered capable of saying, doing and achieving, and this was connected to wider relations of gendered power at the time. That sense of viewing excess as linked to alterity led to a rearticulation of rights and their subject to challenge that which was dominant. In addition, migrant rights, in articulating a conception of rights in contrast to the state-centric conception of international human rights, demonstrated rights concepts to be in excess of articulation to advance the aims of Western states. It did so by beginning with the fact that migrants and their experiences lay outside the discourses and usage of rights that appeared dominant and linked this to the wider experiences of marginalisation and alterity that migrant communities face within Western, capitalist economies. Following from understanding the excess characterising human rights in a more critical way, in line with experiences of alterity within current dominant regimes of power, each of these instances involved a rearticulation of human rights, capitalising on the fact that human rights are not only characterised by excess – capable of reappropriation – but also driven by excess – offering opportunities which are built into their politics for rearticulation anew.

Accordingly, excess can be considered as central in driving the politics of human rights and in facilitating moments where rights are utilised in a new way. While the rearticulation of human rights based on excess is not always radical, critical responses to excess, in the sense of viewing such as linked to alterity within a critical approach to power, may allow rights to be conceived of and used in a manner that goes beyond their dominant form and attachment to discourses such as liberalism, capitalism, internationalism and statism. From the examples above it is possible to see how this has taken place in various critical engagements with rights throughout their history. Following this analysis, the question I wish to pose is whether it might be possible to productively focus on human rights as driven by excess and use this as a starting point in alternatively approaching human rights in the contemporary period. It is asserted that this is possible, and when combined with a re-engagement with the underpinnings of human rights, both theoretical and practical, one means of conceiving rights as a discourse which may be exploited for radical ends emerges. To bring this into view, it is important to build upon earlier approaches which have viewed the excess of human rights as linked to alterity and engaged in processes of articulation and rearticulation on this basis by foregrounding one additional and important insight: the fact that human rights will *never* be free from excess linked to alterity. Human rights will always reflect some element of alterity. Embrace of this important insight can subsequently lead to a view of human rights as futural. It is this perspective that the idea of human rights to come seeks to advance as allowing a useful contemporary radical approach to human rights to emerge. Let us consider this further.

To begin with the assertion that human rights may productively be viewed as never free from alterity, radical thinkers are no doubt correct in suggesting that human rights are limited, that such limitations are often linked to wider problematic relations of power and what much radical work wants to achieve cannot be accomplished by the discourse as it presently stands in its dominant or mainstream form. Instead of stopping at this observation, allowing it to lead to a bypassing of the discourse and politics of human rights in radical thought and activism, what happens if we fully accept this assertion and look at it in a new way? The subject, remit and content of any conception of human rights will *always* be exclusive and restrictive in some way, always tied to a particular time, context or view of the world which cannot be fully inclusive. Human rights, no matter how hard we try to make them completely inclusive, will always demonstrate excess linked to alterity, requiring ongoing rearticulation. This fact indeed reflects our wider conditions of existence within relations of power; alterity will always be present. The ineradicable nature of alterity in human rights, instead of a negative attribute, may be perceived as offering opportunities to initiate critical claims responding to power across time and context, so allowing rights to emerge as potential tools of radicalisation. It is important to distinguish what is being advanced here from mainstream conceptions of human rights. Those advancing such conceptualisations may agree that articulation and rearticulation of human rights can never end, that the excess driving human rights can never be eradicated, but this perspective lacks radical impetus in that it is not underpinned by a critical approach to power. In contrast, when excess is understood as linked to alterity within a critical relation to power it is necessary to engage in a deeper and constant scrutinising of currently restrictive regimes and discourses and so enter into a more critical relation to human rights and what they may be perceived as capable of meaning, doing and achieving in such contexts. Importantly for radical activists seeking to utilise human rights in everyday politics, this view of ongoing critical activity engaging with alterity visibilises rights not as top-down concepts but places emphasis on grassroots activism. By conceiving human rights as constantly worked and reworked through a never-ending critical relation to ineradicable alterity, focus returns to bottom-up engagements with rights which draw attention to everyday experiences of exclusion. This holds particular potential to counter the closing off of bottom-up development of human rights in the post-2001 era. Only by transcending the state, the international and the top-down can rights meaningfully engage with alterity and come into view as a discourse or a site capable of effective exploitation by radical politics.

Taking a critical approach to the excess driving human rights and using it to ground a new understanding of human rights to come, therefore, involves approaching rights politics as not about claiming, applying or enforcing already existing articulations of human rights, but about challenging and debating human rights based on the inevitable alterity and exclusion of current rights concepts and ideas. This constant working and reworking of the alterity of current rights concepts which defines rights and their politics must necessarily characterise human rights as an unsettled project. When we foreground the fact that rights can never be free from alterity human rights emerge as unfinished norms to be rearticulated in an ongoing way which may be harnessed to advance the claims of those on the margins. This understanding introduces a fundamentally *futural* conception of human rights and a future for human rights in the futural. This insight is at the heart of the idea of human rights to come. Following on from the view of human rights as driven by excess linked to ineradicable alterity, radical thinkers and activists can be encouraged to understand the politics of human rights as a never-ending activity striving towards achievement of a perfect conception of rights, and relations of living and being more generally, which is freed from alterity. Such a conception is an impossibility forming the horizon of rights politics which, despite its impossibility, must nevertheless be striven towards. Because a fully perfected conception always remains an impossibility, the critical approach to alterity and power can never end. From this the central message of human rights to come emerges; a perfect conception of human rights freed from alterity must always remain 'to come' in the Derridean sense of a self-refuting promise.[21] The 'to come' of human rights is not a reason to abandon rights and their politics but, on the contrary, a reason for radical thinkers and activists to engage in the politics and practice of human rights. It is the very promise and utility of rights, the sustenance of a never-ending critical relation to power and critique of alterity within the politics of rights, and thereby the underlying reason why rights may be reclaimed in and by radical politics. In this view, the temporality of rights is disrupted. Human rights emerge as a becoming, something we are searching for, yet something that we also have, must grapple with, in the present (Douzinas 2007: 296–297). The concept of human rights to come seeks to propose a way in which we may draw out and radically exploit the promise of human rights which, as Anna Grear describes, 'constantly draws the human imagination forwards, but is ever-deferred, always "not yet"' (2012: 26). In approaching human rights as human rights to come, current understandings of rights become undone and it is necessary to engage with rights as never taking a final or settled form, unaware of how they will develop but containing the promise of a perfect future in the present. Again, this does not undermine the power or utility of rights, but enhances their potential to achieve radical change, to be put to various usages in unpredictable and uncontainable ways towards a futural horizon of perfect relations of inclusion and power which always remains 'to come'.

In considering what it means to conceive of human rights as futural concepts which are 'to come', it is instructive to consider previous work that has conceived of human rights as futural in a critical sense, most notably that of Douzinas.[22] Reading the history of human rights from natural law onwards through utopian resources and the writings, in particular, of Ernest Bloch,[23] Douzinas asserts that 'the tradition of human rights, from the classical invention of nature against convention to contemporary struggles for political liberty and human dignity against state law, has always expressed the perspective of the future or the "not yet"' (2000a: 145). Douzinas seeks to recover rights from what he deems 'their dubious respectability' in the modern period (2000a: 376) and consider the way in which 'human rights are the utopian element behind legal rights ... [the] claim to justice [of liberal legal systems] and as such impossible and futural looking' (2000a: 245). From this analysis, human rights hold radical promise because they are futural, always gesturing towards the 'not yet' and critique. Accordingly, in Douzinas's seminal conclusion, 'the end of human rights comes when they lose their utopian end' (2000a: 380). This reading of human rights highlighting the significance of the futural is fundamental in informing the concept of human rights to come. Indeed, the idea of human rights to come may be thought of as taking up possibilities for radically re-engaging human rights after Douzinas, asking more of how it may be possible to further utilise and fully exploit a focus on the futural in human rights for contemporary radical politics. After Douzinas's assertion of the promise of the 'not yet' in human rights how can this be foregrounded and practically acted upon in order to offer meaningful possibilities for re-engaging human rights in radical work? How can we move to, in Douzinas's view, reclaim the utopian promise of human rights from hijack by governments, treaties and ever-increasing formalisation of human rights? These are the questions which the concept of human rights to come seeks to respond to. It aims to bring a conception of human rights as futural, following on from a critical approach to the alterity always haunting rights, into conversation with the theoretical and practical underpinnings of rights more generally to advance a new holistic approach to human rights which is of use in radical thought and politics. In this view both a conception of human rights as futural and the need to underpin rights with alternative resources and ideas to those advanced within mainstream conceptions of rights are important. These elements work together and complement one another.

In the chapters to follow, a futural conception of human rights is thought in conversation with radical re-engagements with the key underpinnings of rights; how rights are approached as a politico-legal activity, how the universality of human rights is understood, the ideas of consensus and conflict in the politics of human rights, the ontological foundations of human rights and, importantly, how we can conceive of and approach the practice of human rights. These elements are reconsidered to begin to elucidate the idea of human rights to come and to radically take up the challenge of the 'not yet' of human rights in the contemporary era. To advance this view and draw the contours of the concept of human rights to come, alternative resources to that of Douzinas will be engaged. While Douzinas draws upon the work of Marxist thought, psychoanalysis and a range of poststructuralist resources, articulation of the concept of human rights to come will, as outlined previously, focus on alternative resources, including critical legal thought, radical democratic thinking and feminist perspectives. I assert that these resources can be used to further productively grapple with the possibility of a futural conception of human rights and expand understanding of what it might mean to engage in a holistic re-engagement with human rights, both their theoretical underpinnings and their practice, on this basis. In this sense while the conception of human rights to come is informed by previous work to radically re-engage rights, it also seeks to move discussion forward, focusing in particular on the intersection between theoretical and practical re-engagements and the way in which alternative resources may assist in a contemporary foregrounding and exploitation of the futural in rights.

Conclusion: the future of the history of human rights

By considering the theoretical, political and legal history of human rights it is clear that these rights have developed in particular ways, aligning with and advancing particular structures, discourses and interests which are not always amenable to the aims of radical politics. Indeed, discourses such as liberalism, capitalism, internationalism and statism which have become integral to the contemporary human rights regime in its dominant form are the very discourses which such politics seeks to challenge and dismantle. However, rather than abandoning human rights following this observation, radical activists and thinkers may productively return to the fact that parallel, non-hegemonic histories of rights can also be detected which demonstrate the radical potential which human rights hold as a discourse always in excess of their dominant articulations. Characterising such alternative histories in terms of excess is important because the excess characterising human rights which these alternative histories demonstrate can be thought of in another way: as also gesturing towards the way in which human rights are driven by excess in their need for ongoing articulation and rearticulation. This drive offers radical possibilities when the excess of human rights is grasped as linked to alterity within a critical approach to power, and such can offer the starting point for a new future for human rights when rights are understood as never free from alterity, always needing to be subject to critical articulation and rearticulation and therefore unsettled concepts which may be understood as futural, directing towards the promise of a perfect horizon which remains self-refuting.

Human rights to come seeks to capitalise on the excess of human rights and work towards a more radical future and possible usages for rights beyond their current mainstream articulation and the state-driven, top-down appropriation of rights discourse which has emerged and been solidified in the modern period. Human rights to come is a concept which may be utilised in radical politics to envisage a new way of approaching the theoretical underpinnings and practice of human rights which foregrounds the futural, the inability for human rights to be finally articulated, and the possibilities for rearticulation to challenge the exclusions and alterity of current rights concepts and discourse. Understanding human rights as human rights to come involves foregrounding that the subject, the meaning, the content of human rights can always be otherwise and envisaging the task of rights politics as being about initiating and sustaining ongoing discussion over what these elements should look like in contingent locations, responding to contextualised restrictive regimes of power. The politics of human rights in this understanding becomes a never-ending and futural politics of excess, of critically reworking the exclusions and alterity which any conception of human rights inevitably contains and which is reflective of dominant regimes of power more generally. In this view, human rights begin to move away from much of what characterises them within liberalism; they begin to escape the containment of international human rights structures and return to offer radical possibilities, to be tools of sedition and challenge. It is to further articulation of the concept of human rights to come in relation to the theory and practice of human rights that discussion will now turn.

Notes

1 See Wendy Brown (2004); Cheah (2006: 145); Baxi (2002: 38–39); Dine and Fagan (2006).
2 See, for example, Ishay (2004); Hunt (2007); Lauren (2011); Donnelly (2013a: 65–91); Herbert (2002).
3 Liberalism is of course a contested concept, as is the nature of the connection between liberalism and human rights. For one perspective on the link between human rights and liberalism, see Donnelly who states that 'the international Bill of Human Rights rests on an implicit model of a liberal democratic (or social democratic) welfare state. The legitimate state . . . is democratic: Political authority arises from the sovereignty of the people. It is liberal: The state is seen as an institution to establish the conditions for the effective realisation of the rights of its citizens. It is a welfare state: Recognised economic and social rights extend well beyond the libertarian rights to property. And all three elements are rooted in the overriding and irreducible moral equality of all members of society and the political equality and autonomy of all citizens' (1999: 68).
4 The link between human rights, capitalism and property has been explored by many, in particular the work of Susan Marks (2008) and wider contemporary Marxist scholars.
5 For further discussion on dispossession and its potential, see Butler and Athanasiou (2013).

6 See further Grear (2010: 50–67).
7 For discussion, see Haas (2014); Donnelly (2013b); Shelton (2014); Hoffmann (2011); Neier (2012); Lauren (2011); Moyn (2010: 176–211).
8 See Pollis and Schwab (1979); Twining (2007).
9 See Baxi (2009: 156–196); Kapur (2006); Goodhart and Mihr (2011); Brysk and Shafir (2007).
10 See Denike (2008); Wilson (2005); Duffy (2015: 543–581).
11 For discussion, see Nolan (2015).
12 A non-exhaustive list of such engagements includes Douzinas (2000a); Brown (2000, 2004); Baxi (2002); Marks (2008); Golder (2013).
13 Rancière (2004: 305–306); Douzinas (2000a: 244); Wall (2014); Zerilli (2005: 120).
14 See, for example, Florian Hoffmann (2012: 82–83); Kapur (2006: 670); Freeman (2011: 11).
15 On this point, see Douzinas (2000a); Wall (2014). Indeed, as Zachary Manfredi comments, 'much of the recent debate about human rights revolves around asking how we are to narrate their history' (2013: 10).
16 See, for example, Winstanley (2009).
17 See further, Hudson (1946); Fields (2003: 8–9).
18 For wider discussion of Olympe de Gouges and thought on the link between women and rights during this period, see Rancière (2004); Scott (1989); Diamond (1994).
19 See further Nyers and Rygiel (2012).
20 These include, for example, Douzinas (2000a); Grear (2010); Wall (2012).
21 See, for example Derrida (2005a; 2005b). For Derrida, the 'to come' – *à venir* – articulated in relation to his thinking of democracy and justice, for example, does not refer to a future that will one day become present but to a structural future, a promise, that will never be actualised in any present. Rather than a future present it refers to the absolute future of pure invention, the order of the impossible (Patton 2007: 772). The 'to come' in Derrida's sense is both constative and performative; an open-ended description of the idea of democracy or justice, but also a demand for more (Patton 2007: 773).
22 See also Golder (2010); Fitzpatrick (2007) and Upendra Baxi's brief footnoted analysis of the declaratory nature of human rights covenants as making statements 'about rights-in-the-making or even human rights "to come"' (2012: 157).
23 See further, Douzinas (2000b). For more on the intersections between human rights and utopia specifically, see, for example, Moyn (2010) and Goodale (2009).

References

Basok, T. (2009) 'Counter-hegemonic Human Rights Discourses and Migrant Rights Activism in the US and Canada', *International Journal of Comparative Sociology*, 50(2): 183–205.
Baxi, U. (1998) 'Voices of Suffering and the Future of Human Rights', *Transnational Law and Contemporary Problems*, 8(2): 125–170.
Baxi, U. (2002) *The Future of Human Rights*, Oxford: Oxford University Press.
Baxi, U. (2009) *Human Rights in a Posthuman World: Critical Essays*, Oxford: Oxford University Press.
Baxi, U. (2012) 'Reinventing Human Rights in an Era of Hyper-Globalisation: A Few Wayside Remarks', in C. Gearty and C. Douzinas (eds), *The Cambridge Companion to Human Rights Law*, Cambridge: Cambridge University Press, 150–170.
Beitz, C. (2009) *The Idea of Human Rights*, Oxford: Oxford University Press.

Brown, W. (2000) 'Suffering Rights as Paradoxes', *Constellations*, 7(2): 230–241.
Brown, W. (2004) '"The Most We Can Hope for ...": Human Rights and the Politics of Fatalism', *South Atlantic Quarterly*, 103(2–3): 451–463.
Brysk, A. and Shafir, G. (eds) (2007) *National Insecurity and Human Rights: Democracies Debate Counterterrorism*, Berkeley; Los Angeles: University of California Press.
Butler, J. (2006) *Precarious Life: The Powers of Mourning and Violence*, 2nd edn, London: Verso.
Butler, J. and Athanasiou, A. (2013) *Dispossession: The Performative in the Political*, Cambridge: Polity.
Chandler, D. (2006) *From Kosovo to Kabul and Beyond: Human Rights and International Intervention*, 2nd edn, London: Pluto.
Cheah, P. (2006) *Inhuman Conditions: On Cosmopolitanism and Human Rights*, Cambridge, MA: Harvard University Press.
Denike, M. (2008) 'The Human Rights of Others: Sovereignty, Legitimacy, and "Just Causes" for the "War in Terror"', *Hypatia*, 23(2): 95–121.
Derrida, J. (2005a) *The Politics of Friendship*, trans. G. Collins, London: Verso.
Derrida, J. (2005b) *Rouges: Two Essays on Reason*, Stanford, CA: Stanford University Press.
Diamond, M. J. (1994) 'The Revolutionary Rhetoric of Olympe de Gouges', *Feminist Issues*, 14(1): 3–23.
Dine, J. and Fagan, A. (2006) *Human Rights and Capitalism: A Multidisciplinary Perspective on Globalisation*, Cheltenham: Edward Elgar.
Donnelly, J. (1999) 'Human Rights and Asian Values: A Defense of "Western Universalism"', in J. Bauer and D. Bell (eds), *The East Asian Challenge for Human Rights*, Cambridge: Cambridge University Press, 60–87.
Donnelly, J. (2013a) *Universal Human Rights in Theory and Practice*, 3rd edn, Ithaca, NY: Cornell University Press.
Donnelly, J. (2013b) *International Human Rights*, Boulder, CO: Westview.
Douzinas, C. (2000a) *The End of Human Rights: Critical Legal Thought at the Turn of the Century*, Oxford: Hart.
Douzinas, C. (2000b) 'Human Rights and Postmodern Utopia', *Law and Critique*, 11(2): 219–240.
Douzinas, C. (2007) *Human Rights and Empire: The Political Philosophy of Cosmopolitanism*, New York; London: Routledge.
Douzinas, C. (2010) 'Adikia: On Communism and Rights', in C. Douzinas and S. Žižek (eds), *The Idea of Communism*, London: Verso, 81–100.
Duffy, H. (2015) *The 'War on Terror' and the Framework of International Law*, 2nd edn, Cambridge: Cambridge University Press.
Fields, A. Belden (2003) *Rethinking Human Rights for the New Millennium*, Basingstoke: Palgrave Macmillan.
Fitzpatrick, P. (2007) 'Is Humanity Enough? The Secular Theology of Human Rights Law', *Social Justice & Global Development Journal*, 1–14, available at: www.go.warwick.ac.uk/elj/lgd/2007_1/fitzpatrick (accessed 2 January 2017).
Freeman, M. (2011) *Human Rights: An Interdisciplinary Approach*, 2nd edn, Cambridge: Polity.
Golder, B. (2010) 'Foucault and the Unfinished Human of Rights', *Law, Culture and the Humanities*, 6(3): 354–374.
Golder, B. (2013) 'Foucault, Rights and Freedom', *International Journal for the Semiotics of Law*, 26(1): 5–21.

Golder, B. (2014) 'Beyond Redemption? Problematising the Critique of Human Rights in Contemporary International Legal Thought', *London Review of International Law*, 2(1): 77–114.

Goodale, M. (2009) *Surrendering to Utopia: An Anthropology of Human Rights*, Stanford, CA: Stanford University Press.

Goodhart, M. and Mihr, A. (eds) (2011) *Human Rights in the 21st Century: Continuity and Change*, New York: Palgrave Macmillan.

Grear, A. (2010) *Redirecting Human Rights: Facing the Challenge of Corporate Legal Humanity*, Basingstoke: Palgrave Macmillan.

Grear, A. (2012) '"Framing the Project" of International Human Rights Law: Reflections on the Dysfunctional "Family" of the Universal Declaration"', in C. Gearty and C. Douzinas (eds), *The Cambridge Companion to Human Rights Law*, Cambridge: Cambridge University Press, 17–35.

Haas, M. (2014) *International Human Rights: A Comprehensive Introduction*, London: Routledge.

Herbert, G. (2002) *A Philosophical History of Rights*, Brunswick, NJ: Transaction.

Hoffmann, F. (2012) 'Foundations beyond Law', in C. Gearty and C. Douzinas (eds), *The Cambridge Companion to Human Rights Law*, Cambridge: Cambridge University Press, 81–96.

Hoffmann, S. L. (ed.) (2011) *Human Rights in the Twentieth Century*, Cambridge: Cambridge University Press.

Hudson, W. (1946) 'Economic and Social Thought of Gerrard Winstanley: Was He a Seventeenth-Century Marxist?', *Journal of Modern History*, 18(1): 1–21.

Hunt, L. (2007) *Inventing Human Rights*, New York: Norton.

Ishay, M. (2004) *The History of Human Rights: From Ancient Times to the Globalization Era*, Berkeley: University of California Press.

Kapur, R. (2006) 'Human Rights in the 21st Century: Take a Walk on the Dark Side', *Sydney Law Review*, 28(4): 665–687.

Kennedy, D. (2002) 'The International Human Rights Movement: Part of the Problem?', *Harvard Human Rights Journal*, 15: 101–125.

Lauren, P. G. (2011) *The Evolution of International Human Rights: Visions Seen*, Philadelphia: University of Pennsylvania Press.

MacPherson, C. (1962) *The Political Theory of Possessive Individualism*, Oxford: Clarendon.

Manfredi, Z. (2013) 'Recent Histories and Uncertain Futures: Contemporary Critiques of International Human Rights and Humanitarianism', *Qui Parle*, 22(1): 3–32.

Marks, S. (ed.) (2008) *International Law on the Left: Re-examining Marxist Legacies*, Cambridge: Cambridge University Press.

Moyn, S. (2010) *The Last Utopia: Human Rights in History*, Cambridge, MA: Harvard University Press.

Neier, A. (2012) *The International Human Rights Movement: A History*, Princeton: Princeton University Press.

Nolan, A. (2015) 'Not Fit for Purpose? Human Rights in Times of Financial and Economic Crisis', *European Human Rights Law Review*, 4: 360–371.

Nyers, P. and Rygiel, K. (eds) (2012) *Citizenship, Migrant Activism and the Politics of Movement*, New York; London: Routledge.

Patton, P. (2007) 'Derrida, Politics and Democracy to Come', *Philosophy Compass*, 2(6): 766–780.

Pollis, A. and Schwab, P. (1979) 'Human Rights: A Western Construct with Limited Applicability', in A. Pollis and P. Schwab (eds) *Human Rights: Cultural and Ideological Perspectives*, New York: Praeger, 1–19.

Rancière, J. (2004) 'Who Is the Subject of the Rights of Man?', *South Atlantic Quarterly*, 103(2–3): 297–310.

Reilly, N. (2009) *Women's Human Rights: Seeking Gender Justice in a Globalizing Age*, Cambridge: Polity Press.

Scott, J. W. (1989) 'French Feminists and the Rights of "Man": Olympe de Gouges's Declarations', *History Workshop*, 28: 1–21.

Shapiro, I. (1989) *The Evolution of Rights in Liberal Theory*, Cambridge: Cambridge University Press.

Shelton, D. (2014) *Advanced Introduction to International Human Rights Law*, Cheltenham: Edward Elgar.

Twining, W. (2007) 'Human Rights: Southern Voices; Francis Deng, Abdullahi An-Na'im, Yash Ghai and Upendra Baxi', *Law, Social Justice & Global Development Journal*, available at: www.go.warwick.ac.uk/elj/lgd/2007_1/twining (accessed 2 January 2017).

Wall, I. (2012) *Human Rights and Constituent Power: Without Model or Warranty*, London; New York: Routledge.

Wall, I. (2014) 'On a Radical Politics for Human Rights', in C. Douzinas and C. Gearty (eds), *The Meanings of Rights: The Philosophy and Social Theory of Human Rights*, Cambridge: Cambridge University Press, 106–120.

Wilson, R. A. (ed.) (2005) *Human Rights in the 'War on Terror'*, Cambridge: Cambridge University Press.

Winstanley, Gerrard (2009) *The Complete Works of Gerrard Winstanley: Volume 1*, T. N. Corns, A. Hughes and D. Loewenstein (eds), Oxford: Oxford University Press.

Zerilli, L. (2005) *Feminism and the Abyss of Freedom*, Chicago: University of Chicago Press.

Chapter 3

(Re)Doing rights
The performativity of human rights to come

Introduction

This chapter begins to explore more of what it means to understand human rights as human rights to come by considering how this involves a particular approach to rights as a politico-legal activity; what is involved in the everyday use of rights, and how this can be theorised. As part of its radical re-engagement, the approach of human rights to come rejects understandings of the activity of human rights as made up of purely legalistic engagements between pre-existing subjects who possess rights as objects. Instead, it advances an understanding of the activity of human rights as a dynamic and generative *doing* that works to bring the content of rights, and the subjects who claim them, into being. Discussion will explore how human rights to come may, drawing from already existing accounts of rights as performative, be characterised as a performative doing. By involving ongoing practices of articulation and rearticulation to rework the limits of dominant human rights concepts and related restrictive regimes of power, human rights to come can be thought of as an inherently performative activity. However, discussion also highlights the way in which the idea advances something more in relation to the performative politico-legal activity of rights and so works to bring into view a slightly different perspective on rights as performative than has been advanced to date.

Following the chapter's first section introducing conceptions of rights as a politico-legal activity, this 'something more' is broken down into two elements. First, as explored in the second section, it is necessary to understand the activity of human rights to come as not just a performative doing but a performative doing *in futurity*. This involves bringing to the fore the interrelation between the present and the future in the performative and, in particular, highlighting the fact that the performative articulation and rearticulation of rights in the practice of human rights to come is towards a future that is self-refuting, characterising critical performative activity as without end. Second, as asserted in the third section, human rights to come involves not only a performative doing but a performative *re*doing of human rights. At its heart this concept seeks to reimagine and rework the discourse of human rights beyond liberalism and other problematic discourses, facilitating new forms, usages and possibilities for rights at a fundamental level. Through Butler's thinking on performative reiteration it is asserted that the performative nature of rights makes such a redoing possible, and that the activity of human rights to come involves reiterating the discourse of human rights to allow more radical conceptions and usages to emerge. By understanding and embracing these two elements the particular way in which human rights to come advances approaching rights as a performative activity comes into view.

From rights as objects to rights as a performative doing

To introduce how the re-engagement with human rights being asserted requires rights to be understood as a politico-legal activity, it is useful to explore how such has been thought more generally. A variety of perspectives on this issue have been advanced. In one such approach, which is usually associated with mainstream conceptions of human rights as international human rights, the activity of rights is conceived of as one where rights holders bring the rights they possess, or are seeking to advance that they possess, to a dispute or an oppressive situation, such an encounter involving either enforcement of those rights or a struggle with the rights of others.[1] In this view rights appear as pre-existing objects and the politico-legal activity of human rights consists of an application of these objects and/or a contest over them. This application or contest often takes place with reference to law, adjudicated on in a way that follows legal provisions and precedent of domestic or international law, and is thus resolved, it is advanced, in a relatively controlled and predictable manner (Douzinas 2000: 231–235). In this process, already existing human rights objects may be moved around or further articulated, one rights holder may receive recognition over another, the application of human rights may compel addressing of an injustice, but this activity is conceived of largely as working within already existing legal and/or social frameworks. This is the conception of the politico-legal activity of human rights that has in many ways been promoted by the increasing legalisation and codification of human rights in international law from 1945 onwards.

Reflecting on this approach, Karen Zivi comments that 'there is a tendency – common to both academic and everyday understandings of rights – to treat rights as objects or things that we have, the way we have arms or legs, and that we put to use for various purposes' (2012: 10). From the perspective of work seeking to utilise human rights for the ends of radical social transformation, this appears problematic. As Zivi continues, this approach demonstrates an accompanying tendency 'to reduce rights claims to statements about the world that can be verified or falsified or to depict them as purely instrumental claims whose democratic effect and outcome we can or should be able to control' (2012: 10). From this perspective both human rights and the subject who engages or claims rights pre-exist the practice of human rights and are not necessarily changed through this activity. Human rights, in this sense, are presented as primarily legalistic, relatively devoid of politics, or even 'above' politics.[2] This conception limits radical possibilities for rights by invisibilising the important way in which the politico-legal activity of rights is one that is generative, bringing certain effects into being through its doing, and how it shapes, even holds power to radically alter, our sense of self and the world around us at a fundamental level (Zivi 2012: 24).

While an understanding of rights as objects and the practice of rights as a primarily legalistic activity has dominated much mainstream thinking on human rights, this is not the only approach that has been advanced. An understanding of rights as a generative activity, in the way gestured towards above, is one that has increasingly emerged, especially in critical thinking on rights. In this contrasting approach, the politico-legal activity of human rights does not involve application of or contest over objects that pre-existing subjects possess; rather, this activity is a 'doing' which brings the effects rights describe, and the subjects who claim them, into being. This understanding has gained much traction and derives from performative theorising which began with the work of linguistic theorist J. L. Austin (1975). Austin's concept of performative utterances worked to illustrate how particular speech acts do more than just describe or reflect, but actually form a part of producing or constituting the world around us. In doing so, Austin highlighted the distinction between constative utterances – which express some state of affairs and are either true or false – and performative utterances – which in their uttering actually perform an action (1975: 1–11). Now famous examples of the latter from Austin's work include the utterance 'I do' in the context of a marriage ceremony as performatively bringing the marriage contract into being, and the utterance 'I name this ship . . .' in a ship-naming ceremony performing the act of naming (1975: 5–6).

Austin's work has been taken up and expanded in diverse ways; one of the most significant of these is found in the work of Judith Butler which has been particularly important in developing a concept of the performative in critical and radical thought.[3] In what is by now the most widely renowned element of her work, Butler appropriates Austin's idea that language is performative and uses this to theorise gender as a performative activity. The idea that performatives are concerned with effect through repetition forms the basis of Butler's consideration of the constituting and subjectivising workings of discourses of gender (2006: 198). Butler suggests that any subject's social persistence is premised on ongoing repetition of culturally acceptable norms of gender. These performative repetitions do not serve to reinforce a natural or innate gender identity but constitute the identity that they purport to be, so that 'gender is always a doing, though not a doing by a subject who might be said to pre-exist the deed' (Butler 2006: 34). Butler's use of performativity characterises gender as not a noun or a static cultural marker, but an incessant and repeated action within the everyday, contingent and performative construction of meaning (2006: 151).[4]

It is by no means an understatement to say that the term 'performativity' and the idea of the performative has proliferated across boundaries and disciplines and has proved a fruitful tool for critical analysis.[5] Thinking on human rights has not been immune to this trend, and various characterisations of the politico-legal activity of rights as a performative doing have been advanced. Commentators have drawn upon work such as that of Austin and Butler to demonstrate and think through the dynamic and generative doing that is involved in rights practices, using this to directly counter ideas of rights as pre-existing objects which are merely applied or drawn upon by pre-existing subjects. For example, Arabella Lyon asserts that,

> the utterance 'all human beings are born free and equal in dignity and rights' shares similarities with Austin's conforming performatives. Here through the felicitous criteria of an international procedure of ratification by a particular kind of people, the speech act constructs norms of freedom, equality and dignity.
>
> (2013: 76)

In this perspective, the assertion made through a right is a doing, working to bring effects into being, as opposed to a static legal provision contained within the confines of international treaties and used in a legalistic way. The right does something through its utterance. Taking a similar perspective, Linda Zerilli characterises rights as 'not things to be distributed from above, but a demand for something more made from below. Rights are not things, but relationship. As such they are not something we *have* but something we *do*' (2005: 122, emphasis in original).[6]

Perhaps the most comprehensive exploration of the relationship between rights and performativity can be found in Zivi's account of rights claiming as a performative practice.[7] For Zivi, 'to approach rights and rights claiming from the perspective of performativity means . . . asking questions not simply about what a right is but also about what it is we do when we make rights claims' (2012: 8). Zivi's characterisation of claiming rights as a performative doing, primarily through Austin although also utilising Butler, Derrida (1988) and Stanley Cavell (1976), means:

> attending to the ways in which the making of a claim such as 'I have a right to X' does far more than accurately (or perhaps inaccurately) represent a pre-existing moral, legal or political reality . . . A performative perspective on rights moves us from an almost exclusive focus on questions about what rights are to a more careful consideration of what it is rights do.
>
> (2012: 8)

This account allows us to see how claiming a right involves more than invocation of an object which the subject inherently possesses, but in fact works to bring relations of living and being into existence, serving to (re)create the world and subjects within it. In Zivi's view 'it is through the making of rights claims that we contest and constitute the meaning of individual identity, the contours of community, and the forms that political subjectivity take' (2012: 7). From this, the politico-legal activity of rights is a fundamentally interrelational activity that serves to 'not only constrain but also enable us in our relations with others' (Zerilli 2004: 82), a performative understanding of rights reminding us 'that our speaking is a social practice' (Zivi 2012: 8). Legalistic understandings often overlook this important intersubjective element of the practice of rights and its significance (Zivi 2012: 10). Rights, performatively conceived, hold important potential to shape how we relate to one another and who is understood as an intelligible subject.

This work exploring how performative theorising can be engaged to (re)consider rights as performative has been of use in facilitating moves beyond the dominant, legalistic understandings of rights which have accompanied the increasing codification of human rights. After such work it can no longer be said that rights are objects to be used or applied. The question that must be asked is how does this understanding fit with the idea of human rights to come? Engaging with the performative dynamic involved in human rights as a politico-legal activity is indeed central in beginning to understand the alternative approach to rights which human rights to come gestures towards, and the radical possibilities it may offer. Part of the work and the utility of this concept is to visibilise, and capitalise on, the important generative aspect of human rights which emerges when rights are considered a performative activity. When rights are reapproached as human rights to come, involving ongoing articulation and rearticulation to meet the ineradicable limits of currently dominant rights provisions, an inherently performative element comes to the fore. In making rights claims that look different, that contest the limits of the present, those engaging in the practice of rights are working to performatively bring such new conceptions into being. The process of articulation and rearticulation which is central to human rights to come can be conceived as performatively recreating rights ideas to become more expansive, to meet their present limitations. Such making of new rights claims also aims to performatively rework relations of alterity and power, bringing into being new possibilities for those who are marginalised or excluded from current rights concepts and/or wider conditions of intelligibility through the process of rearticulation. For example, when feminists assert that the right to life involves more than just the physical protection of life, but also attention to the conditions supporting life which may require women to have access to abortion provision, and never-ending societal reassessment of what is needed for a viable gendered life, they are performatively reworking not only how the right to life is understood but also how women as subjects are understood within wider relations of heteronormative and repronormative power.[8] While of course the performative activity of human rights to come may not always be successful in fully reworking dominant rights concepts or relations of power, this does not take away from the performative drive of this activity.[9] The idea of human rights to come, accordingly, engages and capitalises on the performativity of human rights to rework rights beyond their current limits, and to rework related restrictive relations of power, through processes of articulation and rearticulation that never end.

Resultantly, human rights must be understood as a dynamic doing that is constitutive, and holds potential to be radically disruptive, of the ideas and values human rights represent and of relations of living and being more generally. Approaching human rights as human rights to come stresses the creative and dynamic element of rights and their practice and, moreover, focuses attention on how it may be exploited in ways that allow human rights to become a vehicle to challenge restrictive regimes of power and advance the aims of radical politics. This understanding of human rights to come as a fundamentally performative activity involves drawing from earlier work such as that of Zivi to foreground how rights performatively serve to (re)create the world around us; however, it is important to note that it also involves something more. To understand how the idea of human rights to come enables a specifically futural approach to human rights that facilitates a radical rethinking of rights, it is necessary to extend beyond what has already been thought in relation to human rights and performativity and consider some elements of performativity as yet under-theorised in existing accounts of rights as performative. Human rights to come involves visibilising and foregrounding rights as a performative activity, but it also involves visibilising and foregrounding rights as a performative doing *in futurity* and as a performative *re*doing. In what follows, this assertion is explored considering, first, the productive relationship that may be conceived between the performativity of human rights to come and futurity, and, second, the way in which a conception of rights as a performative doing assists in advancing the overall aim of human rights to come which is to radically *re*do the discourse of human rights beyond their current form. By considering these two elements the idea of human rights to come as a performative politico-legal activity comes into greater view and it is also possible to see how this concept involves something more than just a taking up of existing thought on the performative nature of rights.

The performativity of human rights to come: a 'doing in futurity'

The articulation and rearticulation which serves to rework the limits of human rights, and their link to experiences of alterity more generally, defines human rights to come as a performative doing. However, when we add the fact that human rights can *never* be free from limitations, complete eradication of alterity remains to come, something more must be understood about the performative doing of human rights to come; it must be understood as having a futural element. As a result, this concept can be thought to foreground human rights not just as a performative doing, but also as a *doing in futurity*.[10] Understanding human rights to come as a performative doing that is definitively futural does not involve straying far from the underpinnings of performative thinking. Rather, on the contrary, it involves bringing into view the interconnection between the present and the future which is central to the performative, albeit not yet fully explored in performative accounts of rights. In what follows, this inherent link between the performative and the futural is considered as is the way in which human rights to come seeks to foreground this link.

The present and the future in the performative

At a basic level, the idea of performativity emerging from the work of Austin and Butler evidences a simultaneous interrelation between the present and the future. The act of making a performative utterance, for example, saying 'I do' for Austin, embodying particular bodily gestures that cohere with dominant ideas of masculinity/femininity for Butler, can be conceived of as doing something that is both now, a speech act or a gesture in the present, and futural, bringing something new into being (be it a marriage contract or a sexed/gendered identity). More than this, following Butler's conceptualisation of performativity, the concept of the performative doing can be seen to not only describe or provide an account of the generative activity in everyday life, it can also carry a sense that it is possible to do things *differently* and, therefore, holds the promise of a better future – utilising the performative nature of gender, for example, to imagine and bring into being a new, less limiting future of living and being sexed/gendered that is facilitated by doing the performative in a slightly different way in the present (2006: 187–193). Performativity must be understood as caught up with the everyday present – the here and now, revealing and critiquing its limitations – but also operating to bring something futural into being, even potentially working towards a future of better relations of living and being in the performative doing. It is in this way that the performative connects the present and the future, by its very nature acting in the present for the future, offering the promise of something beyond the here and now and working to bring it into being. Some further points emerge from this interrelation between the present and the future in the performative which must be considered.

When considering the futurity that is at the heart of the performative doing, it is important to note that the future that the performative gestures towards, and works to bring into being through performative activity in the present, is not one that is fully determined (Butler 2004: 190–191). The performative can never be utilised to facilitate the futural in a predictable sense. This idea of an uncertain future, one that evades full control, threads through performative thinking in different ways. In Austin's seminal account, the performative is not always guaranteed to succeed; conditions may not permit the performative to be felicitous. The performative doing can, for example, misfire, can suffer from some infelicitous condition that fails to bring into effect performative consequences, even where such was intended by the maker of the statement (Austin 1975: 12–24). In Butler's thinking, the unpredictability of the performative is an element that particularly comes to the fore. Butler highlights from her early work onwards the 'excitability' and temporality of performative speech acts which renders them out of control, unpredictable, citational and continually in need of repetition in order to maintain their dominant meaning (Butler 1997a; Jagger 2008: 14). Following from Butler's rejection of the sovereign subject, it is never possible to be fully in control of our performative utterances or doings, how they will be heard, taken up and, potentially, (re)appropriated.[11] Thus, while the performative doing in the now is always interrelated with the future, this interrelation is one that is itself unpredictable and always beyond sovereign control.

It is clear to see how the futurity of the performative holds much potential for radical politics, offering possibilities to challenge restrictive relations of power in the present and bring better futures into being, albeit these futures cannot be fully determined or controlled. However, additionally, while performativity as a critical tool in the Butlerian sense does serve to provide opportunities to bring into being a form of better relations of living and being, for example a broader range of ways to be sexed/gendered that violate the heteronorm, there is no indication that such critical performative work can ever end. A perfect form of sociopolitical relations of gender can never be finally achieved; alterity will always remain in some form.[12] While the performative act does bring something new, something of the future, into being, at the same time the overall vision of the future it gestures towards may be conceived of as always 'to come', possessing what Douzinas describes as 'the co-presence of present and future in the structure of the promise' (2007: 296). The futural, and utopian, promise of performativity is something that has been considered by José Muñoz. In his work, Muñoz highlights the performative as a doing for and towards the future or, in other words, 'a doing in futurity' (2009: 26). Viewing performativity as having a futural, utopian character, Muñoz comments that 'utopian performativity is often fuelled by the past. The past or at least narratives of the past, enable utopian imaginings of another time and place that is not yet here but nonetheless functions as a doing for futurity, a conjuring of both future and past to critique presentness' (2009: 109). The critique of the present in the performative for a better future is always ongoing, working towards a utopian horizon that is naturally self-refuting.

Futurity, performativity and rights

Following the above, the idea of performativity can be thought as intimately caught up with the futural; a doing that brings the future into being in the present and, when used as a critical tool, gesturing towards an idea of a future which is better than the present, a broader utopian horizon that may guide and drive the doing of the present. However, can this futural element of performativity be detected as informing thinking on human rights as a performative politico-legal activity? To some extent the link between the present and the future in the performative is detectable in work considering the politico-legal activity of rights using performative thinking. For example, Zivi states that a performative perspective on rights:

> means appreciating that a seemingly simple utterance such as 'the people have a right to self-governance' is always far more than a single sentence; it is, instead, a complex activity more akin, perhaps to telling a story or crafting a particular perspective on the present *and future*.
>
> (2012: 9, emphasis added)

From this, to claim a right is to performatively bring into being a new narration of the past, present and the future in contexts of power, and even, it might be added, to performatively bring a new future into being which is less restrictive, a future where alternative subject identities are recognised or where fewer people are denigrated and oppressed. Zivi's performative account of rights claiming also demonstrates an understanding that the conception of the future that rights work to bring into being cannot be fully controlled or determined, but rather is subject to the unpredictable process of performative utterances, what she terms the 'messy or uncontrollable elements of speech activity' (2012: 42). This renders the future rights envisage and work towards always beyond sovereign control. Thus, the concept of futurity and the relation between futurity and the performative as explored above has been somewhat present in performative understandings of rights. However, this is not a theme that has been reflected on fully or explicitly, and space remains to consciously build upon the link between the performative and the futural in conceptualising the politico-legal activity of rights to re-engage rights as offering more radical possibilities. Let us consider how this may be initiated via the concept of human rights to come.

In many ways, human rights to come seeks to further what can be gathered of the relation between performativity, futurity and rights in Zivi's account. When radical thinkers or activists engage in this activity they are performativity re-narrating the past, present and the future and bringing new futures into being that challenge restrictive regimes of power. It is also true that the future which this activity works to bring into being cannot be controlled or predicted; no activist or group can fully determine the outcome of performative rearticulation or guarantee a particular outcome in advance. It is not the case that the 'to come' of human rights is filled with a set content which is steadily worked towards in a linear fashion. On the contrary, the 'to come' emerges as a driving force which retains the instability and the uncontainable possibility of always being otherwise which derives from the performative nature of rights. As a result, understanding human rights as human rights to come encourages visibilisation of the way in which making rights claims does performatively bring into being new futures within contexts of power and involves an acceptance of the uncertainty of such a future, an abandonment of attempts to render the practice of human rights predictable and contained, sanitised of the inherent uncertainty which comes into view when we engage with human rights as a performative doing. However, this idea advances that it is necessary to further explore the relation between performativity, futurity and the politico-legal activity of rights.

Human rights to come, first, requires a foregrounding of the futural in the performative to a greater extent than has been the case in other performative accounts of rights. It requires an understanding of rights not only as a performative doing but as a performative doing *in futurity* at a fundamental level. The interrelation of the present and the future must be viewed as central to the radical possibilities for rights as a performative practice and must be at the fore of what it means to understand human rights to come as a performative activity.

More than this, the approach of human rights to come also involves foregrounding a particular aspect of the futural in the performative which is not evident in Zivi's account. This aspect, highlighted in the relationship between performativity and futurity outlined above, is the fact that the performative activity of human rights must be conceived of as working towards a futural horizon of living and being that will always remain self-refuting. The future engaged in the performative doing in futurity will never be perfect or fully realised; alterity cannot be eradicated. As a result, the performative activity of rights involves working towards a future that must be grasped as 'to come' and performative work to this end can never cease, this element being what makes the activity of human rights a useful site for an ongoing critical, performative reworking of current relations of power and alterity. Re-engaging human rights as human rights to come, therefore, involves embrace of the fact that in the performative practice of rights radical thinkers, activists and groups are bringing into being a future through the performative doing, but one that will always fall short, and so critical performative work must continue. This characterises the politico-legal activity of rights as an ongoing struggle towards a futural horizon which is impossible and self-refuting. This conception of the futural and the performative is one that has not yet been fully thought through, yet it is an element that provides a key reason why the doing of rights may be re-engaged productively in radical politics.

Accordingly, the performative doing of human rights to come is one that capitalises on the interrelation between the present and the future in performative practice and seeks to foreground an element of this interrelation that has not yet been fully foregrounded – the fact that the future driving the performative practice of rights will always remain 'to come'. In doing so it is possible to see a relationship between performativity and futurity that is complementary. Performative understandings may be of use to think through a futural conception of human rights, and a futural conception of human rights may be furthered through conceptualising human rights as performative. Performativity can be understood as at its heart a futural activity, and from this a futural and a performative conception of human rights may to work together. This is an important insight, and one that it is necessary to grasp in order to begin to consider the performative doing that is central to approaching human rights as human rights to come. Understanding human rights as a performative politico-legal activity via this idea does not just mean understanding human rights as a performative doing; it means embracing and foregrounding the futural that is central to the performative. In doing so, human rights to come both fits within already existing work to reconceptualise the politico-legal activity of human rights beyond rights-as-objects, and also seeks to bring something new to this work by highlighting how rights may productively be conceived as a doing in futurity towards a self-refuting horizon that sustains the critical. When radical thinkers and activists engage in the practice of human rights to come which gestures towards the promise of a fully perfected and complete idea of rights, and of our sociopolitical lives together, they are working towards the bringing into existence of such futural possibilities through the present performative utterance but also foregrounding the fact that this future-looking activity can never be fully finished. It is in this sense that the futural form of human rights to come links to, and may be facilitated and sustained through, the performative doing of human rights and the two become intertwined.

Human rights to come as *re*doing human rights

To return to the assertion outlined above, human rights to come involves visibilising and foregrounding rights as a performative doing, but it also involves visibilising and foregrounding rights as a performative doing *in futurity* and as a performative *re*doing. In this section, the latter claim of this statement is explored; the politico-legal activity of human rights to come as involving a performative redoing. To introduce what is meant by this, the idea of human rights to come is characterised by an aim to reimagine and rework human rights to bring into being an alternative discourse of rights that is more amenable to the aims of radical social transformation. An understanding of human rights as a performative doing can help to facilitate this. Performativity does not only offer possibility to understand human rights to come as a doing, bringing alternative rights ideas into being through articulation and rearticulation, and a doing in futurity, such performative articulation and rearticulation being directed towards a self-refuting horizon, but it also offers possibility to understand human rights to come as involving a *re*doing of human rights as a discourse itself. This goes beyond rearticulation of particular rights concepts and their relation to restrictive regimes of power – the 'human', 'life', 'equality' and so on – and gestures towards utilising the performativity of rights to undertake a deeper redoing of human rights, their form and usages.

To date, thinking on the performative nature of rights as a politico-legal activity has focused on a number of key ideas. For example, the idea that claiming rights – the utterance that 'I have a right to X' – actually works to bring that right into being on some level, often where that right previously did not exist, and the idea that the subject of rights is also brought into being through such utterances, potentially in new or resistant ways. In this way, as Zivi states, rights claims 'both reference and reiterate social conventions and norms' (2012: 19). While such assertions have characterised rights as having a radical and disruptive potential, less prominent in this thinking has been the idea that *rights themselves* can be reworked as a discourse via their performative nature; their form altered, their alignments changed through performative activity. While human rights to come does involve, and seeks to visibilise, the possibility of reworking individual rights ideas via the performative doing, it also seeks to highlight how the radical, disruptive nature of the performativity of rights can be extended to ground new, alternative conceptions of human rights more generally. As performative concepts, human rights involve not only an everyday doing, encompassing processes of articulation and rearticulation, but may potentially be approached to undertake a larger macro *re*doing of rights that works to bring alternative meanings of human rights into being beyond those currently imaginable. To understand how performative theorising may be engaged to visibilise this possibility, it is useful to return to the work of Butler and, in particular, her concept of performative reiteration which provides a vehicle to think through the redoing of rights via human rights to come.

Performative reiteration

Performativity understood via Butler, as acknowledged previously, is not merely a descriptive account of how certain activities are generative in their doing. Rather, performativity also carries a sense that it is possible to do things *differently* through such activities (Butler 2006: 187–193).[13] This gives performativity a radical edge which Butler has developed through the Derridean concept of iteration. To grasp how this concept may help think through the possibilities of redoing human rights, it is necessary to explore how it is used by Butler. In her performative account of gender, while Butler does see subjects as compelled to repeat hegemonic scripts of gender to persist socially, an equally important element of her account is the assertion that the performative scripts of dominant gender are not completely fixed. For Butler, opportunities exist to disrupt these scripts and create space for subversive performances of gender which differ from the norm (1993: 121–140). However, as also indicated above, performative agency in Butler's account does not rely on a sovereign subject who possesses the capacity to perform differing repetitions at will.[14] It is here that the idea of reiteration becomes significant.

Addressing criticism that her account of performativity could be understood as a voluntaristic performance, Butler responded by employing Jacques Derrida's concept of iterability to greater emphasise the constraints and limitations that underpin performativity (Butler 1993: 12–16). Iterability in Derrida's work refers to the possibility of repetition in alterity which any sign exists through.[15] To have an identity, to function as a sign, every singularity must be iterable (Derrida 1988: 12). Signs cannot be only used once, but must necessarily be repeatable (Derrida 1973: 50); however, their repetition is never a complete, pure sameness, but is haunted by alterity and absence in their presence. By virtue of its haunting alterity – the trace of the other 'absent' element in any sign which constitutes its iterability – signs are alterable, possible of, in Derrida's words, 'being weaned from the referent or from the signified' (1988: 10). Following from this, signs are never fully fixed, but exist in a constant state of becoming, and new possibilities for meaning and communication are opened up.

Butler characterises gender as an iterable concept – the citation of a set of conventions which have a prior meaning rather than a fixed or innate identity, the effectiveness and intelligibility of these conventions lying in their continual repetition (1993: 107). Where Butler sees radical potential in the iterability of gender is that in its repetition gender is amenable to alternative significations that haunt, and indeed constitute, its currently restrictive form. Yet, the iteration of gender is not without restraint. Intelligible gender has been restricted to certain forms (namely binarised and asymmetrical ideas of masculinity/femininity) and is an effect of the 'forced recitation of norms' (Butler 1993: 94). The iteration of gender is not performed *by* a subject, but is what *enables* a subject, and enables a subject under conditions where dominant gender norms are cited forcibly because of their imbrication in relations of power (Butler 1993: 95). However, what prevents Butler's account from being a determinist position is her view of how subjects constituted by and through the restrictive and forcible iteration of gender are, nevertheless, able to act to *re*iterate gender.[16] The iterability of gender, its need to be repeated to maintain its dominant meaning or signification, makes gender inherently unstable and vulnerable to citations that challenge the norms they are intended to reinforce so that 'this instability is the *de*constituting possibility in the very process of repetition' (Butler 1993: 10, emphasis in original). The subjectifying operation of power, which Butler derives from Foucault, creates opportunity for the subject to do something with what is done to them and do gender anew (Butler 2004: 3). This cannot be viewed as a sovereign activity; rather, it involves employing constituting power to produce citations which are subversive, which *re*iterate gender and challenge the norms by which subjects are brought into being.[17]

Reiterating rights

Engaged in the context of a performative understanding of human rights and the radical possibilities such may offer, reiteration reveals how it may be possible to subtly alter the meaning of individual human rights concepts. However, it may also be used to go further and explore how rights as a discourse itself may be reiterated – redone – in ways compatible with meaningful challenge to restrictive regimes of power. It is this deeper, more radical, redoing of how human rights can be understood and used that drives the idea of human rights to come. The possibilities for this redoing can be considered through highlighting two crucial things about human rights. First, *human rights maintain their dominant form and meanings within discourses such as liberalism, capitalism, internationalism and statism through ongoing iteration.* The discourse of human rights must be continually repeated in certain ways to maintain its current meaning and authority. For example, Jarrett Zigon considers how the repetition of the core 'truth' of inalienable human rights stemming from inherent human dignity

> can be considered in terms of performativity, and as that which lends legitimacy and authority to an international system that otherwise remains groundless . . . The performative nature of human rights language renders it a moral language that ultimately works to maintain limitations of possible political action within the limits of the currently configured state-systemic-matrix.
>
> (2014: n.p.)

Zigon points towards the 'recognising', 'affirming' and 'reaffirming' that the majority of contemporary international human rights texts begin with as a performative iteration of the particular liberal, internationalist and state-centric notion of contemporary human rights, an attempt to maintain it as 'truth'. The felicity conditions of 'the flow of international funding, media support, and international and transnational government rhetoric and policy all aimed at disseminating the transnational moral "truth" of human rights' in this form make these iterations more likely to be successful (Zigon 2014: n.p.)

However, Zigon, following Butler's approach outlined above, also points to the fact that the need for constant repetition – iteration – of this particular discourse of human rights not only works to bolster its legitimacy and authority but also indicates its vulnerability to alternative iterations. This vulnerability – the trace of the-other-in-the-same – is revealed in particular instances of slippage where questions are raised about the dominant view of human rights and its coherence. Thus, as with Butler's conception of performative gender, the performativity of current conceptions of the discourse of human rights, in Zigon's terms, 'not only works to maintain its "truth", but also [to] simultaneously maintain the limitations established by this truth' (2014: n.p.). In their need for ongoing iteration to maintain their authority, dominant meanings of human rights are by their nature vulnerable.

This leads to the second point that may be asserted following Butler's account of performative reiteration, and it is this that in many ways forms the central kernel of the idea of human rights to come; *human rights as a discourse can, by nature of their iterability, be reiterated, or redone, in new ways*. The need for currently dominant understandings of human rights to be continually iterated to maintain authority offers possibilities for reiterations which give rights meaning in alternative ways. This includes radical reiterations which respond to the restrictions and limitations dominant iterations of human rights work to maintain. It is here that human rights to come seeks to capitalise on the iterability of rights to undertake a performative redoing of rights. Through such work the discourse of human rights, its usages and what it is capable of may be rethought and reworked in ways that are more compatible with the aims of radical politics. How can this reiterative activity be conceived? What would its undertaking involve? Moreover, what would its challenges be for radical thinkers and activists engaging in the politico-legal activity of rights? The remainder of this section considers these questions.

To begin with questions of how to conceive activity to radically reiterate rights and what this might involve, when thinking about how it may be possible to envisage or begin the reiterative redoing of rights advanced via the idea of human rights to come, thoughts may turn to the work of Seyla Benhabib whose conception of 'democratic iterations' at first glance appears to advance a similar idea.[18] Outlining this concept Benhabib states that

> by *democratic iterations* I mean complex processes of public argument, deliberation and exchange through which universalist rights claims are contested and contextualized, invoked and revoked, posited and positioned throughout legal and political institutions as well as in the associations of civil society. In the process of repeating a term or a concept, we never simply

produce a replica of the first intended usage or its original meaning: rather, every repetition is a form of variation.

(2009: 6, emphasis in original)

Benhabib's conception of democratic iterations foregrounds the iterability of human rights and seeks to explore how such may be capitalised on. However, this idea does not quite encapsulate what is involved in work to redo rights via the practice of human rights to come. Benhabib's reflection on the iterability of rights differs in one crucial element – it characterises those who seek to work towards alternative iterations of rights as 'authors of the law' (2011: 15–16). Such a characterisation of reiterative work is not possible in the practice of human rights to come following the critique of the sovereign subject which a performative approach informed by Butler's reiteration involves. It might be said, in the words of Pheng Cheah, that we cannot view rights as '*our* instruments as rational actors, for we are their product-effects rather than their originators' (2006: 175, emphasis in original). However, the idea of human rights to come does still assert that reiteration of human rights in radical politics is possible: how can this be thought to be so? How can radical activists and groups understand and undertake reiteration of human rights in the practice of human rights to come? As a practice which seeks to capitalise on the vulnerability inherent in human rights following from their need to be continually iterated in particular ways to maintain their dominant meaning, human rights to come does not propose a naive picking up of human rights entirely anew through the action of sovereign agency. Radical reiteration of human rights does not equate to a wilful redoing of human rights that poses a discourse of rights entirely unrecognisable from its current form. Such wilful action is not possible after the sovereign subject is erased and, moreover, such a radical new citation of human rights would most likely not be successful – enjoy the felicity conditions to be an intelligible iteration. Rather, what the concept of human rights to come advances to reiterate rights is, to echo Butler's thinking on reiterative gender, 'a taking up of the tools where they lie, where the very "taking up" is enabled by the tool lying there' (2006: 199). This indicates the subtlety and incremental nature of the reiteration involved, and the need to eschew the human rights thinker or activist as a completely free sovereign action rearticulating rights. Rather, only through beginning with current human rights concepts, discourses and resources available and initiating new conversations, dialogues, exchanges which undertake unpredictable political work to subtly reiterate these in ways which challenge the restrictions inherent in dominant conceptions of rights, can an alternative approach to human rights that is beyond their form within liberalism, capitalism, internationalism and statism begin to emerge.

Accordingly, the redoing of human rights to come involves a rejection of the rights thinker or activist as sovereign, but rather an engaging in the redoing of rights as a discourse through slow, steady and incremental performative reiteration of resources already available. A further question that must be addressed is: what would the challenges of such activity be? What may pose as a stumbling block for those seeking to engage in such an activity? One potential challenge or stumbling block that radical thinkers and activists may encounter in this work is the close relationship between dominant discourses of human rights and the state. The assertion has been made that such a link makes it difficult for human rights to be reiterated and rendered of use in contemporary radical politics. For example, while in his account Zigon highlights the inherent vulnerability of dominant iterations of human rights, he concludes that the performative maintenance of discourses of rights that privilege the state and its authority means that human rights are fundamentally limited 'as a language for radically progressive politics' (2014: n.p.). For Zigon, 'every repetition of rights language further solidifies this necessary link between rights and the state-systemic-matrix' (2014: n.p.). While strategic engagement with rights by radical politics may have short-term usages in drawing attention to particular issues, abuses and injustices, 'in the long run the historically accumulated limitations this language carries with it significantly decreases possibilities for imagining, articulating, and ultimately acting in ways to address these issues, abuses, and injustices that go beyond the current configuration of the state-systemic-matrix' (Zigon 2014: n.p.). In this view, the foundational link between human rights discourse and the state from the mid-twentieth century onwards makes reiteration ineffectual, even impossible, for radical groups seeking to utilise human rights as a vehicle of challenge to restrictive regimes of power. All human rights can do is to operate within the given order of institutional power.

Human rights to come takes a directly opposing view. At the core of this idea is an assertion that human rights *can* be performatively reiterated in alternative ways despite the powerful relation between currently dominant human rights discourse and state. To understand why this assertion is possible it is necessary to stay with Butler's account of reiteration, albeit this time to engage critique of it. In Butler's view, law and state, often characterised as closely intertwined, are regarded as largely unproductive sites for radical activity (1997a: 101). This appears a pessimistic account for contemporary work to radically reiterate human rights as a discourse closely connected to the state, often directly articulated by states. However, such work can be viewed as possible when the underpinnings of reiteration are returned to. For example, Paul Passavant and Jodi Dean point towards the citationality of state discourse which, following Butler's own conception of reiteration, should mean that such discourse is amenable to reiteration like any other (2001: 379–385). Passavant and Dean also stress the need to acknowledge that the law and the state are not the same thing, but can be disarticulated to expose both as 'possible sites of resistances that ought not to be ruled out *a priori*' (2001: 381–382).[19] Following such comments, while the state does wield significant power in defining and controlling human rights discourse, there is, arguably, no reason to perceive this relation as some kind of anathema to radical politics. It is, undoubtedly, not an easy task to challenge state discourse, nor the close relationship between human rights and the state as solidified in contemporary times, and such challenges will not bear fruit overnight. However, there appears to be no need to determine the relationship between human rights and state as prohibiting reiteration of dominant ideas of human rights or as itself immune to reiterative possibilities. The implications of this view for the work of human rights to come is that while the relationship between human rights and the state maintained through dominant iterations of human rights is powerful, it does not mean that human rights can never be rethought and reused by radical politics. Indeed, part of reiterating human rights in more radical ways may conceivably encompass new conceptualisations of what human rights could mean and look like beyond the state, disarticulated from discourses of statism. Through sustained hard work, work that may not always be successful, radical activists and groups may begin to challenge dominant conceptions of human rights and question the appropriation of the discourse of rights by state. Approaching human rights as human rights to come involves rejecting an understanding of the possibilities for the discourse of human rights that allows the state to limit its usages. Such a limit on iteration cannot be concretely set, and, indeed, although powerful, is vulnerable through its own very need for iteration.

From the above it is possible to see how, as an iterative discourse which requires ongoing repetition to maintain dominance in line with discourses such as liberalism, capitalism internationalism and statism human rights are open to reiterative redoing in the performative practice of human rights to come. In this activity, radical activists cannot be viewed as sovereign agents wilfully doing rights anew, but are involved in the activity of picking up the tools of human rights in a slightly different way and committing to a long-term, incremental process of articulation and rearticulation – now understandable as iteration and reiteration – towards alternative forms and usages of rights that may redo human rights as a discourse. While this performative redoing is not an easy or a quick-fix solution – demonstrated in particular by the strong relationship between dominant conceptions of human rights and the state which must be reapproached – there is no reason why performative thinking cannot be used to initiate the process and help to begin to think through this central aim of the concept of human rights to come.

Conclusion

This chapter has begun to further consider what it means to approach human rights as human rights to come by reflecting on how this idea advances the politico-legal activity of rights as a performative doing. Moving beyond understandings of human rights as objects and the practice of human rights as a legalistic activity, human rights to come draws attention to human rights as a fundamentally political, dynamic and generative activity, a doing in the performative sense. Already existing accounts of rights as performative assist in understanding the articulation and rearticulation of rights concepts and associated regimes of power which is central to human rights to come as a performative doing; bringing new possibilities for rights concepts and living and being more generally into being through the doing. More than this, however, the performative element of the politico-legal activity of human rights to come involves understanding this activity as not just a performative doing but a doing in futurity and also, at a fundamental level, advancing a redoing of the discourse of human rights beyond its currently dominant form.

Discussion has explored how through foregrounding the inherent interrelation between the present and the future which is central to the performative – a doing in the now for an uncertain, and never fully perfected, future – the activity of human rights to come can be considered a doing in futurity towards a horizon of perfect relations of living and being that remains self-refuting. In addition, performativity also allows possibilities to rework the discourse of human rights in new ways more capable of challenging restrictive regimes of power via the practice of human rights to come. Focusing on Butler's concept of performative reiteration allows us to see how human rights are fundamentally iterable concepts, continually repeated in certain ways to maintain the authority and dominance of their understanding. Visibilising and engaging in such practices of reiteration, human rights to come advances redoings of the discourse human rights in ways which are more amenable to the aims of radical politics. While this approach does not advance that radical activists as sovereign, rational actors are able to utilise human rights in an entirely different way; performative theory does point towards more subtle, incremental practices of reiteration whereby the vulnerability of human rights as an iterable discourse is capitalised upon, including their current relationship with the state and articulation via state discourse. This involves picking up the tools available – human rights in their current form – in slightly modified ways through engagements, debate and dialogue, performatively redoing human rights towards alternative forms, usages and conceptualisations through critical reiterative work.

Notes

1 See Donnelly (2013: 12); Wendy Brown (2004: 455).
2 For discussion on this point, see Ignatieff (2001: 292); Mutua (1996: 629–630); Klug (2005).
3 See Butler (2006). For commentary exploring Butler's work on gender performativity and its usages, see Lloyd (1999); Vicki Kirby (2006: 19–107); Loizidou (2007: 157–168); Chambers and Carver (2008: 34–50); Salih (2002: 43–72, 137–152).
4 Butler's work has since gone on to explore more diverse elements of performative politics and the way in which making political claims does something, and something potentially radical, in the very utterance. See, for example, Butler (2015) where she explores the performative nature of recent political activism involving public assemblies, protests and other similar activities.
5 See, for example, Bell (1999); Parker and Sedgwick (1995); Harris (1999); Loxley (2007); MacKenzie, Muniesa and Siu (2007); Glass and Rose-Redwood (2014).
6 For further elaboration of Zerilli's conception of rights in this sense, see Eleveld (2015).
7 See Zivi (2008; 2012; 2014a; 2014b).
8 For further discussion of this particular example, see McNeilly (2015).
9 The idea of performativity as working towards a future that cannot be controlled, and the foundation of this idea in performative thinking, is explored further below.
10 Here I am drawing from the words of José Muñoz (2009: 26) discussed further below.

11 For further discussion on this part of Butler's work, see Butler and Bell (1999). Butler's account of the excitability of speech, the inability of the subject to control the effects of their speech, is based on a critique of the sovereign subject. Butler rejects the idea of a sovereign subject with full agency, outlining instead via Foucault that 'if I have any agency, it is opened up by the fact that I am constituted by a social world I never chose' (2004: 3). For more on Butler's reworking of Foucault in this way, see Butler (1997b), and for commentary McNay (1999); Mills (2003); Jagger (2008: 89–114).
12 This position can be gathered from Butler's work generally, especially her comments on the ineradicable alterity of the universal outlined in Butler, Laclau and Žižek (2000).
13 For more on the disruptive potential of performativity and the link between performativity and power, see Allen (1998).
14 See further Lloyd (2007a: 57–61).
15 For commentary, see, for example, Bennington (1993: 56); Loxley (2007: 88–111).
16 See further Lloyd (2007a: 64).
17 For more on reiteration and the politics of resignification in Butler's work, see Lloyd (2007b); Mills (2000).
18 See Benhabib (2004: 171–212; 2006; 2009; 2010; 2011: 73–75). For more on Benhabib's use of this concept, see Thomassen (2011).
19 See also Lloyd (2005). These criticisms are largely responding to Butler's earlier work. In her more recent engagements, Butler, indeed, does demonstrate awareness of the broad and dominantly pessimistic account of the state which emerges from her work. In *Undoing Gender* she clarifies that she does not see the state as reducible to law nor as a unilateral monolith and confirms that 'I think the state *can* be worked and exploited' (2004: 116, emphasis added).

References

Allen, A. (1998) 'Power Trouble: Performativity as Critical Theory', *Constellations*, 5(4): 456–471.
Austin, J. L. (1975) *How to Do Things with Words*, 2nd edn, Oxford: Clarendon.
Bell, V. (ed.) (1999) *Performativity and Belonging*, London: Sage.
Benhabib, S. (2004) *The Rights of Others: Aliens, Residents and Citizens*, Cambridge: Cambridge University Press.
Benhabib, S. (2006) 'Democratic Iterations: The Local, the National, and the Global', in S. Benhabib with J. Waldron, B. Honig and W. Kymlicka, R. Post (eds), *Another Cosmopolitanism*, Oxford: Oxford University Press, 45–82.
Benhabib, S. (2009) 'Claiming Rights across Borders: International Human Rights and Democratic Sovereignty', *American Political Science Review*, 103(4): 691–704.
Benhabib, S. (2010) 'Human Rights, Sovereignty and Democratic Iterations', session 6, Keynote Lectures: Human Rights – Global Culture – International Institutions, Our Common Future, Hannover, 4 November 2010, available at: www.ourcommonfuture. de/fileadmin/user_upload/dateien/Reden/Benhabib.pdf (accessed 2 January 2017).
Benhabib, S. (2011) *Dignity in Adversity: Human Rights in Turbulent Times*, Cambridge: Polity.
Bennington, G. (1993) *Jacques Derrida*, Chicago: University of Chicago Press.
Brown, W. (2004) '"The Most We Can Hope for . . .": Human Rights and the Politics of Fatalism', *South Atlantic Quarterly*, 103(2–3): 451–463.
Butler, J. (1993) *Bodies That Matter: On the Discursive Limits of 'Sex'*, New York; London: Routledge.

Butler, J. (1997a) *Excitable Speech: A Politics of the Performative*, New York; London: Routledge.
Butler, J. (1997b) *The Psychic Life of Power: Theories in Subjection*, Stanford: Stanford University Press.
Butler, J. (2004) *Undoing Gender*, New York; London: Routledge.
Butler, J. (2006) *Gender Trouble: Feminism and the Subversion of Identity*, 2nd edn, New York; London: Routledge.
Butler, J. (2015) *Notes Toward a Performative Theory of Assembly*, Cambridge, MA: Harvard University Press.
Butler, J. and Bell, V. (1999) 'On Speech, Race and Melancholia: An Interview with Judith Butler', *Theory, Culture & Society*, 16(2): 163–174.
Butler, J., Laclau, E. and Žižek, S. (2000) *Contingency, Hegemony, Universality: Contemporary Dialogues on the Left*, London: Verso.
Cavell, S. (1976) *Must We Mean What We Say?*, Cambridge: Cambridge University Press.
Chambers, S. and Carver, T. (2008) *Judith Butler and Political Theory: Troubling Politics*, London; New York: Routledge.
Cheah, P. (2006) *Inhuman Conditions: On Cosmopolitanism and Human Rights*, Cambridge, MA: Harvard University Press.
Derrida, J. (1973) *Speech and Phenomena, and Other Essays on Husserl's Theory of Signs*, trans. D. Allison, Evanston: Northwestern University Press.
Derrida, J. (1988) 'Signature Event Context', in G. Gaff (ed.), *Limited Inc*, trans. S. Weber, Evanston: Northwestern University Press, 1–24.
Donnelly, J. (2013) *Universal Human Rights in Theory and Practice*, 3rd edn, Ithaca, NY: Cornell University Press.
Douzinas, C. (2000) *The End of Human Rights: Critical Legal Thought at the Turn of the Century*, Oxford: Hart.
Douzinas, C. (2007) *Human Rights and Empire: The Political Philosophy of Cosmopolitanism*, New York; London: Routledge.
Eleveld, A. (2015) 'Claiming Care Rights as a Performative Act', *Law and Critique*, 26(1): 83–100.
Glass, M. and Rose-Redwood, R. (2014) *Performativity, Politics and the Production of Social Space*, New York: Routledge.
Harris, G. (1999) *Staging Femininities: Performance and Performativity*, Manchester: Manchester University Press.
Ignatieff, M. (2001) *Human Rights as Politics and Idolatry*, A. Gutmann (ed.), Princeton: Princeton University Press.
Jagger, G. (2008) *Judith Butler: Sexual Politics, Social Change and the Power of the Performative*, London; New York: Routledge.
Kirby, V. (2006) *Judith Butler: Live Theory*, London; New York: Continuum.
Klug, F. (2005) 'Human Rights: Above Politics or a Creature of Politics?', *Policy & Politics*, 33(1): 3–14.
Lloyd, M. (1999) 'Performativity, Parody, Politics', *Theory, Culture & Society*, 16(2): 195–213.
Lloyd, M. (2005) 'Butler, Antigone and the State', *Contemporary Political Theory*, 4: 451–468.
Lloyd, M. (2007a) *Judith Butler: From Norms to Politics*, Cambridge: Polity.
Lloyd, M. (2007b) 'Radical Democratic Activism and the Politics of Resignification', *Constellations*, 14(1): 129–146.

Loizidou, E. (2007) *Judith Butler: Ethics, Law, Politics*, London; New York: Routledge-Cavendish.

Loxley, J. (2007) *Performativity*, London; New York: Routledge.

Lyon, A. (2013) *Deliberative Acts: Democracy, Rhetoric and Rights*, Pennsylvania: University of Pennsylvania Press.

MacKenzie, D., Muniesa, F. and Siu, L. (eds) (2007) *Do Economists Make Markets? On the Performativity of Economics*, Princeton: Princeton University Press.

McNay, L. (1999) 'Subject, Psyche and Agency: The Work of Judith Butler', *Theory, Culture and Society*, 16(2): 175–193.

McNeilly, K. (2015) 'From the Right to Life to the Right to Livability: Radically Re-approaching "Life" in Human Rights Politics', *Australian Feminist Law Journal*, 41(1): 141–159.

Mills, C. (2000) 'Efficacy and Vulnerability: Judith Butler on Reiteration and Resistance', *Australian Feminist Studies*, 15(32): 265–279.

Mills, C. (2003) 'Contesting the Political: Butler and Foucault in Power and Resistance', *Journal of Political Philosophy*, 11(3): 253–272.

Muñoz, J. (2009) *Cruising Utopia: The Then and There of Queer Futurity*, New York: New York University Press.

Mutua, M. (1996) 'The Ideology of Human Rights', *Virginia Journal of International Law*, 36: 589–657.

Parker, A. and Sedgwick, E. K. (eds) (1995) *Performativity and Performance*, New York: Routledge.

Passavant, P. and Dean, J. (2001) 'Laws and Societies', *Constellations*, 8(3): 376–389.

Salih, S. (2002) *Judith Butler*, London; New York: Routledge.

Thomassen, L. (2011) 'The Politics of Iterability: Benhabib, the Hijab, and Democratic Iteration', *Polity*, 43: 128–149.

Zerilli, L. (2004) 'Refiguring Rights through the Political Practice of Sexual Difference', *differences*, 15(2): 54–90.

Zerilli, L. (2005) *Feminism and the Abyss of Freedom*, Chicago: University of Chicago Press.

Zigon, J. (2014) 'Maintaining the "Truth": Performativity, Human Rights, and the Limitations on Politics', *Theory & Event*, 17(3): n.p.

Zivi, K. (2008) 'Rights and the Politics of Performativity', in T. Carver and S. Chambers (eds), *Judith Butler's Precarious Politics*, New York: Routledge, 157–171.

Zivi, K. (2012) *Making Rights Claims: A Practice of Democratic Citizenship*, New York; Oxford: Oxford University Press.

Zivi, K. (2014a) 'Performing the Nation: Contesting Same-Sex Marriage Rights in the United States', *Journal of Human Rights*, 13(3): 290–306.

Zivi, K. (2014b) 'The Practice and the Promise of Making Rights Claims: Lessons from the South African Treatment Access Campaign', *African Legal Theory and Contemporary Problems*, 29: 173–198.

Chapter 4

Universality as universalisation
The universality of human rights to come

Introduction

In this chapter thought turns to consider a second underpinning theoretical element which must be rethought in the approach of human rights to come: the universality of human rights. Understanding human rights as fluid concepts continually articulated and rearticulated without end, means moving beyond traditional ideas of universality, thought within the universality–cultural relativity binary as a static characteristic of rights to be endorsed or rejected. Instead, human rights to come encourages an understanding of universality as an ongoing process of universalisation which aims to rid the universal of alterity. The 'to come' characterising human rights signals towards the need to conceptualise a universality that is also 'to come', an ongoing and futural striving which drives the politics and practice of human rights more generally. In this view, universality becomes a site where the futurity of human rights is sustained, and reapproaching universality in such a way emerges as central to the project of radically re-engaging human rights.

This chapter explores this re-engagement with universality in three sections. The first section considers existing thought on the universality, or otherwise, of human rights as providing a context for the re-engagement with universality that human rights to come advances, indeed making such re-engagement possible. While many attempts have been made previously to re-engage the universality of human rights, what the particular perspective of human rights to come seeks to foreground is a futural conception of universality which may offer more radical possibilities for universal human rights in politics that seeks to critically reveal and respond to alterity. As is asserted, even thinking that conceives rights in a futural sense has not explored a potentially productive relationship between universality and futurity. This is what the concept of human rights to come seeks to do. In the second section, thought turns to consider what this futural conception of universality would involve by thinking the universality of human rights as *an ongoing process of universalisation*. This concept is informed by the work of Butler. Her thinking is drawn upon to explore the idea of universality as universalisation, a futural-focused process premised on a universality which remains inevitably 'to come' and one that holds possibility to be thought in the context of a radical politics of human rights. In the third section of the chapter, discussion moves to consider more concretely what it means to approach the universality of human rights as a process of universalisation by engaging two universal human rights concepts: the universal *content* of human rights and the universal *subject* of human rights. These concepts are viewed through the lens of universality as universalisation to outline more of how human rights to come involves a different approach to the key tenets of universal human rights, which in turn leads towards more radical usages for the discourse and practice of human rights.

Engagements with the universality of human rights

The issue of universality has been a persistent and, more often than not, a controversial issue throughout the history of human rights (Brown 1997: 41). Universality has remained such a staple point of contention it has been commented that in the present era debate about the universality of human rights has become 'rather tired' (Goodhart 2013: 31). While many may agree that this assessment is fair, the overwhelming attention dedicated to the question of universality nevertheless demonstrates the continuing importance of this concept to contemporary human rights discourse as well as the stumbling block that universality has posed to human rights throughout their history, including, in recent years, in the context of increasing globalisation.[1] Universality, it is asserted, is also important in the context of work to radically re-engage rights, albeit as a concept it must be thought beyond its traditional frame. To a great extent, traditional discussion on universality has been driven by one of the most fundamental debates on human rights: the deepseated divide between universality and cultural relativity which has dominated what can be seen and heard about universality.[2] However, while this binary forms a starting point for discussion, as elaborated below, it has not necessarily been perceived as an ending point for contemporary engagements with the universality of rights, in particular those which seek to recover rights as a radical discourse. This is an essential point to note. Understanding human rights as human rights to come indeed involves picking up on this idea. In thinking through a radical and futural approach to human rights there is a need to transcend traditional debate on universality to allow differing possibilities for universality, and subsequently for rights themselves, to come into view. Human rights to come advances a particular way in which universality can be productively understood and re-engaged which furthers the futural-focused approach to human rights it proposes. Before exploring this idea further, it is necessary to consider how the universality of human rights has been understood to date, both traditionally and in alternative engagements with rights, and such engagements, the latter in particular, as assisting in bringing into view opportunities to rethink universality in the project of human rights to come.

To begin with traditional understandings of universality, the discourse of human rights has been asserted as universal in a number of respects. First, universality has been advanced in relation to the subject of human rights. Echoing natural law underpinnings, the Universal Declaration of Human Rights asserts in its opening Article that 'all human beings are born equal in dignity and rights'. All possess rights, it is submitted, by virtue of their basic humanity; rights protection extends universally across humankind. In addition to a universal subject, the content of human rights is also presented as universal (Donnelly 2007: 282–283). Certain content, representing the historically specific basic protections that subjects of rights require, has been presented in the form of universal norms. These core protections have been positivised, enshrined in treaties and declarations applying across borders, nations and cultures and are characterised as an authoritative list of what universal rights entail. The universality of human rights is also advanced on a broader conceptual level (Donnelly 2007: 281–282). This refers to the sense that human rights are actively endorsed worldwide, leading to an adoption of the language of human rights not only at the level of international and national law but also as a language to articulate injustices at the grassroots level across countries and continents.[3] In this line of thought, human rights have become embraced as a universal discourse which is available almost everywhere, a broadly utilised way of speaking about and addressing experiences of suffering and wrongdoing that is widely recognised.

The assertion stemming from this – that human rights are universal concepts that apply to all human subjects and consist of a set core content of protections applicable across borders and contexts – broadly summarises the universalist position on human rights (Donnelly 2013: 94–97). This has constituted the position from which human rights law and politics progressed from 1945 onwards. Indeed, strong emphasis on universality in the creation of human rights in international law can be perceived as stemming from the historical conditions at the time, a galvanising narrative following the atrocities of the Second World War (Donnelly 2007: 282). However, while the universalist approach to human rights has been strong, the challenge to it has been equally strong, particularly from voices in the 'Global South' asserting that a universalist understanding of human rights and the associated politico-legal crusade to extend the profile and reach of human rights in the post-Second World War era is problematic. In the latter decades of the twentieth century, coinciding with the rise in postcolonial thought, the universalist position was increasingly articulated as representing:

> A new form of imperial aggression, with the assertion of human rights fulfilling the function of Christianity and civilisation in bygone ages namely the latest way in which a rapacious west covers its selfish tracks, hiding its naked self-interest in a shabby ethical coat.
>
> (Gearty 2008: 5)

The subject of human rights according to such perspectives is not a universal human but a Western construct and the universal content of rights articulated in international law appears as an all too familiar assertion of colonial power, inattentive to cultural particularities, promoting a Eurocentric approach to human life and its flourishing.[4] Following such logic, human rights cannot take a universal form and, indeed, to assert a universalist position renders rights not only of limited utility but is also a potentially damaging assertion linked to global discourses of power which privilege the West. In response, a universal idea of human rights has been rejected, or at least treated with scepticism, as a product of the 'West to the Rest' (Kennedy 2002: 114–116).

This traditional binarised perspective on the universality of rights will be familiar to anyone with even a cursory knowledge of human rights discourse and politics. However, in the context of present work seeking to re-engage the underpinnings of human rights, it is important to note that this binarised discourse, while significant, has not been completely dominant. In recent years, engagement with the universality of human rights has favoured a more nuanced articulation of the nature of the universal and particular in rights, and so alternative understandings have emerged. Thoughts have turned to consider how the universality of human rights can be approached in a way which transcends the universality–relativity frame. This has taken a variety of forms. Some have sought to maintain the universality of human rights while simultaneously seeking to temper the colonialising and more sinister elements it can give rise to.[5] Others have taken a contrasting route, rejecting universality as of any use in the contemporary era, and urging towards alternative understandings of rights.[6] Others still have proposed a return to the universality of human rights albeit in a new form, one which is quite different from the universality envisaged by traditional universalist approaches found in international human rights law.[7]

In the context of present work aiming to envisage new usages for rights in radical politics, how do these existing traditional and alternative engagements with universality fit? Where can the approach advanced by human rights to come be located in this context of thought on universality, and how can it add to such? In beginning to consider this, it is interesting to note that Douzinas, outlined previously as also working to foreground the futural in rights,[8] falls into the category of thinkers who have rejected the characterisation of human rights as universal. For Douzinas 'in postmodernity . . . the discourse of rights has lost its earlier coherence and universalism' (2000: 6). In this view, it is not useful, or even possible, to talk of universal human rights, and so Douzinas's futural conception of rights appears to reject any meaningful recourse to universality. It appears that for Douzinas the universalist–cultural relativist binary does not offer a convincing basis for human rights in the current conjecture:

> The claim that human rights are universal, transcultural and absolute is counterintuitive and vulnerable to accusations of cultural imperialism; on the other hand, the assertion that they are creations of European culture, while historically accurate, deprives them of any transcendent value. From the perspective of late modernity, one can be neither a universalist nor a cultural relativist.
>
> (2000: 12)

Indeed, other problems emerge with the concept of universality. For example, approaching the universality of human rights in the traditional manner, via a universalistic perspective in particular, treats universal human rights as 'claims about moral truths' pertaining to the world around us (Goodhart 2013: 32). As discussion in Chapter 3 highlighted, however, human rights can be considered in a different way; not as universal truths corresponding to an already existing reality, but as performative doings which assist in (re)creating the world through their practice. The 'universal truth claims' of rights from this view emerge as in fact unstable concepts maintained through ongoing performative iteration which both sustains and conceals dominant regimes of power.[9] Traditional approaches to the universality of human rights can also be considered inadequate because they serve to reinforce mainstream conceptions of human rights. The universalist–relativist binary has been closely associated with international human rights law and debate over rights as conceived within it in a liberal, state-driven way. In this respect, discussion of universality within the traditional frame of universality–relativity serves to unwittingly reference and reinforce such conceptions of human rights, potentially obscuring how it may be possible to move beyond endorsing or rejecting universality to conceive the idea of universality, and universal human rights themselves, differently. Accordingly, traditional understandings of universality may be unhelpful in attempts to radically reapproach human rights because such understandings obscure the performative dimension of rights, and also because such approaches, and their monopoly on what the term 'universal' means when thought in relation to rights, hinder possibilities to think human rights beyond their current mainstream conceptualisation and to utilise human rights for the ends of radical social transformation.

From this, it may be said that universality is a limited and limiting concept, and that the drawbacks of universality within the traditional universalist–relativist frame do appear to go some way towards endorsing the position taken by Douzinas that this concept must be abandoned. The futural approach of human rights to come does indeed urge for a critical understanding of universality and how this concept has often served to reinforce currently dominant conceptions of human rights. However, it does not gesture towards the need to give up on universality altogether; it asserts that radical possibilities can be found within a conception of rights as universal. Indeed, as noted above, not all engagements with the universality of human rights have rejected it outright; this includes some who seek to consider a place for rights within radical politics. In such approaches universality is rethought in alternative ways that serve to eschew its more problematic elements. In many ways, this reapproaching of universality has been informed by the trend in contemporary critical and poststructuralist thinking moving from a dismantling of universalism in the twentieth century to, in more recent times, a re-evaluation of this dismantling.[10] In such thinking, the universal emerges anew, in the words of Ernesto Laclau, for example, as 'both an impossible and necessary object' (Butler, Laclau and Žižek 2000: 58). Such re-evaluation does not seek to reject universality as irreparably exclusive and problematic, nor seek to assert a 'new universal' which is all inclusive, but considers the potency of engaging with universality as inherently unfixed, open and fundamentally in contrast to liberal discourses of universalism's transcendence and truth, being attentive to the political possibilities which such unfixity may offer. The return to the universal in this new way in contemporary critical work marks, as Linda Zerilli states, 'a homecoming to Enlightenment ideals – purified of their more poisonous elements, of course – and a reconciliation of sorts between those who refuted those ideals and those who sought to realise them' (1998: 1). From this the universal comes into view as not a transcultural or transhistorical concept to be encountered but a site for politics whereby political engagement with universal concepts and their limits creates and mediates the universal, and can do so in potentially radical ways.

It is this theoretical landscape that makes it possible to see how contemporary engagements with the universality of human rights need not remain within traditional confines, that universality may be re-engaged to imagine new possibilities for rights. Various attempts have been made to bring such re-evaluation of universality into conversation with the theoretical underpinnings of human rights.[11] As Domna Stanton asserts, the critical project to reconceptualise universality 'must undergird any examination of human rights universalism, not only its ambiguous and ambivalent meanings and reach, but also the degree to which it is, always already was, or has become through ongoing contest inflected by plural claims' (2016: 28). The idea of human rights to come can be thought of as part of this work, facilitated by it, a concept that stresses that universality can be reapproached in productive ways that go beyond its conception as a static concept or 'truth claim' and thereby offer alternative possibilities for human rights to be understood. As an inherently futural conception of rights, of human rights to come requires a particular perspective be taken on universality. The re-engagement of universality it advances must be one which facilitates and foregrounds the futural striving central to human rights to come, and the need to maintain a never-ending critical approach to alterity in human rights politics. It is here that a different route is taken from Douzinas's consideration of rights as futural and a conception of rights as universal is retained. It is asserted that only through a futural approach to universality can rights be conceived as futural concepts generally; the universal facilitating the 'to come' which is central to the radical potential of human rights. Thus, while the idea of human rights to come does seek to make visible the limitations of traditional, mainstream approaches to universality, it also seeks to reveal that in radically reapproaching human rights as a process of ongoing and futural articulation and rearticulation, universality does not need to be rejected altogether, and can indeed offer sustaining possibilities for this work.

For a futural conception of the universal: universality as universalisation

To review the position reached so far: understanding human rights as human rights to come necessarily requires a rejection of traditional approaches that characterise universal human rights as truth claims pertaining to a pre-existing world or universality as a fixed attribute of rights to be endorsed or rejected due to how such approaches foreclose the scope that exists to think human rights more radically. However, it does not involve rejecting the idea of universality outright. On the contrary, human rights to come seeks to retain a perception of human rights as universal but asserts that this must be a universality which is reconceived to be thought in a fundamentally futural sense. However, what does this alternative approach to universality look like? What is involved in taking a futural approach to universality? Moreover, how does reapproaching universality in such a way allow human rights to be thought differently to offer something of use to radical politics? In this section, the first two of these questions will be addressed before, in the section to follow, turning to the third.

To return to the fundamental underpinnings of human rights to come, the approach it advances outlines that attention to, and ongoing exposure of, ineradicable alterity in the articulation and rearticulation of rights can offer radical potential when such a process is purposefully undertaken towards a futural horizon of relations of power that remains to come. Through being attentive to this alterity and utilising it as a means to engage in ongoing struggle towards better, more inclusive conceptions of human rights and relations of living and being more generally, possibilities for radical social transformation emerge. It is possible that the universality of human rights may be conceived in a way that facilitates this process of ongoing, futural articulation and rearticulation when thought in the sense of a universality that is 'to come'. This concept characterises universal concepts as concepts that cannot rest but are constantly worked and reworked by the alterity which haunts any universal. Instead of viewing universality as a static attribute or characteristic of rights, this approach brings the universality of human rights into view as a process of *ongoing universalisation*. This ongoing and futural working and reworking of universal concepts and values can be considered as the very heart of the politics of human rights and helps to perceive potential for universality as driving and sustaining never-ending challenge to restrictive regimes of power. Accordingly, understanding human rights as human rights to come involves conceiving universality as a *process, an action, a doing* which takes place through everyday politico-legal engagements with rights, and forms the very lifeblood of human rights as a potentially radical discourse.

This understanding of universality as a futural concept, itself 'to come', which facilitates the overarching aim of human rights to come draws from the general re-evaluation of universality in critical work which foregrounds openness and unfixity, but it is the work of Judith Butler that allows a specifically futural universal to be envisaged.[12] To explore more of what it may mean to understand the universality of human rights to come as a futural process of universalisation it is instructive to engage with Butler's thinking on the universal. For Butler, while static conceptions of universality may be comforting, they are problematic. The problem emerges 'when the meaning of "the universal" proves to be culturally variable, and the specific cultural articulations of the universal work against its claim to a transcultural status' (Butler 1996: 45). In this respect, the universal proves itself to be, in fact, less than universal. However, this is not a reason to abandon all recourse to universality for Butler, 'on the contrary. All it means is that there are cultural conditions for its articulation . . . and that the term gains its meaning for us precisely through these less than universal conditions' (1996: 45–46). It follows that any universal concept is 'only partially articulated, and that we do not yet know what forms it may take' and, as Butler continues,

> the contingent and cultural character of the existing conventions governing the scope of universality does not deny the usefulness of the term *universal*. It simply means that the claim of universality has not been fully or finally made and that it remains to be seen whether and how it will be further articulated.
> (1996: 46; emphasis in original)

Thus, for Butler, the universal always emerges within cultural contexts, is shaped by them, and is necessarily limited and always haunted by its own alterity. However, importantly, where the one who is outside of the legitimating structure of universality nevertheless speaks in its terms 'such a claim runs the good risk of provoking a radical rearticulation of universality itself' (Butler 1996: 46). This process of rearticulation is an ongoing necessity, maintaining universality as a permanent site of contest, of the 'not yet', or the 'to come' (Butler 1996; 48: Butler, Laclau and Žižek 2000: 47). In Butler's words, 'the excluded, in this sense, constitutes the contingent limit of universalization. And the universal . . . emerges as a postulated and open-ended *ideal* that has not been adequately encoded' (1996: 48, emphasis in original). From this outline, Butler asserts that it would be a mistake to think that 'conventional formulations exhaust the possibilities of what might be meant by "the universal"' and that insisting on more expansive reformulations of universality cannot hold a commitment to honouring only the 'provisional and parochial versions of universality' (1996: 47). Instead, exposing the parochialism and alterity characterising the universal is part of extending and rendering substantive the notion of universality, indeed, such is the process of universalisation itself.

Crucial to this ongoing rearticulation of the universal through exposure of its limits is what Butler outlines as the 'performative contradiction' posed by those who speak in the name of the universal while being excluded from it; 'claiming to be covered by that universal, they expose the contradictory character of previous conventional formulations of the universal' (1996: 48). The performative contradiction not only exposes the limits of current notions of universality, but performatively reworks such limits in more expansive and inclusive ways. In this way, 'the universal begins to become articulated precisely through challenges to its existing formulation, and this challenge emerges from those who are not covered by it . . . but nevertheless demand that the universal as such ought to be inclusive of them' (Butler 1996: 48). Through this process, the universal emerges as an open-ended ideal which can be rearticulated and is not restricted to its current legal or normative form. In this process of universalisation, the universal 'can be articulated only in response to a challenge from (its own) outside', from the unspeakable that it has produced through exclusion (Butler 1996: 49). This characterises universalisation as a never-ending process that 'has the capacity to sustain differences . . . [and] to remain permanently open-ended' (Stanton 2016: 28).

It is clear from this outline how Butler's conceptualisation of universality may be of use in advancing a futural conception of the universality of human rights which is compatible with the aims of radical politics. Drawing from Butler to articulate the universality of human rights as a futural-focused process of universalisation involves viewing current universal rights concepts as articulated within cultural contexts which makes them necessarily limited, always haunted by alterity. However, these universal concepts are not static or fixed but are constantly worked and reworked anew in an ongoing process of universalisation – politico-legal work taking place in various locations and contexts to seek to fix the subject, content and remit of rights through constant articulation and rearticulation. This process, which itself defines the work of human rights to come, must be understood as taking place, for example, when current rights concepts are challenged by those they exclude through the assertion of a performative contradiction which exposes the limits of the current universal and reworks it in a new, more expansive, way. Because the universal is articulated within culture, competing accounts of universal concepts always exist at any one time (Butler, Laclau and Žižek 2000: 136–181). The assertions made by those with alternative conceptions of what universal human rights should mean, say or look like, who appropriate the language of rights to challenge the restrictions of the current universal, are advancing a competing universality which enters into dialogue with the dominant universal in the process of universalisation.[13] This dialogue between existing universal concepts and people or groups viewing such concepts as inadequate in some way, advancing new understandings of them, characterises rights politics and is the never-ending working out of the universality of rights. It is this futural process of universalisation which human rights to come seeks to visibilise and harness to allow the alterity haunting universal human rights to be productively engaged towards more critical ends.

Following from the above, in the approach of human rights to come the universality of human rights is not an overarching value that rights possess, nor understood as defined by a universal subject or content that transcends contexts and borders; rather, it is understood as the process of ongoing universalisation revealing and responding to alterity that is rights politics. The universality of human rights is characterised by a constant fixing and unfixing of what universal rights concepts are, what they can be used to do and say, and what they represent which takes place in the diverse politics of human rights. This never-ending process renders universality itself 'to come', capable of sustaining and driving a futural approach to human rights more generally. Aiming towards an ultimately unachievable settled and all-inclusive universal conception of human rights through contestatory political engagement with alterity emerges as the *raison d'être* of universal human rights when universality is understood as a process of universalisation. It is clear how this approach differs from, and actively seeks to break with, traditional conceptions of universality and universal human rights. Understanding universality as a process of universalisation does not involve endorsing or rejecting the universality of human rights, or even framing debate in such terms, but requires immersion in its process. While traditional approaches may involve a limited view of universality as a process – for example, being open to the idea that universal rights norms may change over time – this does not view universality as being defined at a basic level as a process, nor does it foreground the central element of contest over alterity which defines the process of universalisation. Such approaches lack the critique of power, the critical scrutiny of the dominant universal and its relation to current restrictive regimes of power, staged by those excluded from the dominant, that universalisation gestures towards. In contrast, the idea of universality as universalisation requires the universality of human rights to be understood as a futural process of revealing and contesting power, part of what allows rights to be capitalised on in radical politics. Accordingly, this futural conception of the universal holds much potential, and this is what makes it compatible with the aims of human rights to come. Understanding universality in this way can be thought to involve encountering the idea of universality in the discourse of human rights as a foothold to begin to think through human rights as human rights to come, a key site where the work of this concept can be initiated and, indeed, sustained.

Universalisation and the radical: the universal content and subject of human rights

Discussion so far has considered the context for re-engagement with universality in the approach of human rights to come and what is involved in adopting a futural conception of universality. It has been asserted that an understanding of universality 'to come', as a futural-focused process of universalisation, is part of allowing for new possibilities for human rights to emerge. In order to think through more concretely what approaching universality would look like, and how it may allow human rights to be thought differently, discussion now turns to engage with two 'universal' elements of human rights: the universal content of human rights and the universal subject of human rights. These concepts are considered through the lens of universalisation to further bring into view the different approach it advances. As outlined at the outset of this chapter, the universalist position on human rights stems from an assertion that human rights are universal concepts that apply to all human subjects and consist of a core set of protections applicable across borders and contexts. From this, the content of human rights and the subject of human rights appear central to what has traditionally been understood as the universality of human rights. It is possible, however, that these two concepts may be conceived of as universal in a different way, as sites of ongoing, futural-focused universalisation, to allow the discourse and practice of human rights to offer radical possibilities. Central to this is the way in which thinking universality as universalisation enables the foregrounding of alterity in these concepts in a way traditional conceptions of universality cannot, and thereby allows universal human rights to be used in a critical politics of revealing and responding to restrictive relations of power.

The universal content of human rights

Beginning with the universal content of human rights, the first question that must be asked is how may the approach of universalisation facilitate a different view or perspective on such? This can be considered through contrast with two other understandings of this content. The first of these is a traditional universalist approach. In this perspective, human rights content is thought of as universal in the sense of consisting of a set of defined provisions, codified via international law, which enjoy universal authority and application across time and context. This universal content is generally perceived as located in the Universal Declaration of Human Rights, later added to by the two International Covenants to form what is now known as the 'International Bill of Human Rights' (Donnelly 2013: 24). The universal status given to this content, particularly its civil and political rights elements, has taken on an often quasi-sacred character.[14] For example, the Universal Declaration has been characterised, in the words of former UN Secretary-General Kofi Annan, as the 'yardstick by which we measure human progress' and, by Nadine Gordimer, as 'the essential document, the touchstone, the creed of humanity that surely sums up all other creeds directing human behavior' (cited in Ignatieff 2001: 53). The content of human rights, therefore, is presented as universal because it contains timeless provision of the rights inherent to 'human beings' and their conditions for dignity and well-being wherever they are situated and whatever time period they are living in. It is clear that a futural understanding of universality as a process contrasts sharply with this strict universalist approach. In contrast to fixed, the universal content of human rights in this analysis is foregrounded as made up of universal concepts which are by nature inherently unfixed due to the alterity that haunts them and as constantly worked and reworked through processes of rearticulation. Understanding universality as a futural-focused process of universalisation involves embrace of the fact that there can never be any final, settled universal content to human rights, no list engrained in stone, only temporary and contingent meanings. This understanding does not seek to undermine the importance of universal content as laid down in sources such as the International Bill of Human Rights, but seeks to untie human rights politics from a strict adherence to such content as representing the epitome of what human rights are or how they can be understood.

Such content marks only a starting point for human rights politics where attention must be paid to the limits of universal content and such content thought anew when it acts to further or invisibilise oppressive regimes of power. In this view, the universal content of human rights as articulated in international human rights law is not the ultimate articulation of rights but rather only the beginning for ongoing processes of universalisation critically engaging with such content and how it can be understood and used more broadly.

A second understanding which can be contrasted with the approach of universalisation falls into the category of approaches which have sought to modify or provide a more nuanced account of the universal content of human rights than that advanced by a strict universalist understanding. It is the approach of 'relative universality' advanced by Jack Donnelly. In Donnelly's view, human rights are both universal and relative. This relativity does not undermine their overarching universal status, but does have implications for how rights and their practice are understood. Donnelly elaborates that

> rather than see a two-dimensional space of universality and relativity, I suggest that we think of a multi-dimensional space of different forms and mixtures of different types of universality and relativity . . . The crucial work, then, is to identify the ways in which human rights both are and are not both relative and universal – and to avoid treating the universal as if it were relative or falsely universalizing the particular.
>
> (2013: 104)

In particular, Donnelly makes clear the way in which 'relative universality' relates to the universal content of human rights. He states that an authoritative list of human rights is the product of historically and contextually situated political struggles that shape dominant understandings of human dignity, threats to it and what is necessary to protect it (2013: 97–98). For Donnelly, the core list of universal human rights 'has evolved, and will continue to change, in response to social and technological changes, the emergence of new political forces, and even past human rights successes' (2013: 98). This evolution does not take away from their universal content, but forms part of the relativity which is inherent to 'relatively universal' human rights.

While Donnelly's account has been important in negotiating the complex universality of human rights and their content, it does not quite go far enough in offering the opportunities to re-engage human rights that the idea of universalisation offers. The latter differs from Donnelly's characterisation in a number of respects. First, while Donnelly does seek to debunk the idea of universal human rights as timeless, unchanging concepts with fixed content which persists across time and context, the concept of 'relative universality' remains within a traditional frame. In contrast to the aim of human rights to come and its futural understanding of rights, Donnelly's understanding of universality does not aim to radically rethink human rights as a discourse at a fundamental level. Rather, through 'relative universality' Donnelly seeks to further understand, even reinforce, human rights within the confines of international human rights law. Thus, while a 'relative universalist' understanding of the content of human rights does depart from traditional universalist accounts, it does not have in mind a critical rethinking of human rights and their foundations in the same way that universality as universalisation does. Second, understanding the universal content of human rights via the lens of universalisation involves fully eschewing the confines of universality–relativity, something which Donnelly does not do. Where Donnelly stresses the limits of universality – where universality intersects with, or gives way to, relativity – universalisation highlights the need to understand the universal in an entirely different way which begins by also accepting the cultural shaping of any universal content but characterising the working and reworking of such content not as relativism, but as the process of universalisation which opens up space to articulate universal content in new ways. The process of relative interpretation and evolution of universal content which Donnelly identifies may be reframed as the very process of universalisation, of responding to the alterity haunting any universal concept through its shaping in cultural contexts, modifying it through political engagement. This alternative approach moves focus from universality as an attribute to universality as an ongoing process.

From the above, understanding the content of human rights as universal does not involve advancing a list of timeless human rights which apply across time and context, nor does it involve understanding such content as 'relatively universal'. Rather, it involves seeing the content of human rights as always existing in a process which foregrounds it as temporary and limited, existing in a constant process of working and reworking in contexts of power. It is this that allows for the foregrounding of alterity and the facilitation of a human rights politics which is based on the visibilisation and contesting of the limits of universal content to meet the needs of those on the margins. In this respect, it is possible to see not only how universalisation allows the universal content of human rights to be thought differently, but also why such an understanding allows for more radical possibilities for human rights as a discourse and practice. While Donnelly's understanding highlights the contingent nature of the content of human rights – the fact that it is open to contextual reworking – the futural-focused understanding of universalisation goes further than this and foregrounds the contingent nature of universal content but also the fact that because of this contingency the universal content of human rights is always exclusive and shaped by alterity. In the latter approach the focus is not on contingency alone – the responsive development of universal content as laid down in sources such as the International Bill of Human Rights – but on the alterity that flows from the fact that universal human rights content is contingent. The politics of human rights, therefore, may come into view as a process of universalisation in the sense of reworking the alterity of the contingent content of human rights based on its exclusions, facilitating an ongoing critical relation to such content.

Understanding the universal content of human rights via the lens of universalisation also facilitates more radical possibilities for human rights because it allows for an alternative approach to how the 'success' or 'achievement' of human rights content is understood which may provide a more liberating perspective in rights politics. Re-engaging universality as universalisation necessarily means that it is no longer possible to quantitatively measure compliance with the timeless principles of human rights. The universal content of human rights has not failed, or can no longer be considered 'truly universal', because many still suffer human rights violations, because states still fall short of their obligations to ensure the core universal content of human rights is upheld in their jurisdiction. Rather, the 'achievement' of any universal content must remain as futural as the final settlement of that content itself. Universal human rights have not let down those on the margins because universal content is still exclusive or because human suffering still proliferates in various locations across the globe. If the point of universal human rights is to encourage engagement in an ongoing process of universalisation, continual making and remaking of human rights in a way that can never achieve a perfect realisation, we see that it is *engagement in this process in itself* which holds possibilities for those on the margins, rather than the (impossible) output of a final realisation of a core, timeless content of rights. Human rights can never be finally 'achieved' as an answer to the diverse political, social and economic problems facing world populations. The universal content of rights cannot be approached as objects or moral truths which can straightforwardly emancipate or juridically guarantee liberty, security and equality in the liberal sense. Importantly, what human rights to come seeks to visibilise is the fact that the process of contesting and continually rearticulating the universal content of rights to challenge the limits of the currently dominant universal is what holds emancipatory potential. Entering into this process of ongoing contest offers the opportunity to work towards a better vision of our living and being, to performatively bring such into being, albeit this is a vision that can never be *fully* realised. This view, rather than leading into inertia, should push radical thinkers, activists and groups towards a never-ending striving for the enhanced concretisation of the values that universal human rights content represents and the conception of our lives together that it promotes which is achieved through the very process of ongoing working and reworking of universal concepts and ideas.

The universal subject of human rights

A second key universal element which approaching universality as universalisation requires a re-envisaging of is the universal subject of human rights. Again, it is useful to begin by asking how an understanding of universality as universalisation may allow this concept to be thought differently from existing perspectives. The universal subject has been characterised in traditional approaches to human rights in biological terms as relating to an idea of the 'human being' (Donnelly 2013: 10). As Anthony Langlois comments this, indeed, is the force of the 'human' in the term human rights – the idea that these rights accrue to all people simply by virtue of their being human. They do not need to belong to a particular class or religion, their sex or race has no impact, their wealth or status is neither here nor there. Under a human rights regime, it is their *humanity* which serves as the basis for their recognition and the basis for the universalism of the human rights doctrine.

(2005: 371, emphasis in original)

From this perspective, the universal subject of human rights is a straightforwardly pre-existing and easily identifiable being; every member of the human race, in juxtaposition to all other living and non-living beings and objects. Approaching this concept through the lens of universalisation involves rejecting such an approach to the 'human'. Instead, it requires attention be drawn to the fact that the human also exists in a process of universalisation whereby its limits are constantly redrawn by its exclusions. This assertion draws from the by now well-established retort to the universalist position that the 'human' as a universal concept utilised in mainstream rights discourse does not pertain to biology, nor can the 'human' be thought to have a static and timeless character. As Douzinas states, 'what history has taught us is that there is nothing sacred about any definition of humanity and nothing eternal about its scope. Humanity cannot act as an *a priori* normative principle' (2000: 188). The 'universal' human has proved variable, from the early American and French revolutionary origins of contemporary human rights, where rights were the rights of 'man', to 1945 and the creation of modern human rights when, as lesbian, gay, bisexual, transgender and intersex, feminist and postcolonial activism has demonstrated, the 'human' of human rights took the form of a white, Western, heterosexual male. Accordingly, there is no reason to suspect that the universal 'human' who is the subject of contemporary mainstream discourses of human rights should be approached or understood as a fully inclusive and settled universal concept.

Douzinas continues his statement above by asserting that the function of the 'human' 'lies not in a philosophical essence but in its non-essence, in the endless process of re-definition and the continuous but impossible attempt to escape fate and external determination' (2000: 188). From this perspective, the universal 'human' subject of human rights can be conceived as a 'floating signifier'. By this, Douzinas means that 'it is just a word, a discursive element that is not automatically or necessarily linked to any particular signified or concept. On the contrary, the word "human" is empty of meaning and can be attached to an infinite number of signifieds' (2000: 255). By characterising this signifier as 'floating' Douzinas outlines that

> the 'humanity' of human rights is not just an empty signifier; it carried an enormous symbolic capital, a surplus of value and dignity endowed by the revolutions and the declarations and augmented by every new struggle for the

recognition and protection of human rights . . . this symbolic excess turns the signifier 'human' . . . into something that combatants in political, social and legal struggles want to co-opt to their cause.

(2000: 255)

This accounts for how rights have proliferated in line with new, additional subject identities in recent decades as the floating signifier of the 'human' is attached to women, migrant workers, disabled people, children and others (Douzinas 2000: 256). Thus, for Douzinas 'the common aim of human rights campaigns is to link the floating and symbolic signifier to a particular signified, to arrest its constitutive indeterminacy and to achieve the – partial – bonding of human nature with a regional conception of humanity which will bestow upon the latter the symbolic value of the core concept' (2000: 259).

Accordingly, the universal 'human' resists any attempt to be permanently fixed or determined; it is not an all-inclusive concept pertaining to 'human beings', but a non-essence. It is important to highlight that understanding the universal human of human rights via the idea of universalisation involves beginning with this assertion, although it does not involve finishing with it. Again, a distinction must be drawn between this existing approach and that of human rights to come. To foreground the universal human as existing in a futural-focused process of universalisation, it is necessary to build on Douzinas and connect the idea of the human as a floating signifier with futurity. Human rights politics is indeed a politics whereby radical thinkers, activists and groups seek to temporarily fill the floating signifier of the 'human' of human rights but, adding to Douzinas, this floating signifier must be viewed as futural in that it always gestures towards a fully inclusive and complete idea of the human, relating to a futural condition of relations and being rid of alterity, which always remains 'to come'. Viewing the universal subject of human rights in this way involves challenging biological accounts of the universal 'human', but also requires understanding that articulation and rearticulation of this subject gestures towards a self-refuting conception of the human, lest the radical opportunities to challenge restrictive regimes of power shaping who is considered human and who is not that are offered by an ongoing critical attention to alterity be lost.

From this, it can be understood that the practice of human rights to come and its advancement of universality as universalisation encourages staying with the alterity that will always haunt the universal subject of human rights, foregrounding the human as a futural-focused concept that can never be perfected but one that by this fact holds potential to stimulate ongoing debate on alterity in the process of universalisation. It is this that allows the approach of universalisation to offer radical potential. The idea of the human existing in a process of universalisation towards a future of perfect relations of living and being that remains self-refuting encourages those interested in human rights politics to embrace the site of the universal human as one of permanent unsettlement, and this unsettlement as one which holds unsettling potential to rework who counts as human more generally (Butler 2004: 36–39). It allows this concept to be maintained despite its demonstrated shortcomings, and, moreover, provides impetus to keep on critically investigating the human in human rights politics. After considering the human of human rights through the lens of human rights to come the universal subject must also be conceptualised as 'to come', as a concept which can never be fully perfected; in fact the universality of the subject when viewed as universalisation involves actively refusing an illusion of such with a futural focus on the human. From this perspective, there is no universal subject of rights; rather, the universality of the human emerges as a politically productive site to engage in ongoing debate on the meaning of this subject and reveal, in a way that liberal conceptions of human rights currently cannot, the role of power in the creation of notions of the human which will always remain exclusionary.

Significantly, this view of the human and its assertion that there is not, and can never be, a fixed universal subject of universal human rights does not take away the protection contained in the assertion that 'all humans have rights'. On the contrary, it holds radical potential by seeking to enhance the position of those subjects who are often on the margins – women, ethnic communities, those identifying as lesbian, gay, bisexual or transgender, disabled communities – by highlighting the universality of the human as a place where radical politics is able to contest the current power regimes shaping and restricting such subjects, power regimes which are hidden in the straightforward assertion that 'all humans are born equal in dignity and rights'. In this respect, the alternative approach to universality envisaged through human rights to come allows universal human rights to come into view as a vehicle which can be consciously exploited to reveal and contest subjectifying relations of power as opposed to merely reifying them. It highlights the politics of human rights as a space centred on the ongoing contestation of such power and its definition of the subject of rights and thus allows the politics of human rights and its relation to the subject to facilitate a deeper troubling of the power relations that shape us.

Conclusion

In understanding human rights as human rights to come, a reapproaching of the universality of human rights is central. Universality need not be abandoned, but, on the contrary, can be re-engaged to form the very driving force of this project to re-engage rights. While the concept of universality has demonstrated a number of flaws and limitations when thought within the traditional frame of universality–relativity, a place can still be found for human rights as universal in radical politics. The approach of human rights to come encourages radical thinkers, groups and activists to continue already initiated work to reclaim the site of universality, to consider the space to rework the traditional flaws and limitations of universality when thought in relation to rights and to not give up on the idea of universality, albeit this idea must be thought of and approached in a different way.

Butler's conception of universality as a process of universalisation where the 'not yet' of the universal is sustained is of use in articulating the futural approach that human rights to come seeks to foreground, and demonstrates how the 'to come' of the universal can be thought of as central to a radical approach to human rights. While traditional approaches to human rights have tended to present universality in the sense of closure or settlement – pinning down the meaning, content and subject of rights – the futural approach of universality as universalisation reveals both the illusion of such approaches – universal content always being temporary and unfixed – and brings universality into view as a tool to begin to reveal and challenge the alterity of human rights concepts such as the universal content and subject of rights. Understanding universality as universalisation, a futural-focused process, gestures towards the imperative to resist closure, to always sustain attention to the 'not yet', the impossibility of final completion, the 'to come' of any universal as shaped within contexts of power. This, in turn, is an approach which is more amenable to use of human rights to contest restrictive regimes of power and to advance the claims of those on the margins.

Notes

1 For further discussion on this issue, see Ibhawoh (2000); Engle Merry (2003); Dahan Kalev (2004).
2 For authors writing on this debate, see Renteln (1990); Donnelly (1984); Halliday (1995); Brems (1997); Perry (1997); Tilley (2000); Ackerly (2008).
3 See Henkin (1990: ix).
4 See Twining (2007); Mutua (1996; 2001); An-Na'im (1992); Binder (1999).
5 To provide some examples: Conor Gearty advances a re-narration of human rights, 'one that is more convincing and better able to appeal to the global community as a truly universal discourse' (2008: 6); Jack Donnelly advances a recognition of human rights as both universal and relative in various ways (2013: 104); Abdullahi Ahmed An-Na'im has worked to show how universal human rights may be compatible with Islamic law and how the latter can be reworked to produce a better relationship between the two (1999; 2009); An-Na'im et al. (1995).
6 These authors include Douzinas (2000: 12); Brown (1997); Rorty (1998: 170).
7 Among these, Dianne Otto (1997a; 1997b; 1999) utilises poststructuralist resources to consider how it may be possible to approach universality in a way which recognises the transformative critique of rights emerging from non-elite groups such as feminists, lesbian, gay, bisexual and transgender communities, critical race theorists and indigenous groups and is defined by 'continuous political and ethical struggle between differences and across incommensurabilities' (1997a: 34).
8 See discussion in the final section of Chapter 2, where Douzinas's futural conception of human rights is considered.
9 See Zigon (2014).
10 Thinking on this area is diverse in approach and scope. See, for example, Butler (1993); Zerilli (1998); Laclau (1992); Anderson (1998); Balibar (1995).
11 See, for example, Otto (1997a; 1997b; 1999) noted above, Lloyd (2007) and Stanton (2016).
12 Butler's comments on universality are mainly outlined in 'Universality in Culture' (1996), *Excitable Speech* (1997: 86–92) and *Contingency, Hegemony, Universality*

alongside Ernesto Laclau and Slavoj Žižek (2000). For discussion on Butler's universal and its futural element, see Moreiras (2002).
13 This is a process that Butler terms 'cultural translation' explored further in Chapter 7. For further discussion see Butler, Laclau and Žižek (2000: 35–41).
14 See, for example, Mutua (1996: 604–605) and Ignatieff (2001: 53).

References

Ackerly, B. (2008) *Universal Human Rights in a World of Difference*, Cambridge: Cambridge University Press.
Anderson, A. (1998) 'Cosmopolitanism, Universalism and the Divided Legacies of Modernity', in P. Cheah and B. Robbins (eds), *Cosmopolitics: Thinking and Feeling Beyond the Nation*, Minneapolis: University of Minnesota Press.
An-Na'im, A. A. (ed.) (1992) *Human Rights in Cross-Cultural Perspectives: A Quest for Consensus*, Pennsylvania: University of Pennsylvania Press.
An-Na'im, A. A. (1999) 'Universality of Human Rights: An Islamic Perspective', in N. Ando (ed.), *Japan Past, Present and Future: International Symposium to Mark the Centennial of the Japanese Association of International Law*, The Hague; London; Boston: Kluwer Law International, 311–325.
An-Na'im, A. A. (2009) 'Toward a Cross-Cultural Approach to Defining International Standards of Human Rights', in M. Goodale (ed.), *Human Rights: An Anthropological Reader*, Chichester: Wiley-Blackwell, 68–85.
An-Na'im, A. A., Gort, J., Jansen, H. and Vroom, H. (eds) (1995) *Human Rights and Religious Values: An Uneasy Relationship?*, Grand Rapids, MI: Eerdmans.
Balibar, É. (1995) 'Ambiguous Universality', *differences*, 7(1): 48–76.
Binder, G. (1999) 'Cultural Relativism and Cultural Imperialism in Human Rights Law', *Buffalo Human Rights Law Review*, 5: 211–221.
Brems, E. (1997) 'Enemies or Allies? Feminism and Cultural Relativism as Dissident Voices in Human Rights Discourse', *Human Rights Quarterly*, 19(1): 136–164.
Brown, C. (1997) 'Universal Human Rights: A Critique', *International Journal of Human Rights*, 1(2): 41–65.
Butler, J. (1993) 'Poststructuralism and Postmarxism', *diacritics*, 23(4): 3–11.
Butler, J. (1996) 'Universality in Culture', in M. Nussbaum, with respondents, J. Cohen (ed.), *For Love of Country?: A New Democracy Forum on the Limits of Patriotism*, Boston: Beacon Press, 45–52.
Butler, J. (1997) *Excitable Speech: A Politics of the Performative*, New York; London: Routledge.
Butler, J. (2004) *Undoing Gender*, New York; London: Routledge.
Butler, J., Laclau, E. and Žižek, S. (2000) *Contingency, Hegemony, Universality: Contemporary Dialogues on the Left*, London: Verso.
Dahan Kalev, H. (2004) 'Cultural Rights or Human Rights: The Case of Female Genital Mutilation', *Sex Roles*, 51(5–6): 339–348.
Donnelly, J. (1984) 'Cultural Relativism and Universal Human Rights', *Human Rights Quarterly*, 6(4): 400–419.
Donnelly, J. (2007) 'The Relative Universality of Human Rights', *Human Rights Quarterly*, 29(2): 281–306.
Donnelly, J. (2013) *Universal Human Rights in Theory and Practice*, 3rd edn, Ithaca, NY: Cornell University Press.

Douzinas, C. (2000) *The End of Human Rights: Critical Legal Thought at the Turn of the Century*, Oxford: Hart.

Engle Merry, S. (2003) 'Human Rights Law and the Demonization of Culture (And Anthropology Along the Way)', *Political and Legal Anthropology Review*, 26(1): 55–76.

Gearty, C. (2008) 'Are Human Rights Truly Universal?', available at: web.archive.org/web/20130511071932/http://www.conorgearty.co.uk/pdfs/Chapter_29_Universality FINAL.pdf (accessed 2 January 2017).

Goodhart, M. (2013) 'Human Rights and the Politics of Contestation', in M. Goodale (ed.), *Human Rights at the Crossroads*, Oxford: Oxford University Press, 31–44.

Halliday, F. (1995) 'Relativism and Universalism in Human Rights: the Case of the Islamic Middle East', *Political Studies*, 43(1): 152–167.

Henkin, L. (1990) *The Age of Rights*, New York: Columbia University Press.

Ibhawoh, B. (2000) 'Between Culture and Constitution: Evaluating the Cultural Legitimacy of Human Rights in the African State', *Human Rights Quarterly*, 22(3): 838–860.

Ignatieff, M. (2001) *Human Rights as Politics and Idolatry*, A. Gutmann (ed.), Princeton: Princeton University Press.

Kennedy, D. (2002) 'The International Human Rights Movement: Part of the Problem?', *Harvard Human Rights Journal*, 15: 101–125.

Laclau, E. (1992) 'Universalism, Particularism and the Question of Identity', *October*, 61: 83–90.

Langlois, A. (2005) 'The Narrative Metaphysics of Human Rights', *International Journal of Human Rights*, 9(3): 369–387.

Lloyd, M. (2007) '(Women's) Human Rights: Paradoxes and Possibilities', *Review of International Studies*, 33(1): 91–103.

Moreiras, A. (2002) 'A Thinking Relationship: The End of Subalternity – Notes on Hegemony, Contingency, Universality: Contemporary Dialogues on the Left', *South Atlantic Quarterly*, 101(1): 97–131.

Mutua, M. (1996) 'The Ideology of Human Rights', *Virginia Journal of International Law*, 36: 589–657.

Mutua, M. (2001) 'Savages, Victims, and Saviors: The Metaphor of Human Rights', *Harvard International Law Journal*, 42(1): 201–245.

Otto, D. (1997a) 'Rethinking the "Universality" of Human Rights Law', *Columbia Human Rights Law Review*, 1(1): 1–46.

Otto, D. (1997b) 'Rethinking Universals: Opening Transformative Possibilities in International Human Rights Law', *Australian Yearbook of International Law*, 18: 1–36.

Otto, D. (1999) 'Everything is Dangerous: Some Poststructuralist Tools for Rethinking the Universal Knowledge Claims of Human Rights Law', *Australian Journal of Human Rights*, 5(1): 17–47.

Perry, M. (1997) 'Are Human Rights Universal? The Relativist Challenge and Related Matters', *Human Rights Quarterly*, 19(3): 461–509.

Renteln, A. D. (1990) *International Human Rights: Universalism versus Relativism*, London: Sage.

Rorty, R. (1998) *Truth and Progress: Philosophical Papers Volume 3*, Cambridge: Cambridge University Press.

Stanton, D. (2016) 'A New Universal for Human Rights? The Particular, the Generalizable, the Political', in S. McClennen and A. Schultheis Moore (eds), *The Routledge Companion to Literature and Human Rights*, New York; London: Routledge, 27–36.

Tilley, J. (2000) 'Cultural Relativism', *Human Rights Quarterly*, 22(2): 501–547.

Twining, W. (2007) 'Human Rights: Southern Voices; Francis Deng, Abdullahi An-Na'im, Yash Ghai and Upendra Baxi', *Law, Social Justice & Global Development Journal*, (1): 1–63.

Zerilli, L. (1998) 'This Universalism Which Is Not One', *diacritics*, 28(2): 3–20.

Zigon, J. (2014) 'Maintaining the "Truth": Performativity, Human Rights, and the Limitations on Politics', *Theory & Event*, 17(3): n.p.

Chapter 5

Beyond consensus

The agonism of human rights to come

Introduction

In this chapter, the ideas of consensus and conflict, their place in human rights politics, and the approach of human rights to come requires such to be re-engaged, are considered. While in their mainstream form human rights have been to a great extent driven by consensus and consensus-forging, understanding human rights as human rights to come involves foregrounding and actively embracing rights and their politics as characterised by conflict. It is only when conflict and its ineradicable place in the politics of human rights is embraced that the radical possibilities of human rights can be pursued in terms of sustaining a futural conception of rights which is never settled, never fully within grasp and thus facilitates ongoing critical engagements with power. An approach to human rights which aims towards consensus cuts off the promise of the 'to come' and is incapable of facilitating conflictual engagements with the alterity constitutive of current rights concepts and regimes of power more generally. As is explored, human rights to come requires radical thinkers, activists and groups not only to reject a consensus-based approach and understand conflict as at the centre of human rights and their potential for radical politics, but, by its nature, this idea promotes an understanding of the conflict defining human rights politics as a specifically *agonistic* form of conflict. Through engagement with the work of Chantal Mouffe, this chapter explores human rights to come as an agonistic approach to rights, and, moreover, how such an approach allows human rights to emerge as a location where agonistic democracy is sustained more generally and human rights to come may be intimately intertwined with the wider idea of an agonistic democracy 'to come'.

In the first section of the chapter, the idea of consensus in human rights politics is engaged and why understanding human rights as human rights to come requires radical thinkers and activists to not only eschew a consensus-based approach, but to actively embrace conflict in human rights and their politics. The second section turns to the idea of agonism to explore how this approach to conflict is one of agonism. It considers the conflict between adversaries, the critical relation to power and the conflictual consensus at the heart of human rights to come as rendering it a fundamentally agonistic activity. In drawing from Mouffe's concept of agonism to articulate a radical, futural conception of human rights, discussion seeks to add to Mouffe's own work; thinking through more of how human rights may facilitate, as opposed to hinder, engagement with the conflictual nature of the political and so fit with the wider project of agonistic democracy. In the final section, this assertion is taken further in exploring the parallels between the way in which this concept of democracy must inevitably remain 'to come' – sustaining conflict, rejecting completely achieved pluralism and remaining inevitably self-refuting – and human rights to come. This allows a link to emerge between the radicalisation of human rights and their relation to consensus/conflict and the radicalisation of democracy more generally.

Consensus and the politics of human rights

Before turning to the particular agonistic approach that human rights to come can be thought to gesture towards, it is important to understand where the idea of consensus has traditionally emerged in relation to the discourse and politics of rights, and what the particular limitations of a consensus-based approach are. A number of consensus-focused narratives can be detected as characterising mainstream understandings of human rights, particularly in their form as international human rights. For example, Sally Engle Merry suggests that the international human rights system as a whole is defined and driven by 'transnational consensus building' whereby 'states and civil society negotiate a consensus across differences in ideology, politics, and cultural practices' (2006: 19).[1] The creation of treaties and key international human rights documents such as the Universal Declaration of Human Rights and the Vienna Declaration and Programme of Action are frequently described in terms of consensus achieved through reasoned dialogue and discussion between states and their conflicting interests, values and cultural perspectives.[2] Indeed, the legitimacy of the international human rights framework, and the treaties, conventions and other documents resulting from it, is bolstered by the fact that such has been produced through consensus, that states have been willing to put aside differences and reach a position that is acceptable to all. The discourse of human rights is upheld as unique in its ability to facilitate international consensus between diverse states, nations and cultures and this ability appears closely linked to the politico-legal significance and authority of human rights in the contemporary era (Donnelly 2013: 57–60). In addition to the ability of human rights to facilitate consensus and 'transnational consensus building', international human rights law and the UN mechanisms and processes associated with it also promote a focus on consensus via the conception that international consensus has been reached *on* human rights in their current form. This consensus narrative intersects with the universalist approach to human rights encountered in the previous chapter: because global, cross-cultural consensus has been evidenced in key treaties and human rights documents human rights can, and should, be viewed as a universal discourse.[3] Human rights in their present international format are presented as a 'settled norm' over which consensus has been found which, taken together with 'the still prevalent naturalist account of human rights', suggests 'the discovery of a final "truth"', a true universal (Evans 2005: 1051). Thus, discourses of consensus on, and the ability to build consensus through, human rights characterise modern international human rights, their scope, remit and authority at a foundational level.

An emphasis on consensus can also be detected in the politics and use of human rights at a more local level. Human rights are often perceived as a common language that brings people together, an inclusive discourse that draws on what people have in common, and therefore a site where a consensual solution can be reached (Tambakaki 2010: 89). This consensus may be reached by amicable means where one rights-based argument persuades the opposing side of its value, where a compromise is reached between the two through rational discussion or, indeed, it can take the form of a forced consensus where human rights serve to close political debate down based on what rights, or a particular rights concept, represents more generally. This latter approach can be linked to the idea of 'rights as trumps'[4] where, as Michael Ignatieff summarises, 'rights are introduced into a political discussion [and] they serve to resolve the discussion' (2001: 300). This forced resolution occurs because human rights represent something particularly important – a 'universal' truth – that has already been agreed upon and therefore should always take priority over other ideas, arguments or claims. The idea of rights as trumps links to a general liberal fear of majoritarian decision-making, which it is asserted that rights provide a limit to, thereby offering protection for the liberal individual.[5] An approach to rights as trumps capable of forging a consensus by virtue of their inherent value can be detected in many contemporary accounts of and engagements with rights. As Karen Zivi asserts, political actors drawing on the language and provisions of rights often do so assuming – although not always correctly – that such will allow them to supersede other arguments and allow their particular position to 'win' the political battle and facilitate a political consensus in their favour (2012: 28). In this view, political actors frequently approach the practice of rights with the clear end of bringing debate to a close using the powerful moral and politico-legal authority of rights, to forge a consensus that their perspective, backed by rights provision, offers a clear solution to the particular problem at hand, as opposed to viewing human rights as themselves unsettled and debatable ideas.

These narratives demonstrating the various ways in which human rights are often perceived as based upon, or serving to facilitate, consensus among diverse interests have been central to the power of human rights in the contemporary period. In many respects, such narratives link into the classical liberal origins of human rights which promote focus on discussion to resolve conflicts of opinion and a foregrounding of rational argumentation and persuasion, ideals which have remained within mainstream discourses of human rights both internationally and in local political engagements. However, this focus on consensus must be perceived as accompanied by considerable limitations, especially for work seeking to engage human rights in a more radical way, as in the project of human rights to come. For example, understanding the politics of human rights as about reaching consensus through rational discussion or forging consensus through pre-existing agreement on what rights concepts represent obscures elements such as the messiness and unpredictability of the politics of human rights, the ineradicable nature and importance of political disagreement, the performativity of the practice of rights and cements problematic elements such as ideas of 'winners' and 'losers' in the local politics of rights trumping and an intense focus on the outcome of rights politics as opposed to the process itself and the value this may have (Zivi 2012: 24–42). In addition, the focus on consensus in human rights, especially in their form as codified in international law, often serves to obscure important disagreements and the conflict which nevertheless persists within the discourse and practice of rights. It invisibilises, for example, the divergent interpretations of human rights which exist challenging the dominant which include postcolonial perspectives, those revealing the limits of human rights in relation to particular subjects, and those contesting the liberal parameters of rights (Evans 2005: 1054). Indeed, if mainstream conceptions of human rights are presented as emerging from consensus or driven by consensus-building their power is bolstered and, subsequently, so too is the particular vision of human rights they promote, namely a vision which is based on liberal negative freedoms, the bounded individual and free market economy (Evans 2005: 1054–1062). Understanding human rights as human rights to come draws attention to these critiques of a consensus-based approach and involves rejecting focus on consensus in rights politics.

In contrast to the narratives outlined above as characterising mainstream understandings of human rights, an approach foregrounding consensus is not productive, or even possible, in the practice of human rights to come. When rights are understood as existing in processes of articulation and rearticulation responding to their ineradicable limits focus moves from the outcome of rights politics – whether a consensual outcome was, or can be, achieved as the measure of success in human rights politics – and toward the process of such politics, placing emphasis on its performative dimension and the utility this may offer to (re)think the world around us. Furthermore, and importantly, focusing on processes of never-ending articulation and rearticulation draws attention to the fact that rights are always unsettled, rejecting the urge towards settlement that narratives of consensus build into human rights, often in line with particular interests which benefit from containment of political contest (Evans 2005: 1051). This is where a rejection of consensus is necessary to facilitate the futural in the practice of human rights to come. Human rights in this perspective are not ideas characterised by consensus and consensus-forging underpinned by an assumption that bringing political debate to an end is desirable, but ideas that are continually conflictually made and remade in political engagement within a critical relation to power towards a futural horizon of perfection. The particular critique which human rights to come asserts at consensus-based understandings is that such understandings fundamentally obscure the futural nature of human rights; that human rights, and debate over them, will never be finished or settled but in order to be of use rights must remain a self-refuting project. By this very nature human rights cannot be utilised to seek an end to, closure in, or a 'solution to' political debate. The 'to come', which is central to understanding human rights in a radical way, requires the politics of rights to be viewed not as an exercise in consensus-building but as driven by critical engagements with alterity and power which always delay a final settlement or closure. When focus is not on the futural and human rights are viewed as a site or vehicle for forging political consensus, human rights lose their radical potential to sustain futural-focused debate attentive to the ineradicable limits of rights and regimes of power more generally. In this respect, it is necessary to question ideas of consensus detectable in mainstream conceptions of rights to facilitate a never-ending politics of human rights which maintains the promise of the 'to come'.

It is important to note, however, that understanding human rights as human rights to come does not only entail a problematisation of consensus, it also requires an *active embrace of conflict*. A focus on consensus is not the only way that rights politics can be characterised. As outlined above, consensus narratives invisibilise the conflict that nevertheless persists surrounding the discourse of human rights, the conflict that lies just below the surface of rights (Ignatieff 2001: 299). Conflict is, therefore, always a part of human rights. This idea of conflict can be brought into view as one that can be productively harnessed in and through the practice of human rights to come. Indeed, it is only through an active embrace of conflict that the radical possibilities of human rights can be facilitated and an ongoing critical relation to alterity may be productively fostered. To think through how conflict can assist in facilitating the radical in this way, it is possible to draw insights from the thought of Jacques Rancière. For Rancière, consensual processes that aim to regulate plural passions and lead to a rational agreement in terms of our common coexistence are 'post-democratic' in the sense of effacing the *demos* and reducing democracy to 'the sole interplay of state mechanisms and combinations of social energies and interests' (1999: 102). In contrast, democratic politics is defined by conflict, consisting of acts of disruption or dissensus to the existing order staged by the part that have no part, those who are on the margins (Rancière 1999: 11). Following from this, consensus leads to the 'disappearance of the miscount', where those who have no part in the social order stake a claim and take part in it (Rancière 1999: 102). It may be said then that conflict, following the insights of Rancière, must be actively embraced to sustain a radical politics critical to power and alterity.

It is clear that approaches to human rights which foreground consensus are incapable of facilitating the disruptive contest of the part that has no part, and therefore are incapable of sustaining a radical politics of human rights attentive to alterity. For this reason Paulina Tambakaki characterises a consensus-based view of human rights as 'post-democratic'. She outlines that human rights in their mainstream form, focusing on disputes as problems which can be rationally resolved and a privileging of law over politics, problematically aim to realise what cannot be realised; 'to redress the constitutive wrong of politics', to eradicate the alterity which facilitates the political (2010: 89–90). However, while Tambakaki does not consider currently dominant discourses of human rights capable of facilitating productive political conflict in the sense outlined by Rancière, characterising liberal human rights as 'anti-political',[6] it is my assertion that the practice of human rights to come can allow for such possibilities to come into being by facilitating a radical politics of rights that embraces conflict to allow for critical engagements with alterity. This practice involves visibilising the integral part of conflict in human rights and embracing it as a driving force in the everyday politics of rights. To understand this assertion, it is necessary to return again to the foundations of this approach. When human rights are approached as an ongoing and never-ending process of articulation and rearticulation responding to the ineradicable alterity constituting human rights concepts, the purpose of rights politics comes into view as being to challenge existing consensus, to expose its limits based upon the conflictual claims of those on the margins. The activity of articulation and rearticulation is at heart a conflictual one that involves contest over power and existing ways of viewing the world. This practice can be thought of as serving to stage a dissensus, a division in the 'common sense', through asking provocative and critical questions about current inequalities and relations of power (Rancière 2004: 304). Through foregrounding conflict human rights to come carries out its aim of visibilising alterity and the 'part who have no part', thereby offering a means of moving beyond post-democratic, consensus-driven approaches to allow human rights to become a vehicle of use to those interested in radical politics which sustains a critical relation to alterity.

Thus, the concept of human rights to come involves a rejection of the consensus approach to human rights in favour of a foregrounding of the futural and the unsettlement or lack of closure that is central to rights and their politics. Indeed, in order to re-engage human rights in a more radical way, which facilitates a never-ending critical engagement with alterity and power, an active embrace of conflict is required that moves beyond the 'anti-political' and 'post-democratic' tendencies of consensus-based approaches and their invisibilisation of alterity. In doing so, new possibilities for human rights in radical politics are facilitated. However, it is necessary to ask more about this rejection of consensus and embrace of conflict. What form can this be thought to take? What does it mean to embrace and sustain the futural through the idea of conflict in the politics of human rights? Are there any resources that may be of assistance in this repositioning of consensus and conflict? In articulating the nuances of the particular approach to embracing conflict human rights to come seeks to foreground, I assert that the idea of *agonism* is of use, characterising human rights to come as an *agonistic practice of human rights*.[7] Moreover, in this way, human rights to come may be understood as linked to and of use in sustaining something that consensus-based approaches to human rights are incapable of sustaining: an agonistic approach to democracy more generally which is also futural in nature.

From consensus to agonism: human rights to come as an agonistic politics of rights

To understand what it means to advance the practice of human rights to come as an agonistic practice, it is necessary to consider more of the idea of agonism. Broadly speaking, agonism has been developed in critical thought as a concept that gestures towards a constellation of commitments such as contestation of basic principles, respect for difference and attention to the informal operation of power (Wingenbach 2011: xi). The idea is a diverse and complex one, often closely intertwined with work such as that of William Connolly, James Tully, David Owen, Bonnie Honig and Aletta Norval,[8] but it is the work of Chantal Mouffe and her articulation of agonism within the wider context of agonistic democracy that discussion here will draw upon as offering particular possibilities to think through the radical re-engagement with human rights and their relation to consensus and conflict that human rights to come advances.[9] In turn, through this discussion Mouffe's thinking on agonism, the political and human rights may be itself be added to by being brought into conversation with the idea of human rights to come.

Alongside Ernesto Laclau, Mouffe was integral to the origins of radical democratic thought and its focus on the ineradicable nature of antagonism within the political and the social, advancing engagement in hegemonic politics, based upon this ineradicable antagonism, to expand the key tenets of liberal democracy in breadth and depth towards the transformation of existing relations of power (Laclau and Mouffe 2001: 122–127). Mouffe has developed on many of the issues explored in her collaborative work with Laclau in her own subsequent work. Central to Mouffe's thinking is the assertion that liberal democracy is characterised by a fundamental tension between liberalism, and its emphasis on individual liberty and universal rights, on the one hand, and democracy, which privileges equality and popular sovereignty, on the other (2000: 2). Mouffe critiques liberal and deliberative approaches as unable to fully grasp the confrontation between these two elements and, in their search for rational consensus, as missing the conflict and antagonism which is central to any modern democracy, thereby providing an inadequate account of modern democratic politics (2000: 7). For Mouffe, rather than seeking to 'democratise democracy' consensus-based approaches actually create the problems that democratic institutions are currently facing (2005a: 2). Instead of pursuing institutions and means through which supposedly 'impartial' politics reconciling all conflicting interests can take place, Mouffe advances the creation of a vibrant public sphere of contest where different political struggles may productively confront each other in what she terms agonistic pluralism (2005a: 3). In this view, as opposed to seeking rational consensus, liberal and deliberative approaches should 'dedicate their attention to the different ways in which [the] dimension of conflictuality could be played out in ways compatible with a democratic order' (2002: 616).

In understanding this assertion and how it may be engaged in the arena of human rights via the idea of human rights to come, it is necessary to understand how Mouffe draws upon the distinction between 'politics' – the ontic level of political institutions and practices – and 'the political' – the ontological dimension of politics concerning the way in which society is instituted (2005a: 9–10).[10] Mouffe seeks to reveal how 'the political' cannot be grasped by liberal rationalism because it requires negating the antagonism always present in human existence. Mouffe draws from Carl Schmitt's friend/enemy distinction in the political, stating that this distinction reflects our wider ontological condition as we/they, always constituted by that which is outside of us (Mouffe 2000: 16).[11] For Mouffe, 'when we accept that every identity is relational and that the condition of existence of every identity is the affirmation of a difference, the determination of an "other" that is going to play the role of a "constitutive outside", it is possible to understand how antagonisms arise' (2005b: 2). The 'constitutive outside' of the 'they' always holds potential to threaten the 'we' and becomes the locus of antagonism (Mouffe 2005a: 15–16; 2005b: 2–3). Resultantly, Mouffe explains that 'the political cannot be restricted to a certain type of institution, or envisaged as constituting a specific sphere or level of society. It must be conceived as a dimension that is inherent to every human society and that determines our very ontological condition' (2005b: 3). Instead of spurning this always underlying presence of antagonism, efforts should be made to direct it in a way that is politically productive.

The way in which this can be done for Mouffe is by turning relations of antagonism into *agonism*. Mouffe explains the distinction between these two terms by stating that 'while antagonism is a we/they relation in which the two sides are enemies who do not share any common ground, agonism is a we/they relation where the conflicting parties, although acknowledging that there is no rational solution to their conflict, nevertheless recognize the legitimacy of their opponents' (2005a: 20). In foregrounding agonism 'we' and 'they' are not viewed as enemies, but adversaries who share commonality in the sense of being committed to the symbolic space in which the conflict between them takes place.[12] For Mouffe, 'the task of democracy is to transform antagonism into agonism' (2005a: 20). Mouffe asserts that if properly understood, liberal democracy does hold the possibility to productively channel antagonism into agonism (2005a: 5). To achieve this, Mouffe advances the establishment of institutions and practices through which antagonism – as inescapable and fundamental to the ongoing sustenance of democracy – can be played out in an agonistic way. Democracy is in peril, following Mouffe's account not only when there is insufficient consensus and allegiance to the values it embodies, but also when agonistic dynamics are confounded by an apparent excess of consensus. In contrast, 'a healthy democratic process calls for a vibrant clash of political positions and an open conflict of interests' (2005b: 6). So, while consensus is central to democratic politics in the sense of allegiance to the broader ethico-political principles of democracy, any consensus in radical democratic terms is bound to be a 'conflictual consensus', a temporary result of a provisional hegemony which is never fully inclusive and is created though confrontation between adversaries (Mouffe 2000: 103). As opposed to liberal consensus-based approaches, agonistic democracy recognises that there is no such thing as a rational consensus that is not based on any form of exclusion (Mouffe 2000: 32). Antagonism reveals the very limits of any rational consensus (Mouffe 2005a: 12). What is required in the project for agonistic democracy is a drawing of the we/they distinction in a way that is capable of recognising the pluralism which constitutes modern democracy (Mouffe 2005a: 14).

What I assert is that Mouffe's agonism is of use in further conceptualising human rights to come and its embrace of conflict to sustain a futural, critical relation to alterity and power in the politics of rights. To a significant extent, the foundational elements of human rights to come align with the understanding of agonism as outlined above. There are a number of elements driving this assertion. First, in grasping human rights politics as fundamentally characterised by conflict – taking place in processes of articulation and rearticulation where competing interests and ideas of rights meet – human rights to come is capable of recognising the relation of friend/enemy which Mouffe sees as constitutive of the political (2005a: 14–19). However, instead of urging competing interests and ideas of rights towards rational consensus or characterising their contest as a purely antagonistic engagement between 'enemies', human rights to come seeks to encourage antagonistic political engagement on rights to be reapproached, as per Mouffe, as a practice of agonistic engagement between adversaries. The concept of the adversary encourages participants in politics to view themselves not as enemies but as joined together through commitment to the same key ethico-politico elements, and is crucial in transforming current antagonistic relations into agonism (Mouffe 2005a: 20–21). It is only through meaningful engagement with alternative conceptions of rights articulated by others and responding to the limits of such within a shared framework of rights politics that the work of human rights to come can proceed. Participants in this process must not be understood as enemies seeking to destroy one another, but as legitimate adversaries who must tolerate each other and enter into conflictual engagement on this basis in the politics of rights. By encouraging participants to see one another in this way, human rights to come is capable of constructing a we/they in the politics of rights that is compatible with democratic pluralism in Mouffe's sense. Rights politics is visibilised as based on conflict which stems from the antagonism of the friend/enemy distinction characterising the political, and in this conflict all parties take part in political processes of articulation and rearticulation alongside one another as adversaries in contest which must go on without end.

Second, the embrace of conflict central to human rights to come can be understood in agonistic terms due to the way in which it approaches and foregrounds relations of power within the political. The idea of human rights to come aims at a basic level to demonstrate how rights may be re-engaged as a discourse of use in staging meaningful challenge to existing relations of power for those who are marginalised or excluded within dominant power regimes. In doing so, it is compatible with Mouffe's Schmittian-inflected[13] assertion that there can be no political consensus without exclusion (Mouffe 2000: 32), working to keep this insight at the forefront of human rights politics. Human rights to come foregrounds the need for political engagement, contest and conflictual dialogue over current rights concepts, but, importantly, it goes beyond deliberative approaches such as that of Michael Ignatieff which recognise to some extent the conflictual nature of human rights.[14] The way in which it does so is by stressing how this dialogue takes place within contexts of power and involves taking a critical relation to power which is futural-focused in foregrounding the fact that alterity and exclusion can never be eradicated, and so conflictual work must be undertaken without end towards a perfect future that is self-refuting. This element of visibilising power relations as an ongoing site of contest in the politics of human rights reflects the central impetus of the idea of agonistic pluralism (see Mouffe 2000: 21–22, 45–49). Where liberal and deliberative approaches are, according to Mouffe, incapable of effectively recognising relations of inclusion/exclusion and the way in which conflictual politics takes place within scenes of hegemonic articulation, agonism allows us to see how any consensus will always be 'the expression of a hegemony and the crystallization of power relations' (Mouffe 2000: 49). The concept of human rights to come necessarily involves foregrounding the hegemonic nature of current rights concepts, and how such exclude some as opposed to others, encouraging radical thinkers and activists to engage in the counter-hegemonic articulation of competing conceptions of human rights which aim to engage in a critical relation to power. As a practice of rights which rejects the illusion that all interests can ever be fully included, the conflictual reworking of human rights to come adopts a critical relation to power mirroring that which Mouffe is directing towards in her work. It is this defining feature of human rights to come that takes it beyond the deliberative and towards the agonistic and allows human rights to become a site for visibilisation and ongoing questioning of relations of power and inclusion/exclusion.

A final element of human rights to come which resonates with the idea of agonism as understood via Mouffe is the way in which a conflictual consensus on human rights underpins this concept. When engaging in the practice of human rights to come it is important to note that consensus is not fully abandoned; all participants are in consensus that human rights embody broad principles to be promoted, and that the politics of human rights is a useful endeavour to pursue their respective aims. However, in this practice conflict necessarily exists, and is encouraged, surrounding the particular meanings of these values or what human rights should do, say or look like. This conflictual consensus sustains the futural approach of human rights to come; rights concepts must remain unsettled so conflict surrounding their meaning and content must go on indefinitely within the agreed upon symbolic space of democratic human rights politics which remains respected. This idea of conflict and consensus existing alongside one another is central to what makes human rights to come an agonistic practice and why critical engagement with alterity in the context of power in its practice does not descend into pure antagonism where conflictual political engagements are unproductive, perhaps even destructive. In articulating her conception of agonistic democracy Mouffe comments that

> a well functioning democracy calls for a clash of legitimate democratic political positions . . . Consensus is no doubt necessary, but it must be accompanied by dissent. Consensus is needed on the institutions constitutive of democracy and on the 'ethico-political' values informing the political association – liberty and equality for all – but there will always be disagreement concerning their meaning and the way they should be implemented.
>
> (2005a: 30–31)

Mouffe sees this idea of a conflictual consensus as 'providing a common symbolic space among opponents who are considered as "legitimate enemies"' (2005a: 52). In the politics of human rights to come, participants must acknowledge that they will not fully accept or agree with the positions being put forward by their adversaries, but will engage with these in the spirit of conflictual consensus and a pluralism where competing views cannot be assimilated and are not rejected, but engaged with in order to continually be attentive to relations of power and inclusion/exclusion. This practice rests upon ensuring that a variety of competing voices can always be heard in the politics of rights and making sure that conflict between them takes place within a shared symbolic order, within a broader commitment to the symbolic space of human rights and democratic politics.

Therefore, the particular approach of human rights to come appears compatible with the idea of agonism on a number of levels, and this approach may accordingly be productively conceived as an agonistic conception of human rights. Those seeking to engage in its politics may be encouraged to consciously think of their activity in terms of agonism and to embrace the elements of conflict between adversaries, a critical approach to power and relations of inclusion/exclusion, and the notion of conflictual consensus it promotes as facilitating a specifically agonistic understanding of conflict in rights politics. In making this assertion, however, it is significant to highlight that advancing the practice of human rights to come as an agonistic practice does not merely involve a straightforward application of Mouffe's work to human rights. Rather, such holds potential to add to Mouffe's thinking in this area and feed back into the radical democratic project she envisages. The relationship between the political, agonism and human rights, and potential for development of this relationship in a more radical way, is something gestured towards but not significantly fleshed out in Mouffe's own writings. It is here that the idea of human rights to come as a specifically agonistic conception and practice of human rights may be of use.

Considering the tension between the principles of citizenship and human rights in democratic politics, Tambakaki has gone as far as asserting that 'because Mouffe takes into account the antagonistic dimension of the political, her perspective on democracy does not lead to . . . an argument for prioritising human rights' (2010: 93). On first glance, such an assertion is not surprising, certainly not in relation to human rights as shaped through liberal concepts and ideals. Recalling Mouffe's outline of the tension between liberalism and democracy, it is clear that liberal human rights and their emphasis on individual liberty and universal ideas of equality are at odds with the idea of the *demos* and the relations of inclusion/ exclusion that it necessarily involves (Mouffe 2000: 2). Indeed, Mouffe overtly rejects advancement of a universalisation of liberalism and liberal human rights as the answer to the tension between liberalism and democracy, as she sees in work such as that of Jürgen Habermas (Mouffe 2005a: 83–84). To the extent that human rights promote ideas of rational, fully inclusive consensus Mouffe would be very wary of their use and ability to engage with the antagonism inherent to the political and wider political relations of inclusion/exclusion. However, Mouffe does not rule out the radical potential of human rights altogether. She states that human rights do have a role in challenging the relations of inclusion/exclusion of the *demos* and, in doing so, play an important role in keeping democratic contestation alive (2000: 10).[15]

This possibility for human rights to be used in a way that facilitates the political is also hinted at in Mouffe's engagement with politics at an international level. In *On the Political* Mouffe advances the need for plural modernities at this level in order to move beyond Western imposition of liberal democracy on a worldwide scale, in which human rights have indeed been a central part (2005a: 125–126). Engaging with the work of Boaventura de Sousa Santos, who understands universal human rights as an instrument of globalisation if conceived and imposed from above but holds out possibility for a counter-hegemonic rights discourse articulated around cultural specificity (1995: 337–342), Mouffe asserts that it may be possible to pluralise the notion of human rights to prevent it being an instrument in the imposition of Western hegemony, revealing the Western conception of human rights as merely one possible articulation (2014: 188–192). She states that 'to acknowledge a plurality of formulations of the idea of human rights is to bring to the fore their political character' (2005a: 126). The implication from these comments appears to be that alternative engagements with human rights may be possible, engagements which facilitate agonistic pluralism and, moreover, are potentially capable of challenging existing hegemonic power regimes.

Thus, while in their consensus-focused articulation human rights cannot be part of better engaging with the political in modern liberal democracy, Mouffe does not rule out human rights as part of a radical politics which facilitates the political. However, she also does not pursue to any great extent the question of how this work may proceed. It is here that the concept of human rights to come may be of use. This concept offers an alternative to consensus-based understandings of rights which holds potential to facilitate differing understandings of human rights to those currently dominant and encourages agonistic political engagement with currently hegemonic power regimes. Following discussion above demonstrating the way in which the key tenets of human rights to come reflect Mouffe's conception of agonism, this practice can be conceived of as one which utilises the discourse of rights to better grapple with the tension between liberalism and democracy and may be undertaken to carve out a use for rights in radical democratic politics. In this way, the concept of human rights to come offers a means to continue Mouffe's thinking on human rights in a productive manner.

This concept also holds potential to add to Mouffe's work in an additional respect. One critique that has emerged surrounding Mouffe's conception of agonism is the assertion that while she provides an abstract theoretical approach to agonistic democracy Mouffe's thinking does not provide concrete details of the way in which antagonism may be transformed into agonism (McNay 2014: 94–95). As David Howarth asserts, there is an 'institutional deficit' in such an approach in terms of both critique of existing arrangements and in outline of more positive alternatives (2008: 189–190; Wingenbach 2011: xi).[16] In this sense, it is asserted, an agonistic approach is not directly of use at the level of everyday, tangible political activity. Is it possible that the idea of human rights to come could mark a new development in this regard, providing a means for activists to practically engage with and think through agonism in the everyday politics of rights? While by no means offering an institutional framework, the idea of human rights to come does offer a concrete conceptual and practical framework through which the politics of rights can be re-engaged in an agonistic way.[17] Conceiving of human rights politics as an ongoing process of articulation and rearticulation between adversaries within the shared symbolic space of rights appears a useful starting point in embracing conflict in a way that does not descend into pure antagonism. Resultantly, human rights to come may be viewed as taking Mouffe's insights in a more concrete direction, as a tool which radical activists can use to approach and think through political engagement in a way which allows antagonism to be transformed into agonism in democratic politics. This is not to suggest that the model of human rights to come can be all there is to approaching agonism in a more concrete way, but it does offer one approach specific to the discourse and politics of human rights.

Mouffe's work offers rich resources for rethinking the central elements of consensus and conflict in human rights, although Mouffe herself has not pursued much of the particular way in which human rights may be reconceived as a site for productively recognising and embracing agonism and a critical relation to power in modern liberal democracies. The discussion above demonstrating human rights to come as capable of facilitating agonistic engagement in the politics of human rights offers a rejoinder to this, and allows human rights to begin to come into view as capable of being re-engaged to create space in which confrontation is kept open, power relations are put into question and final closure is always impossible. In promoting an agonistic politics of human rights the approach of human rights to come allows the discourse and practice of human rights to be part of recognising and working through the tension between liberalism and democracy as opposed to merely reinforcing it. Indeed, in opening up agonistic potential within the space of rights and their politics in modern democratic contexts, it is possible that the politics of human rights may emerge not only as an isolated agonistic political activity but as *one site where agonism is sustained in an agonistic democracy more generally*. Therefore, the practice of human rights to come can be viewed as a small part of the wider practice of agonistic democracy, permitting rights to become part of this practice where previously they were not. This is an important point and one that leads us to consider more of the natural link that may be thought between human rights to come and agonistic democracy which can also be perceived as 'to come'. The former can be perceived as linked to a broader project of working towards the latter.

Human rights to come as towards agonistic democracy to come

We have seen so far that foregrounding and sustaining conflict within the politics of human rights – where such conflict takes place between adversaries and exists alongside consensus on the broader value and symbolic space of human rights – allows human rights to come to emerge as advancing an agonistic approach to rights. This approach may also allow the politics and practice of rights to be part of sustaining agonism within democracy more generally; providing another location where agonistic engagement can flourish within modern democracy and democratic politics. It is in this sense that human rights to come adds to Mouffe's articulation of agonistic democracy, bringing human rights potentially within its remit in a way not possible when human rights remain within their current liberal confines.[18] However, the practice of human rights to come may be considered part of sustaining democratic practices of agonism and a conception of agonistic democracy not only because it sustains a conflictual approach to human rights which may help us to better recognise and negotiate the irresolvable tension between liberalism and democracy, but also because the futural 'to come' fundamentally links these two concepts together in a complementary relationship.

As has been explored above, part of the reason why approaching human rights as human rights to come necessarily involves rejection of a consensus-based conceptualisation and practice of rights is because this aims to bring an end or 'solution' to political debate and contest on what human rights are, what their meanings consist of and thereby leads to a heavily weighted focus on the outcome of human rights politics to the exclusion of consideration of its process. In contrast, the 'to come' directs us towards an idea of human rights and their politics which can never be brought to an end, which is fundamentally self-refuting. While temporary ends or settlement may be necessary, it is never possible to fully grasp, settle or close what human rights are and this is part of the very promise of human rights as a discourse which may be utilised to constantly challenge and rework restrictive power relations. Agonistic conflict must be sustained in an unending fashion on human rights, power and alterity, working towards the impossible horizon of a completely settled and achievable concept of human rights and relations of living and being more generally. It is in this way that the agonistic conflict which human rights to come seeks to sustain is inherently futural and it is this futural focus which offers productive possibilities for those interested in radical politics and ongoing challenge to restrictive regimes of power. This futural element of human rights to come holds potential to link into and further an idea of agonistic democracy which is, like human rights themselves, also 'to come'.

The idea of 'democracy to come' underlies much of Mouffe's work and derives its lineage from her early articulation of the project for radical democracy alongside Laclau in *Hegemony and Socialist Strategy* (2001) where it was articulated that, as Mouffe elaborates, 'the experience of a radical and plural democracy can only consist in the recognition of the multiplicity of social logics and the necessity of their articulation. But this articulation should always be recreated and renegotiated and there is no hope of final reconciliation. This is why radical democracy also means the radical impossibility of a fully achieved democracy' (Mouffe 1992: 4).[19] This approach to democracy, where democracy's impossible realisation or constitution constitutes the horizon of democratic politics, echoes Derrida's sense that 'democracy remains to come; this is its essence in so far as it remains: not only will it remain indefinitely perfectible, hence always insufficient and future, but, belonging to the time of the promise, it will always remain, in each of its future times, to come: even when there is democracy, it never exists, it is never present, it remains the theme of the non-presentable concept' (Derrida 2005: 306).[20]

Mouffe engages the concept of 'democracy to come' in her own work by asserting that the complete realisation or perfect instantiation of a pluralist democracy, where all agonisms are fully worked through, would mark its disintegration (2005b: 8). She elaborates that an agonistic pluralist democracy 'should be conceived as a good that only exists as good so long as it cannot be reached. Such a democracy will therefore always be a democracy "to come", as conflict and antagonism are at the same time its condition of possibility and the condition of impossibility of its full realization' (2005b: 8). Mouffe continues elsewhere that

> envisaging the 'to come' of pluralist democracy along similar lines [to Derrida] can help us to grasp the difference between the way democracy is conceived by a rationalist like Habermas and in the agonistic problematic which I am advancing . . . in the second case one acknowledges the *conceptual* impossibility of a democracy in which justice and harmony would be instantiated. Perfect democracy would indeed destroy itself. This is why it should be conceived as a good that exists as a good only as long as it cannot be reached.
>
> (2000: 137 emphasis in original)

Thus, central to Mouffe's concept of an agonistic pluralist democracy is the assertion that a fully inclusive and egalitarian *demos* cannot be attained but, more than this, that it is a self-refuting ideal which both guides political engagement and marks its impossible horizon.

Here a clear link can be drawn between human rights to come and democracy to come. The practice of the former can be viewed as not only one space where agonistic relations can be sustained in democratic politics, but as also reflecting and aiding engagement with the 'to come' which is constitutive of the project for agonistic democracy. The two become caught up in a mutually reinforcing relationship. Both democracy and human rights can be understood as existing as a good so long as they cannot be fully reached; concepts which always depart from themselves before they are completely realised or grasped. The impossible ideal of human rights, as the impossible ideal of democracy, is what guides political engagement and contestation to rework the limits and exclusions of current concepts and ideas such as 'liberty' and 'equality'. In encouraging those interested in radical politics to adopt an agonistic and futural approach to human rights, the practice of human rights to come may be considered as complementary to the wider practice of democracy to come; one way of sustaining futural-focused conflict over liberal ideas such as 'liberty' and 'equality' and their limits, and thereby one part of sustaining the 'to come' of democracy more generally. When radical activists practise human rights to come they are also practising democracy to come in terms of promoting and sustaining conflict on the key tenets of liberal democracy, presenting final settlement of such as the horizon of democratic politics. This allows radical re-engagement with human rights to be placed within a wider project for an agonistic democracy which is also to come, where the values of liberal democracy will be concretely realised within a fully plural and perfect democracy which must remain self-refuting. The practice of human rights to come may be part of working out these values within the wider confines of democracy to come, a micro-practice of democracy to come which too ultimately remains an impossible achievement. Accordingly, the agonistic and fundamentally futural struggle of human rights to come may link with the agonistic practice of democracy to come and facilitate a link between the radicalisation of human rights and the radicalisation of democracy more generally.[21]

Conclusion

This chapter has sought to revisit consensus and conflict in the politics of human rights through the lens of human rights to come and to consider how this understanding requires re-engagement with such. Particularly important in this re-engagement is the concept of agonism which is advanced as a productive conceptual tool those interested in human rights in radical politics can engage to understand the approach to conflict advanced in the idea of human rights to come. This idea can be grasped as encouraging an agonistic approach to human rights, and in doing so facilitates a concrete way of transforming antagonism into agonism. This is done through foregrounding conflict as at the centre of rights politics and directing participants in such politics to engage as adversaries conflicting on what human rights mean and how current concepts relate to relations of power. This approach does not descend into one of pure antagonism because of the consensual commitment which those engaging in human rights politics simultaneously possess to the overarching value of human rights principles and discourse itself in the midst of conflict. Characterising the politics of human rights to come as an agonistic politics allows human rights to be viewed as better able to negotiate the tension between liberalism and democracy in a productive way and, therefore, to be one space where agonism is sustained in agonistic democracy more generally. This is a democracy where pluralism can never be fully realised but, moreover, where the defining concepts of democracy themselves remain unsettled and ungraspable, the subject of ongoing conflictual engagement. It is this element of the futural that links the agonistic practice of human rights to come into a wider leftist struggle for agonistic democracy to come, one part of sustaining hegemonic conflict surrounding power relations on a broader level.

Notes

1 As explored below, this mainstream approach to, and understanding of, consensus in human rights has been questioned and problematised. It is important to note that this is particularly so in the contemporary global context where changing international relations, including the waning of Western hegemony, has rendered ideas of international consensus very precarious.
2 See further Cerna (1994: 740–742); Engle Merry (2006: 42–44); Morsink (1999).
3 For discussion see, for example, Parekh (1999: 139–143); An-Na'im (1992); Taylor (1999).
4 See further Ronald Dworkin's conceptualisation of rights as trumps (1984).
5 For critique of this approach, see Fallon (1993).
6 This assessment appears interesting when considered alongside other areas of Rancière's work where he has commented that the discourse of rights can be used to stage dissensual politics, allowing the part that has no part to speak (2004). For further discussion, see McNay (2014: 148–154); Chambers (2013: 47–50).
7 In this way discussion in this chapter stays with Rancière's critique of the anti-political and post-democratic contained in liberal consensus-based approaches, but departs from Rancière's own approach to politics by drawing on the concept of agonism which is not part of his work. See further Ed Wingenbach (2011: xv–xvi).
8 Connolly (1998; 2004; 2005; 2006); Tully (1995; 2008a; 2008b); Owen (1995); Honig (1993a; 1993b; 1995) and Norval (2007).
9 For discussion and commentary on the various and diverse approaches to agonism, see Schapp (2009).
10 This is a distinction which appears in the work of Carl Schmitt (2007), a key influence in Mouffe's thinking. It was popularised in many ways by Claude Lefort (1988), whose work also fed significantly into Laclau and Mouffe's radical democratic thought, and has also appeared as a theme in the work of others including Jean-Luc Nancy and Jacques Rancière.
11 Here Mouffe also draws from Derrida's concept of *différance*.
12 Although the category of enemy does not completely disappear, being reserved for those who 'do not accept the democratic "rules of the game" and who thereby exclude themselves from the political community' (Mouffe 2005b: 4).
13 Of course, Mouffe's engagement with Schmitt's work is critical and does not embrace, or engage unmodified, all aspects of his work, in particular his views on democratic pluralism. For further, see Mouffe (1999: 1–6).
14 See Ignatieff (2001: 229–301).
15 For further discussion on this point, see Mouffe's comments in Mouffe, Worsham and Olson (1999: 187).
16 For some indication of the tangible way in which Mouffe envisages institutional arrangements capable of transforming antagonism into agonism, see Mouffe (2005a: 21–25).

17 This is articulated more fully in Chapter 7 where discussion explores the practice of human rights to come.
18 Following Mouffe, this does not necessarily mean a complete rejection of liberalism and its tools – such as human rights – but a revision of them to facilitate better, more concrete realisation of liberal principles such as 'equality' and 'liberty'.
19 It is important to note, however, that Wingenbach takes a different approach to the relationship between radical democracy and Mouffe's agonistic pluralism, asserting that the latter involves 'more chastened and contingent aspirations' that cannot be equalled with the radical democratic project (2011: xv–xvi, 31–38). For more on how the relationship between agonism and the radical democratic project outlined in *Hegemony and Socialist Strategy* can be thought, see Howarth (2008: 187–189)
20 Laclau and Mouffe acknowledge the foundational influence of the Derridean tradition on their concept of radical democracy, noting in particular the concept of undecidability (Laclau and Mouffe 2001: xi–xii).
21 For more on the links that can be made between the radical democratic project as articulated by Laclau and Mouffe and practice of rights, see Chambers (2004) and McNeilly (2016).

References

An-Na'im, A. A. (ed.) (1992) *Human Rights in Cross-Cultural Perspectives: A Quest for Consensus*, Pennsylvania: University of Pennsylvania Press.
Cerna, C. (1994) 'Universality of Human Rights and Cultural Diversity: Implementation of Human Rights in Different Socio-Cultural Contexts', *Human Rights Quarterly*, 16(4): 740–752.
Chambers, S. (2004) 'Giving Up (on) Rights? The Future of Rights and the Project of Radical Democracy', *American Journal of Political Science*, 48(2): 185–200.
Chambers, S. (2013) *The Lessons of Rancière*, Oxford: Oxford University Press.
Connolly, W. (1998) 'Rethinking the Ethos of Pluralization', *Philosophy and Social Criticism*, 24(1): 93–102.
Connolly, W. (2004) 'The Ethos of Democratization', in S. Critchley and O. Marchart (eds), *Laclau: A Critical Reader*, London: Routledge, 167–181.
Connolly, W. (2005) *Pluralism*, Durham, NC: Duke University Press.
Connolly, W. (2006) 'Immanence, Abundance, Democracy?', in L. Tønder and L. Thomassen (eds), *Radical Democracy: Politics Between Abundance and Lack*, Manchester: Manchester University Press.
Derrida, J. (2005) *The Politics of Friendship*, trans. G. Collins, London: Verso.
Donnelly, J. (2013) *Universal Human Rights in Theory and Practice*, 3rd edn, Ithaca, NY: Cornell University Press.
Dworkin, R. (1984) 'Rights as Trumps', in J. Waldron (ed.), *Theories of Rights*, Oxford; New York: Oxford University Press, 153–167.
Engle Merry, S. (2006) *Human Rights and Gender Violence: Translating International Law into Local Justice*, Oxford: Oxford University Press.
Evans, T. (2005) 'International Human Rights Law as Power/Knowledge', *Human Rights Quarterly*, 27(3): 1046–1068.
Fallon, R. (1993) 'Individual Rights and the Powers of Government', *Georgia Law Review*, 27(2): 343–390.
Honig, B. (1993a) *Political Theory and the Displacement of Politics*, Ithaca, NY: Cornell University Press.

Honig, B. (1993b) 'The Politics of Agonism: A Critical Response to "Beyond Good and Evil: Arendt, Nietzsche, and the Aestheticization of Political Action" by Dana R. Villa', *Political Theory*, 21(3): 528–533.
Honig, B. (1995) 'Toward an Agonistic Feminism: Hannah Arendt and the Politics of Identity', in B. Honig (ed.), *Feminist Interpretations of Hannah Arendt*, Pennsylvania, PA: Pennsylvania State University, 135–166.
Howarth, D. (2008) 'Ethos, Agonism and Populism: William Connolly and the Case for Radical Democracy', *British Journal of Politics and International Relations*, 10(2): 171–193.
Ignatieff, M. (2001) *Human Rights as Politics and Idolatry*, A. Gutmann (ed.), Princeton: Princeton University Press.
Laclau, E. and Mouffe, C. (2001) *Hegemony and Socialist Strategy: Towards a Radical Democratic Politics*, 2nd edn, London: Verso.
Lefort, C. (1988) *Democracy and Political Theory*, trans. D. Macey, Cambridge: Polity.
McNay, L. (2014) *The Misguided Search for the Political*, London: Polity.
McNeilly, K. (2016) 'After the Critique of Rights: For a Radical Democratic Theory and Practice of Human Rights', *Law and Critique*, 27(3): 269–288.
Morsink, J. (1999) *The Universal Declaration of Human Rights: Origins, Drafting and Intent*, Philadelphia: University of Pennsylvania Press.
Mouffe, C. (1992) 'Preface: Democratic Politics Today', in C. Mouffe (ed.), *Dimensions of Radical Democracy: Pluralism, Citizenship, Community*, London: Verso, 1–14.
Mouffe, C. (ed.) (1999) *The Challenge of Carl Schmitt*, London: Verso.
Mouffe, C. (2000) *The Democratic Paradox*, London: Verso.
Mouffe, C. (2002) 'Politics and Passions: Introduction', *Philosophy and Social Criticism*, 28(6): 615–616.
Mouffe, C. (2005a) *On the Political*, London: Routledge.
Mouffe, C. (2005b) *The Return of the Political*, London: Verso.
Mouffe, C. (2014) 'Democracy, Human Rights and Cosmopolitanism: An Agonistic Approach', in C. Douzinas and C. Gearty (eds), *The Meanings of Rights: The Philosophy and Social Theory of Human Rights*, Cambridge: Cambridge University Press, 181–192.
Mouffe, C., Worsham, L. and Olson, G. (1999) 'Rethinking Political Community: Chantal Mouffe's Liberal Socialism', *JAC*, 19(2): 163–199.
Norval, A. (2007) *Aversive Democracy*, Cambridge: Cambridge University Press.
Owen, D. (1995) *Nietzsche, Politics and Modernity*, London: Sage.
Parekh, B. (1999) 'Non-Ethnocentric Universalism', in T. Dunne and N. Wheeler (eds), *Human Rights in Global Politics*, Cambridge: Cambridge University Press, 128–159.
Rancière, J. (1999) *Disagreement: Politics and Philosophy*, trans J. Rose, Minneapolis: University of Minnesota Press.
Rancière, J. (2004) 'Who Is the Subject of the Rights of Man?', *South Atlantic Quarterly*, 103(2–3): 297–310.
Schaap, A. (ed.) (2009) *Law and Agonistic Politics*, Farnham: Ashgate.
Schmitt, C. (2007) *The Concept of the Political*, trans. M. Konzen and J. P. McCormick, Chicago: University of Chicago Press.
Sousa Santos, B. de (1995) *Toward a New Common Sense: Law, Science and Politics in a Paradigmatic Transition*, London: Routledge.
Tambakaki, P. (2010) *Human Rights, or Citizenship?*, London: Birkbeck Law Press.
Taylor, C. (1999) 'Conditions of an Unforced Consensus on Human Rights', in O. Savić (ed.), *The Politics of Human Rights*, London; New York: Verso.

Tully, J. (1995) *Strange Multiplicity: Constitutionalism in an Age of Diversity*, Cambridge: Cambridge University Press.
Tully, J. (2008a) *Public Philosophy in a New Key: Vol. 1, Democracy and Civic Freedom*, Cambridge: Cambridge University Press.
Tully, J. (2008b) *Public Philosophy in a New Key: Vol. 2, Imperialism and Civic Freedom*, Cambridge: Cambridge University Press.
Wingenbach, E. (2011) *Institutionalizing Agonistic Democracy: Post-foundationalism and Political Liberalism*, Farnham: Ashgate.
Zivi, K. (2012) *Making Rights Claims: A Practice of Democratic Citizenship*, New York; Oxford: Oxford University Press.

Chapter 6

Rethinking paradoxical sovereignty
The ontology of human rights to come

Introduction

In this chapter, focus turns to consider ontology, exploring the way in which understanding human rights as human rights to come requires re-engagement with the ontological foundations of rights in order to expose and reposition the relationship between rights, sovereignty and vulnerability. When engaging in a radical politics of human rights which is based on an ongoing, critical relation to power a different ontological conception of our lives, and what human rights may be capable of offering or doing in relation to them, that departs from the traditional sovereign subject of rights is essential. The sovereign subject has been critiqued from a variety of perspectives as hindering as opposed to facilitating a conception of human rights capable of working towards radical social transformation. However, this problematic sovereign subject may provide a starting point for the alternative understanding of the subject that the approach of human rights to come can be thought to be based upon. Discussion in this chapter foregrounds the sovereign subject of human rights as constituted by a paradoxical relationship between sovereignty and vulnerability that offers possibilities to consider and work towards alternative ontological underpinnings for human rights. While this paradox is not currently approached in a way that is compatible with radical political objectives and engagements with interrelated life in mainstream understandings of human rights, fleeing from vulnerability in favour of advancing an illusion of sovereignty, space does exist to consider the relationship between sovereignty and vulnerability anew in a more radical way in the politics of human rights to come. This consideration would reveal and reimagine our interrelated vulnerability within relations of power.

To bring this perspective into view, I assert that two elements are necessary. First, radical thinkers and activists can foreground the vulnerability that constitutes the paradoxical subject and approach it as a *source of critical engagement with alterity and power* in the politics of human rights. Drawing from the work of Martha Albertson Fineman and Judith Butler I consider how the practice of human rights to come may be conceived as one of foregrounding vulnerability and interrelated life, operating to draw attention to unequal experiences of vulnerability that cause harm to particular subjects within contexts of power and facilitating challenge to such through the politics of rights. The concepts of futurity and rearticulation central to human rights to come offer opportunities for this to take place. Second, the relationship between rights, sovereignty and vulnerability may be rethought in the practice and politics of human rights to come by also foregrounding vulnerability as a *source for resistant action*. This involves returning to the paradox characterising the subject and reapproaching it to envisage a concept of agency and political action in human rights that does not stem from the subject's sovereignty, but in fact from her vulnerability. It is only through her vulnerability that the subject can act resistantly, and do so in a radical politics of human rights to come. Vulnerability, accordingly, appears as that which is essential to re-engage human rights more radically; however, the subject is not a straightforwardly vulnerable subject which erases all trace of paradox. In contrast, paradox continues to define the subject of rights and its possibilities.

The paradoxical sovereign subject of human rights

It is instructive to begin this investigation of the ontological possibilities of human rights to come by considering the current subject of human rights and what may be understood as its shortcomings. Human rights in their presently dominant form are unmistakably characterised by a particular subject: the bounded, autonomous and sovereign subject of liberalism more generally. This subject is rational, self-possessive and agentic, enjoying a negative form of freedom in the traditional liberal sense of freedom from unnecessary or unwanted impingement or interference from the state, and, indeed, other subjects more generally.[1] The protection afforded to this subject is, as MacPherson (1962) has demonstrated, intimately connected with the classical liberal protection of property.[2] The subject's property must be protected from outside interference, and the subject-as-property himself[3] must also be protected from such interference (Naffine 2001). This impetus reflects the Lockean assertion that man is the 'master of himself, and proprietor of his own person, and the actions or labour of it' (1967: ch. V, section 44). Human rights in their contemporary form as international human rights law, as influenced by and developed from classical liberalism and natural law thinking, appear as one discourse which operates to protect and uphold this sovereign liberal subject (Kapur 2006: 675). From the formulation of the fundamental human rights contained in the Universal Declaration of Human Rights, a protection of the sovereign subject-as-property can be detected. Provisions such as the right to life, the right to be free from slavery, the right to be free from inhumane or degrading treatment or torture are afforded to an already existing, fully formed and impermeable subject in order to uphold his sovereign individualism and ability to live and act in the world as an atomised agent. More than this, human rights discourse serves to equate the sovereign legal subject with the 'human' itself (Grear 2010: 45).

This subject has been the focus of much scholarly attention, and has been critiqued as problematic in various ways. Many of these critiques are long-standing and well established in critical thinking on human rights. For example, the sovereign subject enshrined at the heart of human rights, and legal rights more generally, has been revealed as operating to support wider liberal structural arrangements and a capitalist free market economy (Grear 2010: 68–95). This subject has also been critiqued as not fully reflecting the actual human subject and the full conditions of humanity, rather constituting a 'thin caricature' of the human (Douzinas 2000: 237). This assertion has emerged as having a number of facets. In terms of gender, the sovereign subject has been exposed as definitively male, upholding and furthering the interests of masculinity, and the prioritisation of 'masculine' traits such as rationality and atomisation, leading to a form of subjectivity exclusive of women and other gendered identities (Charlesworth 1995; Otto 2006). In addition to reflecting key masculine traits, the sovereign subject, in possessing the ability to be self-sufficient and independent in his actions, also appears to reflect a specifically adult subject, eschewing life experiences such as infancy and old age which are not characterised by sovereign control and self-possession (Fineman 2008: 11–12). As a self-contained, independent subject reproductive life is also invisibilised. The sovereign subject central to modern human rights, therefore, has been revealed as inherently problematic, reinforcing the marginalisation of many aspects of human experience and bolstering existing inequalities, thereby inhospitable to being utilised to facilitate radical social transformation. In this respect, advancing a radical approach to human rights capable of meaningfully challenging existing power regimes, drawing attention to how power works to advance some lives as opposed to others, requires moving beyond the sovereign subject. What I assert is that such an approach can begin to be thought through by engaging with the sovereign subject of human rights as not just problematic, but also as deeply *paradoxical* in nature. While the paradox defining the sovereign subject does not offer radical potential as it is currently approached within dominant human rights discourse, possibilities exist to reapproach this paradox anew and use it as a starting point to consider alternative ontological underpinnings for human rights.

The idea of paradox is by no means unusual in or alien to discussion of human rights. Rather, the paradoxical nature of human rights is a steady theme in critical commentary on rights.[4] For example, human rights appear as a discourse that is defined by paradox in the sense that it both emancipates and dominates, protects and controls (Douzinas 2010: 81), and that it serves to reinforce the subordinated identities of the subjects it seeks to liberate (Brown 2000). The particular paradox that I want to highlight in the present discussion relates to the paradoxical nature of the sovereign subject of human rights. This paradox can be stated as follows: the sovereign subject is presented as invulnerable – atomised and impenetrable in his sovereignty, agency and self-possession – however, this subject, paradoxically, can be considered as having rights only to the extent that he is *non-sovereign* and *inherently vulnerable*: open to injury, pain and suffering from forces outside himself. The sovereign subject needs rights to prevent injury or interference from sources external to his atomised self, injury or interference caused by relations of interdependency which his sovereignty on the face of it denies. In this manner, vulnerability and sovereignty are fundamentally interconnected; sovereignty always implies vulnerability so that the sovereign, atomised rights-holding individual can only exist to the extent that he is vulnerable and in relation with others. The sovereign subject emerges, therefore, as deeply paradoxical; rights do not uphold and recognise the already existing sovereignty of the subject, but the sovereign subject possesses rights to protect against inherent vulnerability.

Within currently dominant human rights discourse this paradox is approached in a particular way which does not fully visibilise the complex relationship between sovereignty and vulnerability. Indeed, on the contrary, a theme of flight from vulnerability runs through the historic foundations of human rights. Returning to the early classical liberal and natural law thinking which underpins human rights, the work of Hobbes is characterised by a fear of insecurity, vulnerability and the 'threat' the other poses to the self (Lorey 2015: 47). For Hobbes, individuals are subject to rule by the state in order to obtain protection and security from the vulnerability experienced in the state of nature. Here vulnerability to forces outside the self is presented as a problem to be solved by contractual agreement and submission to the state and the rule of law. This idea of utilising, turning to, juridical sources to obtain protection from vulnerability has proved to be of lasting resonance. In the later history of human rights this flight from vulnerability is accompanied by an assertion of an illusion of individual sovereignty. A familiar genealogical reading indicates that the contemporary human rights regime emerged as a response to the embodied suffering the human was capable of being exposed to. Drawing from the work of Lynn Hunt (1996), Anna Grear states that the French Declaration of the Rights of Man emerged in an eighteenth-century context characterised by increasing recognition of vulnerability and pain reflected in changing social attitudes to torture and a rise in social empathy (2010: 138). Similarly, modern international human rights law as recognisable today was brought into being following the suffering generated and brought into sharp relief by the Nazi regime in the Second World War period (Donnelly 2013: 170–172). However, the response to such embodied suffering was not an embrace of an embodied vulnerable subject but assertion of a disembodied, abstract and invulnerable subject (Grear 2010: 137; 2007). While the origins of contemporary human rights are rooted in embodied experiences of vulnerability, and many of the founding rights pertain to such – protection from slavery, inhuman and degrading treatment and torture, etc. – the subject of human rights nevertheless emerged as an abstracted, sovereign individual who transcends the structures of bodily experience, vulnerability and interdependence. In this way vulnerability, and an acknowledgement of the potentially injurious relationship between the other and the self, appears central to the discourse of human rights and its subject throughout its history, however, the response to this vulnerability has been a reinforcement of (the illusion) of sovereign invulnerability.

Resultantly, the paradox of the subject of human rights has been approached in dominant rights discourse in a way that seeks to pursue juridical protection of sovereignty, understanding vulnerability as a problem to be solved rather than a wound that exposes being (Wall 2008: 67). In this respect, as Illan Wall comments, 'human rights at once announce a relation between the political and pain [which stems from interrelationality], but at the same time they attempt to flee from it' (2008: 67). In their origins, contemporary human rights have been established in opposition to such suffering done 'to' the subject and foreground a sovereign subject whose autonomy is upheld by law, serving to invisibilise the fact that this subject always exists in an inherently vulnerable condition, impinged upon by his interrelationality to others and the world around him.

Rather than 'solving' the problem of vulnerability, all eschewing vulnerability in favour of sovereignty serves to do is invisibilise the reality of the human subject's interrelated existence and foreclose productive possibilities for revealing, and reimagining, our conditions of vulnerability within relations of power. The currently dominant approach to the paradoxically sovereign subject marginalises space for engagement with how vulnerability may be experienced differentially and how the other's impingement on the self may demand a response, instead of a reinforcement of ideas of sovereign and atomised individuality. This adds to the reasons why the sovereign subject of human rights may be viewed as inadequate to facilitate work towards radical social transformation. Nevertheless, rather than being a reason to disregard human rights in radical politics, this paradoxical nature of the sovereign subject may be used as a starting point to engage in a rethinking of the ontological basis of human rights capable of facilitating an alternative conception of the subject, what human rights are and what they can be used to do or say. This rethinking involves repositioning the relationship between human rights, sovereignty and vulnerability and can be thought to have two elements or strands. First, it is necessary to reimagine vulnerability not as a negative experience or threat but as a *source of critical engagement for and in human rights politics*. This involves engaging with vulnerability in a different way than that dominant in the history of human rights to date; as an ontological reality that does not encourage a retreat to the illusion of sovereignty, but facilitates a critical relation to alterity and power. This reapproaching of vulnerability allows rights to emerge as a site for revealing and contesting currently unequal experiences of vulnerability. Second, following from this, repositioning the relationship between human rights, sovereignty and vulnerability also requires coming to view vulnerability as *a source for resistant action in human rights politics*. This is possible through coming to accept, or becoming more comfortable with, paradox at the centre of human rights, embracing Douzinas's observation that human rights have only paradoxes to offer (2000: 21), and reapproaching the sovereignty–vulnerability paradox to reveal that it is only through vulnerability that the subject may act in a resistant politics of human rights. These two elements, and their relation to the concept of human rights to come, are explored further in the discussion below.

Rethinking ontology: vulnerability as a source of critical engagement with alterity and power

Following from engagement with the paradoxical sovereign subject and how dominant approaches to human rights have promoted a retreat to sovereignty as a response to vulnerability, in beginning to reposition the relationship between rights, sovereignty and vulnerability productive possibilities may be found by staying with the idea of vulnerability and considering how engaging with it in a different way to that traditionally characterising human rights can encourage not a retreat to the illusion of sovereignty, but a critical relation to alterity and power. The concept of vulnerability has been widely engaged in recent years to stimulate more ethical conceptualisations of, and responses to, the interrelated human condition as involving a constitutive relation to the other. Vulnerability, in this view, is a condition common to all human, and indeed non-human, life from which clear political objectives can be drawn. Feminist work has been particularly important in considering the normative significance of vulnerability and its capacity to reframe the underpinnings of much contemporary moral and political thought.[5]

Here it is possible to think of the work of Martha Albertson Fineman which begins from the assertion that 'our current system has been built upon myths of autonomy and independence and thus fails to reflect the vulnerable as well as dependent nature of the human condition' (2008: 19). Fineman, developing her earlier thinking on dependency (2004), seeks to 'claim the term "vulnerability" for its potential in describing a universal, inevitable, enduring aspect of the human condition that must be at the heart of our concept of social and state responsibility' (Fineman 2008: 8). Flowing from realisation of and engagement with this inevitable condition of vulnerability, and how some are positioned differently in relation to vulnerability than others (Fineman 2010: 269), Fineman calls for what she terms a 'responsive state' which would be responsible for the organisation and overseeing of social institutions to provide resources and assets to further meaningful equality in the context of vulnerability.[6] Judith Butler has also dedicated a significant amount of thought to vulnerability. Stemming from the inherent vulnerability which characterises social existence, Butler views all life as precarious (2009a: 25). Precariousness implies 'living socially, the fact that one's life is always in some sense in the hands of the other. It implies exposure both to those we know and to those we do not know; a dependency on people we know, or barely know, or know not at all' (2009a: 14).[7] Precariousness, however, is not simply an existential condition of individuals; instead it is a social condition from which clear political demands and principles emerge (Butler 2009a: xxv). Norms, social and political organisations and other institutions have developed to maximise precariousness for some and minimise it for others (Butler 2009a: 2–3). So, while all life is equally defined by precariousness, not all lives are equally precarious. To meaningfully work towards the flourishing of human life in such contexts Butler does point towards social institutions as perhaps capable of advancing policy obligations which enhance the conditions for life (2009a: 13), but, unlike

Fineman, she does not specifically endorse a role for state. Ethical responses to vulnerability and the interrelated nature of our lives, for Butler, appear best pursued through political forums and action.

Fineman and Butler are of course only two of the many theorists who have considered vulnerability as a concept of critique.[8] Their work offers a rejoinder to the discussion above in that rather than viewing vulnerability as something that happens 'to' the subject which the subject requires protection from and that generates a response of asserting (illusionary) sovereignty, they encourage characterisation of vulnerability as something defining the subject which can never be eradicated without eradicating what it means to be human. This alternative ontological approach appears more amenable to the aims of radical social transformation as it directs attention towards the way in which we *are all impinged upon and vulnerable to injury and harm*, yet, following Fineman and Butler, *not all experience vulnerability in the same way*. Rather, relations of power lead some to experience harm or injury more than others, in Butler's terms, to be more precarious than others. This may include those who lie outside the dominant norm, those who are on the margins of society or are otherwise disadvantaged by prevailing power regimes. Such subjects and their experiences gesture towards the fact that vulnerability and exposure to the other is not encountered uniformly, and may be a site for violence, injury and other harm in line with wider social relations of power. In turn, our interrelation with others in the context of vulnerable life places ethical obligations upon us – individually and collectively – to respond to such experiences and attend to the conditions that generate them.[9] Accordingly, staying with and embracing vulnerability as an ontological concept may be used to draw attention to conditions of inequality and in this way holds potential to facilitate a critical relation to alterity and power. Engagement with such is not possible when we view vulnerability as a threat and respond with an assertion of sovereignty.

Increasingly, thoughts are turning to vulnerability as providing a convincing ontological basis for human rights which displaces the sovereign subject. As Alexandra Timmer outlines, 'the vulnerability thesis is an invitation to reimagine the "human" of human rights as a vulnerable subject, and to redirect (Grear 2010) human rights law in his/her image' (2013: 148).[10] This involves moves away from the sovereignty currently characterising the subject of liberal human rights and also the use of human rights to 'protect' some subjects or groups designated as those who experience vulnerability in favour of foregrounding a shared ontological condition of vulnerability and interrelationality.[11] Particularly significant in this turn of thought is the work of Bryan Turner and Anna Grear. Turner, as Fineman and Butler above, begins from the assertion that 'vulnerability defines our humanity', going on to characterise this definitive condition and experience of human vulnerability as providing 'the common basis of human rights' (2006: 1). In his sociological approach, founded in a specifically embodied conception of vulnerability, Turner develops his thesis that 'rights are enjoyed by individuals by virtue of being human – and as a consequence of their shared vulnerability' (2006: 3). Human rights, which exist themselves within a context of institutional vulnerability, can be defined as universal principles because of the shared human ontology of vulnerability (2006: 6), and so Turner aims to 'develop a robust defence of universalism from the perspective of a social ontology of human embodiment' (2006: 9). Thus, Turner uses ontological vulnerability to justify universal human rights and to defend them against attacks, including those of cultural relativism. While Turner is explicit in his criticism of liberal theory and its ontological insufficiencies, his own re-engagement largely stays committed to what is understood and 'known' about human rights (Wall 2008: 66). Accordingly, while Turner's work is significant in beginning to displace the sovereign subject at the heart of human rights, it does not go far enough in linking ontological vulnerability with a radical rethinking of human rights beyond their current mainstream form.

A contrasting approach may be found in the work of Grear (2007; 2010; 2013). While she agrees with Turner that vulnerability is a shared ontological condition that cannot, and should not, be turned away from, Grear departs from Turner in a number of respects. First, while Turner focuses his account on socioeconomic rights and rights pertaining to the body/health, Grear outlines that 'embodied vulnerability offers a suitable, conceptually compelling and direct theoretical foundation for all categories of human rights, including civil and political rights' (2010: 130). Second, Grear also outlines that it is necessary to take a more positive approach to vulnerability and its possibilities than that presented by Turner who focuses on suffering and pain which follow from ontological vulnerability (2010: 131). However, arguably the most important point of departure from Turner in Grear's work appears in that while Turner seeks to draw on vulnerability to justify universal human rights in their current form, Grear seeks to use vulnerability to *redirect* human rights. In her approach Grear calls for the reconstruction of human rights and their subject based on vulnerability towards a more ethical approach to the self and the other (2010: 163–7). Human rights in this view 'should be conceptualised as juridical instantiations of our shared duty to respond to the fundamental incidents of a human ontic commonality', leading to a reconstruction of rights to draw attention to the particularity of the human in contexts of interrelation, vulnerability and dependency (Grear 2010: 167). Grear's work demonstrates how it is possible to take the repositioning between rights, sovereignty and vulnerability in a more critical direction which does not bolster human rights in their current form but may think them anew and allow for alternative possibilities for rights to emerge in navigating our interrelated living and being together.

Accordingly, to date work has been undertaken to foreground vulnerability as crucial in defining and thinking about the subject of human rights. This work has been important in considering ontological possibilities beyond sovereignty that embrace the subject's inherent vulnerability within interrelational life as opposed to fleeing from it. Of particular note in this is Grear's use of embodied vulnerability 'as a vital concept of resistance to the tendency of human rights to be open to influences that suppress their potential for radical humanitarian critique' and to use vulnerability to open 'law to a range of considerations hitherto systemically suppressed' (2010: 132). The question that attention must turn to now is what does the conception of human rights to come have to add to this intervention challenging the privileging of sovereignty in the subject of human rights? What I assert is needed following such work foregrounding vulnerability as not a threat to the subject to be juridically solved, but an ethical condition to be embraced, including in human rights, is an enhanced focus on one key element of vulnerability theorising emerging from the work of Fineman and Butler highlighted above – the fact that *not all experience vulnerability in the same way*. Relations of power render experiences of vulnerability unequal, a site of harm and injury for some to a greater extent than others. In order to utilise vulnerability as an ontological basis for a radical politics of human rights it is necessary to engage with this element of vulnerability, considering vulnerability as a concept that has a critical impetus, leading to an attention to marginalisation and suffering in interrelated life and challenge to how power operates to lead to differential experiences of vulnerability. It is in this respect that encounters with the subject's vulnerability can move beyond a response of retreating to sovereignty to focus on vulnerability as an ineradicable part of the subject's existence but also one capable of use to stage critical engagements with restrictive regimes of power, rendering rights one site in which to carry out this activity. How can this re-engagement with vulnerability to become attentive to our interrelated nature within contexts of alterity and power productively inform radical re-engagements with human rights? How can the vulnerability which is central to, although invisibilised in, the sovereign subject be focused on and used as a point of departure to facilitate more radical possibilities for human rights to visibilise and intervene in experiences of marginalisation? In what follows below attention turns to consider these questions and how human rights to come may facilitate this.

In many ways, the key elements driving human rights to come are compatible with foregrounding vulnerability and offer opportunities to do so in a manner that facilitates attention to differential experiences of vulnerability and the need to challenge them. The first element capable of facilitating this is the central idea of futurity. While dominant approaches to human rights and the sovereign subject may see the futural horizon of the politics of human rights as an end to vulnerability, or complete sovereign choice and agency for the subject, which amounts to the same thing, the approach of human rights to come puts forward an alternative view. Informed by the assertion of Fineman, Butler and others that invulnerability is not a possible, or productive, end to strive towards,[12] in encouraging an ongoing, never-ending critical relation to alterity and power the 'to come' of human rights may be thought to advance a horizon of a form of living and being where all experience supportive responses to inherent vulnerability and adequate conditions to thrive in interrelational life.[13] While this horizon may never be fully achievable, a 'to come' which remains always self-refuting, it is a futural horizon which is more productive, holding possibility to better direct attention towards the other and its relation to the self as opposed to the futural aim of eradicating vulnerability, which only serves to return to discourses of sovereign individualism and its related problems. As a result, the futural element of human rights to come may be productively harnessed to sustain an ongoing, never-ending critical relation to differential experiences of vulnerability and what this demands, directing the aim of human rights politics towards equality of vulnerability and ethical relations to the other which will never be fully achieved but which, in its ultimate unachievability, places human rights in a more productive relation to vulnerability.

Alongside the possibility to focus on a futural horizon where all have the ability to thrive in interrelated and vulnerable life, the activity of articulation and rearticulation central to human rights to come also offers opportunity to foreground and challenge particular unequal experiences of vulnerability within contexts of power. In the practice of rearticulating human rights the language of rights can be used in modified ways to draw attention to and challenge experiences of vulnerability currently invisible. By reiterating rights in ways previously unimagined or unauthorised, subjects such as women, gender minorities, black and ethnic minority individuals, refugees and asylum seekers may visibilise experiences of harm or marginalisation in the context of vulnerable life and simultaneously assert a right to resources or conditions that would address such. Through this activity human rights can be used to stage more meaningful encounters with vulnerability and the demands it makes upon us as individuals and upon wider social institutions and structures as well as how such vulnerability is experienced within wider contexts of power, encouraging debate on what it means to support all life as vulnerable life. From this, in contrast to Turner who asserts that we 'need human rights to protect us from contingency' (2006: 126), the practice of human rights to come offers the possibility of reappropriating human rights to *draw attention to* contingency and contingent experiences of vulnerability; using the language of rights in new ways that visibilise vulnerability generally but also the particular conditions of vulnerability that various subjects face, foregrounding this particularity within the context of a critical relation to alterity and power. From this, rearticulation of human rights may bring into view experiences of harm and injury, unequal experiences of vulnerability; however, it may also assist in facilitating effective responses to such experiences. At a broad level engaging in practices of ongoing, futural-focused articulation and rearticulation can be understood as a space for encountering the vulnerability of the self and the other. As a practice of contesting the limits of current human rights concepts and regimes of power more generally based on that which they exclude, it involves coming into contact with the other and the other's suffering or marginalisation and the effects this has on the self in interdependent contexts. Therefore, in the work of human rights to come activists must engage in a general opening to the other in order to take part in its activity, acknowledging the demands of the other made upon the self through democratic processes which also may open possibilities for enhanced pain or suffering, may demand a response to the other. In this respect, the process of articulation and rearticulation offers both opportunities to contest differential experiences of vulnerability and to facilitate responses to these experiences by the fact that such processes require political actors to be open and so may encounter the demands of the other on the self.

In addition to rearticulation of rights to bring into view differential experiences of vulnerability and demand a response to them, rearticulation in the practice of human rights to come may facilitate a critical approach to current distributions and experiences of vulnerability within contexts of power in another respect. It may be possible in this practice to rearticulate human rights in ways that intentionally break with individualised ideas of subjectivity; rearticulating rights drawing upon collective forms of subjectivity to better reveal vulnerability and challenge how such interrelated experiences of living and being vulnerable have been obscured by individualised, sovereign ideas of the subject. As a discourse, human rights may be drawn upon in communal, interrelational or group forms revealing how discourses of power have invisibilised how experiences of vulnerability are inherently intersubjective and may require a response that goes beyond the individual subject. There are a number of forms such rearticulations could take. For example, an intersubjective 'right to care' might be articulated whereby attention is drawn to the fact that care activities can only be understood interrelationally, that care is a common experience and cannot be approached in terms of individuality, advancing what Isabel Lorey describes as a 'care community in which our relationality with others is not interrupted but is regarded as fundamental' (2015: 99). Such a right could work to reveal the way in which some lack care, how some carry out care work currently unrecognised, how care should become a greater focus for state activity as an integral part of interrelated life, and so must transcend assertion by an individual subject. Human rights can accordingly be explored and redeployed in ways that draw attention to the interrelationality which rights at their heart presuppose and how conditions to reduce vulnerability in contexts of power must often be addressed or thought through interrelationally.

From this outline, it is clear that the concept of human rights to come provides tools to stress that our ontological condition requires ongoing, never-ending critical interrogations of and responses to vulnerability and the other as opposed to juridical protection aimed towards a 'solution' to the vulnerability of the sovereign subject. This practice offers much scope to visibilise vulnerability as differentially experienced within contexts of power and to challenge the often harmful impacts of such unequal experiences. Through the activity of rearticulating human rights the language and politics of rights become arenas for facilitating engagements with the interrelationality that characterises our lives, allowing the sovereign subject to be displaced, vulnerability thought anew, and rights engaged to reveal, challenge and demand intervention in experiences of unequal vulnerability. In this activity, the vulnerability of human rights to performative reiteration, returning to discussion in Chapter 3, allows the discourse of rights to be harnessed to productively intervene in ontological vulnerability in such a way. Thus, to address ontological vulnerability we need not look to rights in and of themselves, but rather to what it is we can *do with* rights as a vulnerable discourse. In contrast to Turner who uses ontological vulnerability to defend universal human rights, a more radical approach advanced by the practice of human rights to come is to utilise the idea of vulnerability to break apart universal human rights and think through new usages of the language of rights and their politics to address differential vulnerability within contexts of power. This involves a shift from thinking of human rights as protecting from vulnerability to fully embracing ontological vulnerability *and* the vulnerability of human rights themselves, drawing attention to where the two may productively intersect. It is in this sense, therefore, that human rights to come stands as a model capable of providing tangible means for human rights discourse and politics to engage with vulnerability in a more critical way and for human rights to be directed towards an alternative ontological underpinning more amenable to advancing the aims of those on the margins and facilitating radical social change. As noted above, however, this is not the only element that is involved in repositioning the relationship between rights, sovereignty and vulnerability in a way more amenable to the aims of radical politics. It is also necessary to, second, return to the paradox characterising the subject of rights and re-approach this in a different manner to allow vulnerability to come into view as a source for resistant action in a radical politics of human rights.

Reapproaching paradoxical sovereignty: vulnerability as a source for resistant action

It is clear from the above that human rights to come provides a vehicle for reimagining vulnerability as a source of critique, to draw attention to experiences of alterity and inequality. This re-engagement with vulnerability in the discourse and politics of rights may be added to in order to also bring vulnerability into view as a source of resistant action and, accordingly, that which facilitates a radical politics of human rights. It is this second element that discussion to follow explores. To begin to grasp vulnerability as a source of resistant action it is necessary to return to the paradoxical nature of the sovereign subject and approach this paradox in a new way. Before turning to consider this, it is important to note that in this respect the idea of human rights to come must not be thought of as advancing a straightforward replacement of the paradoxical sovereign subject with the vulnerable subject, thereby erasing the paradoxical nature of the subject of human rights. On the contrary, instead of seeking to smooth over, ignore or deny the paradoxical nature of this subject, a more radical approach involves embracing the paradoxical relationship between sovereignty and vulnerability, albeit understanding it differently to facilitate as opposed to hinder radical politics. As a result, human rights to come involves engaging in a politics of rights which is defined by an overtly paradoxical subject but, rather than a paradoxical subject that flees from vulnerability to assert sovereignty, agency and self-possession, one that embraces vulnerability and its relation to agency and political action in an alternative manner.

How can this reapproaching of the paradoxical relationship between sovereignty and vulnerability defining the subject be understood? As outlined above, while the sovereign subject is presented as invulnerable – atomised and impenetrable in his sovereignty, agency and self-possession – this subject is in fact inherently vulnerable, and sovereignty always implies vulnerability. The dominant approach to this paradox has been to flee from vulnerability in favour of advancing an illusion of sovereignty that presents the subject of rights as free to act and choose in the world of his own accord, and rights as upholding the ability to do such. For example, rights such as the right to freedom of movement, to marry and found a family, to free choice of employment, to freedom of expression, conscience and religion are understood in the mainstream view of human rights as international human rights as reflecting and facilitating the agentic choice of the sovereign subject. As Grear observes, 'what emerges as being the most important characteristic of the liberal legal subject is the ability to choose. The liberal legal subject is the origin of his own interests and discourses' (2010: 81). In this approach to the paradox between sovereignty and vulnerability agentic political action, the claiming of rights for example, stems from the subject's sovereignty. The vulnerability invisibilised under the surface of the paradoxical sovereign subject does not prohibit or impinge upon the subject's agentic choice or action; the sovereign subject acts despite vulnerability and interrelation with others. It may be asked, therefore, what concept of action is left when we stay with vulnerability and further foreground it as an integral part of the subject of human rights? How can a resistant politics be initiated by a conception of the subject which foregrounds vulnerability as central to human existence and rights politics?

What I assert is that it is possible that the paradoxical relationship between sovereignty and vulnerability can be reapproached, the nuances between them explored anew, to allow for an alternative account of agency of the paradoxical subject to emerge which is of use in radical politics. This involves inverting the approach outlined above that advances the subject acts and chooses despite vulnerability, that action in human rights politics stems from sovereignty, and stressing instead that *it is only through her constitutive vulnerability that the subject of human rights can act resistantly*. Vulnerability in this view is the starting point for political action to resist problematic regimes of power; the subject can act in radical politics only because she is vulnerable. It is in this way that embrace of vulnerability does not erase the paradox and tension between sovereignty and vulnerability but involves repositioning this paradox. While at present accounts of the subject as an agent acting despite vulnerability serve to further ideas of atomisation which do not effectively capture all human life as ineradicably vulnerable, and exposed to different experiences of injury and harm within conditions of power, this alternative approach is focused on foregrounding an idea of action more amenable to the aims of radical politics. In this approach vulnerability is a source of resistant action, its very starting point. Through reapproaching the paradoxical relationship between vulnerability and (resistant) agency the vulnerable subject of human rights may be understood as not disempowered by experiences of differential vulnerability and harm but capable of action to challenge such. The vulnerable subject's paradoxical agency appears as that which is engaged when undertaking the practice of human rights to come; it is only through a (paradoxical) ontology of vulnerability that radical political action to rearticulate human rights to challenge restrictive relations of alterity and power is possible at all.

To further think through possibilities to reapproach the paradoxical relationship between sovereignty and vulnerability constituting the subject of human rights in this alternative way and the particular radical possibilities that emerge from such, it is instructive to return to Butler's conception of vulnerability. In her more recent work, Butler has sought to consider the relationship between vulnerability and resistance, particularly within the context of radical political action. She comments that when subjects experiencing differential distributions of vulnerability act resistantly in demonstrations, protests and other forms of public assembly 'it is not that vulnerability is converted into resistance, at which point strength triumphs over vulnerability' (2015a: 151), rather, 'vulnerability and resistance can, and do, and even must, happen at the same time' (2015a: 141). Thus, a complex and nuanced interrelation exists between the subject's vulnerability and acts of resistance. The way in which Butler articulates and accounts for this interrelation is by returning to her earlier thoughts on performativity. At a fundamental level, a performative account of the subject assumes interdependency and vulnerability from such interdependency. As Butler outlines, 'when we speak about subject formation, we invariably presume a threshold of susceptibility or impressionability that may be said to precede the formation of a conscious and deliberate "I". That means only that this creature that I am is affected by something outside of itself' (2015b: 1). The 'I', therefore, is shaped by formative relations with others and the impact of social norms whereby 'if I can come to touch and feel and sense the world, it is only because this "I", before it could be called an "I" was handled and sensed, addressed, and enlivened' (2015b: 11). Performativity stresses that the subject is vulnerable to shaping and interpellation, 'certain name-calling from the start' (Butler 2015a: 63), including in damaging or restrictive ways, and indeed that there is no 'I' prior to such processes of shaping and interpellation, these processes performatively bring the subject into being.

However, Butler makes clear that performativity 'describes both the processes of being acted on and the conditions and possibilities for acting, and . . . we cannot understand its operation without both of these dimensions' (2015a: 63). As has been stressed in response to early misinterpretations of Butler's account, performativity does not present an unagentic subject unable to act in resistance but, rather, the subject's vulnerability to performative discourses that bring her into being facilitates action through offering possibility to take 'an oppositional relation to power that is, admittedly, implicated in the very power one opposes' (Butler 1997: 17). This is made possible via subtle processes of reiteration which the subject may engage in. As Butler comments, 'this very domain of susceptibility, this condition of being affected, is also where something queer can happen, where the norm is refuted or revised . . . Precisely because something inadvertent and unexpected can happen in this realm of "being affected", gender can emerge in ways that break with, or deviate from, mechanical patterns of repetition' (2015a: 64). Thus, it is only through being vulnerable to, open to shaping by, discourses, norms and processes of interpellation that the subject can act resistantly, reiterating these discourses in alternative, subversive ways. Considering this approach in the context of embracing ontological vulnerability in and through the activity of human rights to come, it is important to stress that practices of resistant reiteration of rights are not made more difficult because of the subject's vulnerability but, on the contrary, are only possible *because of* such inherent vulnerability to the other, to shaping from normative discourses of power from the start.

Butler's thoughts on the relationship between vulnerability and resistance offer a starting point for new engagements with the idea of vulnerability in human rights to envisage a radical politics of human rights. This thought can be brought into conversation with the paradoxical subject of human rights, and the dominant approach to it, to demonstrate that alternative interpretations of this paradox are possible. Work to reposition the relationship between rights, sovereignty and vulnerability to allow for a politics of human rights to emerge does not involve moving away from the idea of paradox constituting the subject, but embracing the paradoxical relationship between sovereignty – and its related ideas of agency and choice – and vulnerability in a new way which is attentive to the complex relationship between these two ideas, and the way in which vulnerability may offer resources for radical politics. Embrace of the vulnerability constituting the subject of human rights does not erase a notion of agency or political action but can be viewed as in fact opening possibility to foreground a subject who can engage in resistant politics to challenge the restrictive operation and relations of power. When the subject is embraced as inherently vulnerable and such vulnerability is seen as opening up space for resistance, the subject of human rights may be thought of as capable of acting to challenge differential distributions and experiences of vulnerability through practices resistantly rearticulating rights. This is a conception of agency which, in contrast to dominant interpretations of the paradoxical subject, embraces interrelationality and its associated demands and risks as opposed to foreclosing it in favour of an illusion of sovereign action despite vulnerability and the impingement of the other on the self.

It may be asked, however, what possibility is there for integrating, exploring and expanding such a new approach to the paradoxical subject in the politics of human rights? How could the activity of human rights to come begin to bring vulnerability into view as a source of resistant action? The answer to these questions returns to the centrality of rearticulation to this practice within a wider performative conception of human rights as a politico-legal activity. While the sovereign subject and the dominant approach to its paradox that seeks to flee from vulnerability may indeed appear taken for granted and solidified in human rights discourse and practice, such understandings need to be continually asserted. The subject must be placed in a particular position in relation to sovereignty and vulnerability in an ongoing way in order to maintain its authority. Returning to Chapter 3's consideration, however, in such a need for repetition to maintain authority, coherence and truth opportunities arise for an alternative conception of the paradoxical relationship between sovereignty and vulnerability that facilitates more radical possibilities in the sense outlined above. Accordingly, radical activists and thinkers might look for opportunities to break down the dominant iteration of the paradoxical subject, to reiterate it anew and thereby to allow for an alternative politics of human rights to emerge which begins with an alternative approach to the paradoxical subject. Activity to seek to foreground vulnerability as a source of resistant action within this subject must be never-ending. As discussed previously, a future where all experience supportive responses to inherent vulnerability and adequate conditions to thrive in interrelational life must remain one that is self-refuting. Injury to the subject can never be fully removed and vulnerability will always stand to be advanced as a source of resistant action to restrictive and harmful relations of power, the subject and its paradox continually advanced in such a way in the performative, futural work of human rights to come.

It is crucial to note that not only does this alternative account of the paradox defining the subject of rights allow a subject to emerge who is more amenable to taking a critical approach to power in the politics of human rights, but this paradoxical relationship between vulnerability and resistance characterising the subject is an imperative necessity in initiating such a politics; is what facilitates the very practice of human rights to come itself. As a practice of resistant rearticulation, when activists engage in this activity they are engaging the paradoxical relation between vulnerability and resistance that constitutes their subjectivity. Accordingly, by embracing ontological vulnerability human rights politics itself gains a conception of action which is more amenable to the ends of radical social transformation, foregrounding the subject's possibilities for reiterative action which fits with the performative activity of human rights to come itself. When we begin with an account of human rights which foregrounds performativity and practices of reiteration of human rights in radical politics, those engaging in such a politics cannot be understood as sovereign agents, but as vulnerable subjects employing their paradoxical relationship with power and resistance towards more radical ends within the specific arena of human rights and their politics. Human rights to come requires the paradoxically vulnerable–resisting subject and is one means through which resistant reiteration can be engaged in. Embracing the paradoxical nature of human rights, the paradoxical vulnerable subject, in particular, is central to the practice of human rights to come and foregrounding this paradox is part of what makes this approach stand out as distinct as a productive vehicle to reposition the relation between rights, sovereignty and vulnerability. Not only is moving beyond the current approach to the paradoxical subject one element of the re-engagement of human rights that human rights to come advances, but it is also the impetus driving this practice itself, for without reapproaching the subject in such a way the resistant politics of human rights to come would not be possible.

Conclusion

Realigning human rights towards the ends of radical social transformation in the practice of human rights to come requires re-engagement with the current ontological underpinnings of human rights, namely the sovereign subject of rights. This subject is problematic in terms of its bounded, masculine, ablest and ageist nature and has been a key reason advanced for why human rights cannot facilitate radical social transformation. The idea of a paradoxical relationship between sovereignty and vulnerability at the centre of this subject helps to demonstrate both how vulnerability has been invisibilised or retreated from in favour of sovereignty in dominant approaches to human rights but also, importantly, provides a starting point to reconsider the current relationship between rights, sovereignty and vulnerability in a way that renders rights more amenable to critically engaging with power and facilitating radical social transformation. Discussion above has explored the repositioning of this relationship as having two elements: first, moving from viewing vulnerability as a threat that happens 'to' the subject and seeing it as an inherent condition of life which holds potential to draw attention to unequal experiences of vulnerability. In this way vulnerability can be approached as a source of critical engagement with alterity and power in the politics of human rights. Second, following this re-engagement with vulnerability it is also possible to bring vulnerability into view as a source of resistant action in human rights politics. This involves a repositioning of the paradox constituting the subject to reveal how it is through vulnerability that the subject can act resistantly at all.

As an ongoing and futural practice of rearticulating human rights in contexts of power and alterity human rights to come offers possibilities for rights to be utilised in ways that draw attention to the subject's vulnerability as opposed to foreclosing it, and to utilise the discourse and politics of rights to challenge differential distributions of vulnerability and bring into view the demands the vulnerability of the other marginalised by relations of power makes in the context of interrelated life. Indeed, the futural horizon of the 'to come' can be thought of as a relation of living and being whereby vulnerability is equally distributed and the demands that the vulnerability of the other places on the self, and social institutions, are understood and effectively responded to. These possibilities imaginable through the practice of human rights to come are facilitated by the vulnerability of rights themselves that this idea at its centre visibilises – rights are vulnerable to use in ways that advance the illusion of sovereign autonomy, but also in ways that draw attention to the subject's vulnerability, interrelationality and bring us into contact with the other that is constitutive of the self. However, this re-engagement with vulnerability does not seek to straightforwardly replace the sovereign subject and its paradoxes with a vulnerable subject that is free from paradox and contradiction. Rather, the approach of human rights to come involves foregrounding an alternative ontological paradox in that it is only through vulnerability that the subject can act resistantly. This paradox, as opposed to being problematic and hindering radical action as that constituting the sovereign subject, actually visibilises how the vulnerable subject is enabled to act to challenge restrictive formative discourses and distributions of vulnerability. Indeed, human rights to come does not seek to merely foreground this paradoxical idea of vulnerability in the vulnerable subject of human rights, but is dependent on it, its own reiterative practice being facilitated by this very paradox.

Notes

1 See Berlin (1969); Taylor (1985: 211–229).
2 For further discussion of MacPherson, see Chapter 2.
3 I am using the male pronoun to discuss the sovereign subject, given that, as will be explored further below, this subject appears as definitively male.
4 In addition to the work of Douzinas (2013) and Wendy Brown (2000), see Jack Donnelly who refers to a 'possession-paradox' central to human rights in that having a right becomes particularly important when one does not 'have' it (2013: 9). Slavoj Žižek also engages the paradox of 'universal human rights as the rights of those reduced to inhumanity' (2011: 167). Work such as Scott (1996), Hafner-Burton and Tsutsui (2005), Palmer (2002) and Mullins (2012) has also engaged the idea of paradox.
5 For commentary of recent thought in this area, see MacKenzie, Rogers and Dodds (2014).
6 See Fineman (2010; 2013).
7 See also Butler (2009b). For further development of ideas of precarity and precariousness, see Lorey (2015).
8 See also the work of Martha Nussbaum (2001; 2005); Pedar Kirby (2006a; 2006b; 2011); Russell Beattie and Schick (2013); Sánchez-Flores (2010).
9 In this assertion, clear echoes of Emmanuel Levinas appear. Butler indeed directly draws upon his thinking on the ethical relation between the Other and the self in her work on vulnerability and precariousness (2006: 128–151). See, for example, Levinas (1985; 2000; 2001).
10 Here Timmer is referring to Fineman's vulnerability thesis in particular, although the comment can be thought to be true for wider approaches to vulnerability also.
11 See Timmer and Peroni (2013).
12 See Fineman (2008: 10; 2010: 269); Butler (2005: 103).
13 Here discussion is gesturing towards Butler's conception of liveability which can be understood as the ability to sustain a viable social life in conditions of inherent precariousness and the sociopolitical operation of precarity which follow from the vulnerability of human existence (Butler 2004: 39). These conditions include basic socio-economic conditions of physical persistence – shelter, food, warmth, for example – but also by conditions of social intelligibility – and also normative conditions which shape who may be recognised within contingent sociopolitical cultures as a subject capable of living a life that counts.

References

Berlin, I. (1969) *Four Essays on Liberty*, Oxford: Oxford University Press.
Brown, W. (2000) 'Suffering Rights as Paradoxes', *Constellations*, 7(2): 230–241.
Butler, J. (1997) *The Psychic Life of Power: Theories in Subjection*, Stanford: Stanford University Press.
Butler, J. (2004) *Undoing Gender*, New York; London: Routledge.
Butler, J. (2005) *Giving an Account of Oneself*, New York: Fordham University Press.
Butler, J. (2006) *Precarious Life: The Powers of Mourning and Violence*, 2nd edn, London: Verso.
Butler, J. (2009a) *Frames of War: When Is Life Grievable?*, London; New York: Verso.

Butler, J. (2009b) 'Performativity, Precarity and Sexual Politics', *AIBR: Revista de Antropología Iberoamericana*, 4(3): i–xiii.
Butler, J. (2015a) *Notes Toward a Performative Theory of Assembly*, Cambridge, MA: Harvard University Press.
Butler, J. (2015b) *Senses of the Subject*, New York: Fordham University Press.
Charlesworth, H. (1995) 'Human Rights as Men's Rights', in J. Peters and A. Wolper (eds), *Women's Rights, Human Rights: International Feminist Perspectives*, New York; London: Routledge, 103–113.
Donnelly, J. (2013) *Universal Human Rights in Theory and Practice*, 3rd edn, Ithaca, NY: Cornell University Press.
Douzinas, C. (2000) *The End of Human Rights: Critical Legal Thought at the Turn of the Century*, Oxford: Hart.
Douzinas, C. (2010) 'Adikia: On Communism and Rights', in C. Douzinas and S. Žižek (eds), *The Idea of Communism*, London: Verso, 81–100.
Douzinas, C. (2013) 'The Paradoxes of Human Rights', *Constellations*, 20(1): 51–67.
Fineman, M. (2004) *The Autonomy Myth: A Theory of Dependency*, New York: New York Press.
Fineman, M. (2008) 'The Vulnerable Subject: Anchoring Equality in the Human Condition', *Yale Journal of Law and Feminism*, 20(1): 1–23.
Fineman, M. (2010) 'The Vulnerable Subject and the Responsive State', *Emory Law Journal*, 60: 251–275.
Fineman, M. (2013) 'Equality, Autonomy and the Vulnerable Subject in Law and Politics', in M. Fineman and A. Grear (eds), *Vulnerability: Reflections on a New Ethical Foundation for Law and Politics*, Farnham: Ashgate, 13–28.
Grear, A. (2007) 'Challenging Corporate "Humanity": Legal Disembodiment, Embodiment and Human Rights', *Human Rights Law Review*, 7(3): 511–543.
Grear, A. (2010) *Redirecting Human Rights: Facing the Challenge of Corporate Legal Humanity*, Basingstoke: Palgrave Macmillan.
Grear, A. (2013) 'Vulnerability, Advanced Global Capitalism and Co-symptomatic Injustice: Locating the Vulnerable Subject', in M. Albertson Fineman and A. Grear (eds), *Vulnerability: Reflections on a New Ethical Foundation for Law and Politics*, Farnham: Ashgate, 41–60.
Hafner-Burton, E. and Tsutsui, K. (2005) 'Human Rights in a Globalizing World: The Paradox of Empty Promises', *American Journal of Sociology*, 110(5): 1373–1411.
Hunt, L. (1996) *The French Revolution and Human Rights: A Brief Documentary History*, New York: Bedford/St Martin's Press.
Kapur, R. (2006) 'Human Rights in the 21st Century: Take a Walk on the Dark Side', *Sydney Law Review*, 28(4): 665–687.
Kirby, P. (2006a) *Vulnerability and Violence: The Impact of Globalisation*, Ann Arbor, MI: Pluto.
Kirby, P. (2006b) 'Theorising Globalisation's Social Impact: Proposing the Concept of Vulnerability', *Review of International Political Economy*, 13(4): 632–655.
Kirby, P. (2011) 'Vulnerability and Globalisation: Mediating Impacts on Society', *Journal of Human Rights and the Environment*, 2(1): 86–105.
Levinas, E. (1985) *Totality and Infinity*, trans. R. Cohen, Pittsburgh: Duquesne University Press.

Levinas, E. (2000) *Entre Nous: Essays on Thinking-of-the-Other*, trans. M. Smith and B. Harshav, New York: Columbia University Press.
Levinas, E. (2001) *Alterity and Transcendence*, trans. M. Smith and B. Harshav, New York: Columbia University Press.
Locke, J. (1967) *Two Treatises of Government*, 2nd edn, Cambridge: Cambridge University Press.
Lorey, I. (2015) *States of Insecurity: Government of the Precarious*, London: Verso.
Mackenzie, C., Rogers, W. and Dodds, S. (eds) (2014) *Vulnerability: New Essays in Ethics and Feminist Philosophy*, Oxford; New York: Oxford University Press.
MacPherson, C. (1962) *The Political Theory of Possessive Individualism*, Oxford: Clarendon.
Mullins, G. (2012) 'Paradoxes of Neoliberalism and Human Rights', in E. Swanson Goldberg and A. Schultheis Moore (eds), *Theoretical Perspectives on Human Rights and Literature*, London; New York: Routledge.
Naffine, N. (2001) 'The Nature of Legal Personality: Its History and its Incidents', in M. Davies and N. Naffine (eds), *Are Persons Property? Legal Debates about Property and Personality*, Aldershot: Ashgate, 51–74.
Nussbaum, M. (2001) *The Fragility of Goodness: Luck and Ethics in Greek Tragedy and Philosophy*, 2nd edn, Cambridge: Cambridge University Press.
Nussbaum, M. (2005) 'Analytic Love and Human Vulnerability: A Comment on Lawrence Friedman's "Is There a Special Psychoanalytic Love?"', *Journal of American Psychoanalytic Association*, 53(2): 377–383.
Otto, D. (2006) 'Lost in Translation: Re-scripting the Sexed Subjects of International Human Rights Law', in A. Orford (ed.), *International Law and its Others*, Cambridge: Cambridge University Press, 318–356.
Palmer, S. (2002) 'Feminism and the Promise of Human Rights: Possibilities and Paradoxes', in S. James and S. Palmer (eds), *Visible Women: Essays on Feminist Legal Theory and Political Philosophy*, Oxford: Hart, 91–116.
Russell Beattie, A. and Schick, K. (eds) (2013) *The Vulnerable Subject: Beyond Rationalism in International Relations*, London: Palgrave Macmillan.
Sánchez-Flores, M. (2010) *Cosmopolitan Liberalism: Expanding the Boundaries of the Individual*, London; New York: Palgrave Macmillan.
Scott, J. W. (1996) *Only Paradoxes to Offer: French Feminists and the Rights of Man*, Cambridge, MA: Harvard University Press.
Taylor, C. (1985) *Philosophy and the Human Sciences: Philosophical Papers 2*, Cambridge: Cambridge University Press.
Timmer, A. (2013) 'A Quiet Revolution: Vulnerability in the European Court of Human Rights', in M. Albertson Fineman and A. Grear (eds), *Vulnerability: Reflections on a New Ethical Foundation for Law and Politics*, Farnham: Ashgate, 147–170.
Timmer, A. and Peroni, L. (2013) 'Vulnerable Groups: The Promise of an Emergent Concept in European Human Rights Convention Law', *International Journal of Constitutional Law*, 11(4): 1056–1085.
Turner, B. (2006) *Vulnerability and Human Rights*, Pennsylvania: Pennsylvania University Press.
Wall, I. (2008) 'On Pain and the Sense of Human Rights', *Australian Feminist Law Journal*, 29(1): 53–76.
Žižek, S. (2011) 'Against Human Rights', in A. S. Rathore and A. Cistelecan (eds), *Wronging Rights? Philosophical Challenges for Human Rights*, London: New Delhi: Routledge, 149–167.

Chapter 7

On translation
The practice of human rights to come

Introduction

The previous chapters have engaged with the way in which understanding human rights as human rights to come requires approaching the underlying theoretical foundations of rights in a very different way. This has a significant impact on how to think about human rights, and also how to engage in their politics and practice. In this chapter focus turns to consider more specifically the practice of human rights to come; how activists, political groups and others interested in using human rights to advance the aims of radical politics can tangibly approach rights in this way. The concept of human rights to come does not advance a theoretical re-engagement with rights alone; it is also a concept which can be practised. Indeed, this is a crucially important element: to encourage radical social transformation and meaningful reworking of regimes of power that affect daily living and being, re-engagement with human rights cannot be restricted to the level of theorisation but must link into the everyday practice and politics of rights. It is in and through this practice that the actual work of human rights to come takes place; of articulating and rearticulating rights discourse based on a critical relation to alterity, and thereby offering possibilities to advance the claims of those on the margins. Thus, our understanding of this concept must necessarily offer a tangible way to make the theoretical realignments and critical engagements with power it is advancing accessible.

In the discussion which follows, the task of envisaging the practice of human rights to come is undertaken. Recalling the idea of reiteration which is central to the concept, human rights to come can be practised by beginning with what is already taking place in human rights activity and using this as a starting point to engage in a slightly altered practice of rights which facilitates sustained critical engagements with alterity and the 'to come'. The way in which I propose this can be done is by reflecting on the idea of translation. The translation involved in the practice of human rights to come does not seek to stay with existing practices of translation in the sense of top-down translation, or an understanding of translation which focuses on the power of the dominant to integrate the subordinate, but is a practice which has a critical impetus to challenge the dominant and its power at a fundamental level. To practise human rights to come, translation must be understood as taking place between multiple articulations of rights in various locations and contexts, and as an activity that is fundamentally *disruptive* of the dominant and *futural* in nature, foregrounding a critical relation to alterity and power. This understanding of translation may be facilitated by looking to Judith Butler's model of cultural translation which provides effective tools to start thinking through and consciously approaching the practice of human rights to come as a disruptive, and specifically futural, practice of translation.

However, in envisaging such, I also assert that we cannot stay with Butler alone, leaving her concept of cultural translation fully intact. The practice of human rights to come must be viewed as one that is holistic and multivariate, involving different roles, spaces and subjects. To further understand this, and the role actors beyond activists and political groups may have, it is possible to engage with wider critical thinking on translation, such as the work of Homi Bhabha and Gayatri Spivak, to consider the role of the translator. This idea is not present in Butler's account but appears important in thinking through the practice of human rights to come as an activity taking place in more locations than grassroots politics alone, allowing a role to be envisaged for those occupying privileged politico-legal positions who are supportive of using human rights to facilitate radical social change.

The practice of human rights and translation

When initially thinking about the practice of human rights to come it is important to note that, given the concept's function to encourage contextualised and contingent re-engagements with human rights, it is not possible, or indeed desirable, to outline a precise roadmap for activists and other political movements or groups to follow. This would undoubtedly undermine the utility and critical force that the concept holds. However, to be accessible, it is necessary for significant inroads to be made towards envisaging what it would mean to practise human rights as human rights to come. As outlined above, given the emphasis that the concept places on using already given discourses and ideas in a new, more radical manner, it is submitted that those interested in practising human rights in this way may productively begin with what already characterises rights practice and use this as a starting point. As any other reiterative activity, this does not advance a radical break with already existing understandings and practices, but advances subtle shifts, using tools already available in modified ways.

From this, it must be asked what does already characterise the practice of human rights? What activities or forms of engagement are central to everyday interactions with human rights in localised contexts? Undoubtedly the practice of human rights is a complex and diverse phenomenon, differing according to place, time and context.[1] It would be misleading to say that there is one way to practise human rights. Rather, this practice consists of a multitude of diverse activities and actions undertaken by a range of social actors. For example, it involves the claiming of rights to address experiences of marginalisation or oppression, an activity which can take place in political or legal arenas. It also involves practices of lobbying and awareness raising to promote the values that human rights represent and integrate them into legal and policy activities. The practice of human rights is carried out via educational activities to advance rights consciousness or ideas as well as social justice initiatives to facilitate everyday access to rights such as food, water or shelter. In addition to all of these elements, the practice of human rights can be understood to involve processes of translation whereby conversations between the international and the local, or what rights currently represent and what they 'should' or could represent, are undertaken to negotiate how rights can be understood and advanced concretely. It is this latter element that I would like to focus on to identify practices of translation as practices that stand to be usefully exploited – rethought and reapproached – towards more radical ends to offer a foothold to begin a radical practice of human rights to come.

To identify translation as a key part of practising rights is unsurprising given that human rights are transnational norms which are intended to move from the global to the local, from theory to practice, across diverse cultures and sociopolitical contexts. In this respect, human rights require translation on a number of different levels. Indeed, a wide body of literature has developed considering the practice of human rights as one of translation.[2] Seminal among this has been the anthropological work of Sally Engle Merry which explores how the meanings of international human rights norms take effect in localised cultural contexts. Merry advances that 'in order for human rights ideas to be effective . . . they need to be translated into local terms and situated within local contexts of power and meaning' (2006a: 1). This activity is characterised as a process of vernacularisation; human rights are remade in the local vernacular through social and politico-legal engagement which allows for a localised conception of human rights to emerge (Merry 2006a: 1; 2006b: 2009). The translation of human rights in the sense outlined by Merry and others involves both linguistic and extralinguistic forms of translation which are characterised by dialogue between two discourses or languages within a context of power.[3] The result of such translational dialogue is an outcome which strikes a balance between the global and the local, leading to some kind of consensual understanding being reached. Following such work, and its expansion by others within anthropology and in wider disciplines, Jarrett Zigon comments that conceptualisation of the practice of human rights as involving translational processes of vernacularisation has become 'somewhat of a truism' (2013: 55).

In this perspective, the practice of human rights involves an important element of translation between international and local norms and contexts. The practice of human rights to come can also be considered as involving, and indeed is in many ways defined by, an activity of translation. However, space does exist to add to, or modify, the conception of translation with which human rights thinkers and activists are equipped in order to use translation to consciously facilitate and sustain a radical politics of human rights. The concept of translation when thought in relation to human rights has usually been understood in two ways. The first of these is to consider how Western, state-led rights discourse articulated at the international level translates to the local. In other words, how international norms enter the local vernacular. This serves to place focus on, and perhaps unwittingly reinforce, the power of the former as dominant, translating to the latter. Alternatively, a second conception of translation has envisaged a more reciprocal model whereby in translational dialogue the local translates back into the international and shapes it. This is the approach taken by Merry above.[4] This second understanding of translation focuses on the international dominant as also integrating local norms and understandings into itself. While this second approach holds more potential to critique and rework that which is dominant, it still remains within given frames of reference. It remains committed to the international human rights regime and its authority to define human rights, albeit advancing a development of such definitions based on local experience, as opposed to aiming to more deeply challenge and displace this discourse through translational engagements.[5] In this respect, while such mainstream practices of translation have been envisaged as involving an element of speaking back to the power of the dominant international human rights norm, they are not entirely disruptive of this dominant at a foundational level.[6]

The question I wish to explore is whether translation may be approached slightly differently; whether it can be, as noted above, reiterated. This reiteration would involve, first, understanding the practice of human rights as *always* one of translation between competing ideas and articulations of rights which must be negotiated. In this view translation takes place not only between the international/local and Western/non-Western, but between multiple articulations of human rights made by competing political actors in diverse political and legal locations. Accordingly, translation must be thought to define the everyday activity of advancing, claiming and debating rights and is at the centre of rights politics. Second, and crucially, this contrasting understanding of translation must be viewed as fundamentally *disruptive*. It does not remain within the frame of international human rights law as currently conceived, retaining the authority of this discourse as dominant, but aims to engage in a deeper contestation of its foundations and authority. Translation is not approached as discourses translating into the dominant, but the dominant is dislocated as a frame of reference and that which has power to incorporate alternative understandings into itself. Translation, so conceived, would take place among competing ideas of what human rights are, what they mean, what they can be capable of doing or achieving that aims to disrupt the current international human rights regime by rethinking not only its content but its foundational commitments and ability to pronounce on the idea of rights. Thirdly, this critically disruptive practice of translation must be *futural-focused*, foregrounding the element of the 'to come' and the sustained critical relation to the alterity and power of the dominant which such entails. The change from the familiar ideas of translation within human rights here is subtle, indeed intentionally so, but such a subtle shift is powerful. It serves to orientate the work of translation in a different direction; a deeper opening up of human rights and a radical practice of human rights as defined by ongoing critical translation among numerous conceptions of what rights are and what they may be capable of doing which need not remain committed to the current conception of rights articulated in the international human rights regime.

How can such a concept of translation begin to be thought through? Over recent decades the idea of translation has been increasingly utilised across a range of disciplines from postcolonial studies to sociology and ethnography. This has extended beyond an exclusive focus on language and processes of linguistic translation to consider the dynamic process of interaction among cultures and ethnic groups in various contexts from colonialism to globalisation (Young 2012: 156). This latter use of the concept has been termed *cultural translation* and has emerged as a critical tool to talk about and make sense of the world (Pym 2010: 143; Buden et al. 2009). Rather than merely a neutral concept to observe the way in which cultures are transmitted and reinterpreted in different contexts, cultural translation, particularly in postcolonial theorising, has directed attention to questions of power, resistance and domination and the potential to use processes of translation to resist or rework dominant regimes (Young 2012: 156). This is the case in the work of Homi Bhabha and Gayatri Chakravorty Spivak, for example. In Bhabha's use of cultural translation to consider the experience of migrant communities, the practice of cultural translation 'desacralizes the transparent assumptions of cultural supremacy, and in that very act, demands a contextual specificity, a historical differentiation within minority positions' (1994: 327). Drawing from Walter Benjamin (1985), Derrida (1985) and Paul de Man (1985), cultural translation is engaged in Bhabha's work to stage cultural difference, to foreground the 'foreign' and thereby conjure something new, allowing a move beyond the traditional binary options of migrants either assimilating with dominant culture or standing out from it (Bhabha 1994, 339). In her work, Spivak considers translation in postcolonial contexts, outlining how translation can further colonial possibilities, appropriating the voice of the subaltern (1994). However, significantly, Spivak also outlines translation as simultaneously holding counter-colonial possibilities to expose and rework the limits of the dominant culture (1993: 179–200).

Cultural translation, therefore, has emerged as a way of exploring processes of transmission, reinterpretation and realignment within contexts of oppression, foregrounding the potential of translational practices to introduce something new based on alterity, to question and resist already existing regimes of power in a radical way. In such approaches to translation focus is moved from top-down translation, or the power of the dominant to integrate the subordinate, and redirected towards how translational activity may offer a vehicle to challenge the dominant at a fundamental level, to rework currently dominant frames of reference. This way of approaching translation interlinks with the overarching aim of human rights to come as a way of reinterpreting and re-engaging the foundations of mainstream conceptions of human rights and their relation to restrictive regimes of power, and allows us to begin to see how the translational activity involved in the practice of rights may be productively exploited in order to do so. The model of cultural translation can be developed to offer tools for approaching the practice of human rights to come as involving translation between diverse discourses and ideas of rights in a way that is attentive to power and alterity and disrupts dominant conceptions of human rights, their foundations and authority on this basis. In further envisaging such a radical practice of translation, particularly useful tools can be found by staying with the Butlerian influence central to the present re-engagement with human rights and considering Butler's articulation of cultural translation.

Informed by the work of Bhabha and Spivak, Butler views cultural translation as an activity whereby the unfixity of any universal concept is foregrounded and constantly reworked through translational dialogue between its current form and that which it excludes or forecloses, represented in competing conceptions of the universal which exist alongside the dominant. In this perspective, multiple conceptions of the universal exist at any one time and compete with one another. In terms of the disruptive nature of this translation, Butler stresses that 'the task of cultural translation is one that is necessitated precisely by the performative contradiction' whereby the alterity of the current, dominant universal is exposed and that 'the extension of universality through the act of translation takes place when one who is excluded from the universal, and yet belongs to it nevertheless, speaks from a split situation of being at once authorized and deauthorized' (1996: 49–50). However, when competing conceptions of the universal come into translational dialogue in this approach the dominant universal will not merely integrate the demands made upon it to create a 'truer' universal; rather, *both* must change to apprehend the other (Butler 1996: 48). The result of translational dialogue between competing universals is the creation of a new universal which speaks to the limits of the former but which can never be fully complete, inclusive or settled, and so becomes the new, dominant universal which is open to challenge from that which it excludes (Butler, Laclau and Žižek 2000: 11–43). It is interesting to note that Butler indeed envisages this model of cultural translation as relevant to the practice of human rights. For example, she highlights the translational contestation over the universal concept of the 'human' which lesbian, gay, bisexual, transgender and intersex (LGBTI) human rights activism involves (1996: 46). In such activity those who are excluded from the dominant universal pose a performative contradiction which exposes its limits, and the dominant enters into translational dialogue with the competing conception of itself, each giving and receiving from one another, to articulate a new, more inclusive universal. Butler endorses such activism stating: 'how might we continue to insist upon more expansive reformulations of universality, if we commit ourselves to honoring only the provisional and parochial versions of universality currently encoded in international law?' (1996: 47). The ongoing making and remaking of universal discourse via the practice of cultural translation emerges as central to a healthy and democratic human rights politics (2004: 36).[7]

As one way of re-engaging human rights towards the ends of radical social transformation, the practice of human rights to come can be envisaged as involving the activity of cultural translation to advance the claims of those excluded from dominant discourse and to rework such discourse to produce new understandings. The model of disruptive translation committed to a foundational challenge to existing dominant frameworks and regimes found in cultural translation offers a productive starting point for engaging in the practice of human rights to come, disrupting the dominant discourse of human rights and its authority to define rights. However, this practice involves a distinct approach, not commensurable with activism such as that of LGBTI activists referred to above. Such activism, while challenging dominant articulations of rights, did not go as far as challenging the foundational elements of human rights explored in the preceding chapters as central to understanding human rights as human rights to come. In particular, what distinguishes this concept from other radical engagements with rights is the central element of *futurity* and attention to the productive possibilities which may follow from foregrounding this. It is the 'to come' and focus on it which human rights to come advances as offering particular, and unique, possibilities for facilitating and sustaining a practice of human rights attentive to alterity and capable of advancing the ends of radical social transformation. This signals towards the need for a model of cultural translation which not only takes place in multiple locations and is fundamentally disruptive, but allows activists and other radical movements or groups to understand and approach the activity of translation within the wider context of the 'to come'. I assert that the tools to do so can be found by remaining with Butler's theorisation of cultural translation but expanding it to foreground the element of futurity within it which is central to this model but not highly visible in her own engagement of cultural translation and radical practices of human rights. In the discussion below, I explore this and what a tangible practice of human rights to come as a practice of disruptive, futural-focused translation might look like. Following from this, I additionally consider how in envisaging such it is not possible to stay with Butler alone. To bring into view and initiate a holistic practice of human rights to come, resources must also be drawn from wider conceptions of cultural translation.

Cultural translation and a disruptive and futural practice of human rights to come

Before turning to consider what the practice of human rights to come might look like as a specifically disruptive and futural practice of cultural translation, it is important to note that viewing Butler's model as a starting point for such practice provides the means to tie together many of the theoretical re-engagements explored in the previous chapters. For example, Butler's cultural translation appears to offer ways of foregrounding, and capitalising upon, the performativity of rights politics outlined in Chapter 3 as central to understanding the politico-legal activity of human rights to come and opportunities to reiterate rights anew. Cultural translation in Butler's view can be thought of, at a basic level, as a performative activity. As outlined above, focus on the performative contradiction is key to the approach to cultural translation she seeks to advance. The assertion of performative contradictions – revealing dominant discourses to be less universal than they purport, and through this revelation performatively reworking universal discourses themselves – appears as a way to begin the practice of human rights to come, using such performative contradictions to enter into translational dialogue which at its heart is performative, capable of bringing into being the very change it advances.

In addition, Butler's cultural translation is informed by her work on universality which has been explored in Chapter 4 as capable of engagement to advance rich possibilities for reapproaching the universality of human rights, and so offers a means of putting this alternative understanding of universality into practice. Recall that it is necessary to reject universality as a static attribute or characteristic of rights and approach universality instead as a process of ongoing universalisation whereby universality itself remains 'to come', conflictually worked and reworked towards a futural completion that must remain self-refuting. A Butlerian understanding of cultural translation captures the manner in which competing conceptions of the universal come together and enter into dialogue, translating between one another to rework the limitations of the current universal. In this view, no assertion of universality can be made without requiring cultural translation (Butler, Laclau and Žižek 2000: 35). Thus, approaching the practice of human rights as a process of cultural translation is underpinned by, and naturally helps work towards, an alternative view of the universality of human rights which departs from, and indeed challenges, traditional conceptions.

Cultural translation can also be considered as compatible with foregrounding an ontology of vulnerability which has been outlined in Chapter 6 as required to displace liberal notions of bounded individualism and sovereignty traditionally characterising human rights. Practising cultural translation requires activists and others to embrace vulnerability in the practice of human rights. Butler characterises translation between ideas of the 'human' as constituting 'a loss, a disorientation' (2004: 38). Engaging in translational activity involves transcending bounded approaches to our lives as subjects and opening to the other which is constitutive of the self in interrelated life. In cultural translation activists must come into contact with the intersubjective and ecstatic nature of our living and being, and so its practice facilitates encounters compatible with the alternative ontology which human rights to come seeks to advance. Practising human rights to come as cultural translation can also be considered as involving a giving up of the illusion of sovereign control in the sense that it is not possible to approach the work of advancing competing universals with a predetermined goal in mind. There is no guarantee that the assertion of a competing universal or the staging of a performative contradiction will render the desired outcome, or will result in a new universal which is more expansive and attentive to alterity. Activists must give themselves up to be vulnerable in the unpredictable politics of translation and so remind themselves of the ontological approach of vulnerability which re-engaging human rights as human rights to come necessarily involves.

Importantly, Butlerian cultural translation is an inherently agonistic practice, drawing attention towards the value of political conflict which holds possibility to facilitate a rejection of ideas of consensus in the practice of human rights to come. Cultural translation emerges from a conception of universality as a site of contest. As Butler asserts, 'both the form and content of universality are highly contested, and cannot be articulated outside the scene of their embattlement' (Butler, Laclau and Žižek 2000: 37). Approaching the practice of human rights to come as one of translating between competing conceptions of the universal articulated in various spaces and locations of human rights politics, therefore, necessarily leads away from a tendency to seek consensus in the activity of human rights. Instead, activists must engage in contest over the universal as a process of universalisation, a site of contest in the sense that the approach of human rights to come advances. This is not a purely destructive antagonism, but an agonistic process in the sense outlined in Chapter 5 whereby all share a commitment to the values that human rights represent, but promote translational contest over the specific form these values take in particular locations and contexts based on a critical relation to alterity. We can thus understand cultural translation as not a practice of assimilation or the pursuit of consensus, but a practice where the translational encounter between competing universals visibilises the alterity within the dominant norm and thereby 'exposes the failure of the norm to effect the universal reach for which it stands' (Butler 1996: 50). Through this agonistic encounter new articulations of the universal come into being which are 'no more determinative of a "final" reading than the one that is received' (Butler 1996: 51) and cultural translation emerges as a dialectical process which refutes the achievability of full and final synthesis.

From this, Butler's cultural translation provides means to envisage and begin a practice of human rights to come which facilitates the underpinning elements of this concept. In particular, the attention to the 'to come' and the impossible and self-refuting horizon that this establishes for human rights and their politics, while still encouraging a striving towards such a horizon, is central to a Butlerian approach to cultural translation. This model is developed out of an understanding of universality as a 'not yet', and is characterised as a 'future-orientated labour' (Butler 2006: xviii), sustaining conflictual workings and reworkings of the universal without knowing its future in advance. Here Butler too is in conversation with, and indebted to, the Derridean 'to come' (Butler, Laclau and Žižek 2000: 269). This critical focus on futurity is, I assert, unique to Butler's conceptualisation of cultural translation and is key to what recommends it as a starting point for envisaging the practice of human rights to come. In consciously approaching the practice of human rights with a view to the 'not yet' of the universal, activists may resist ideas of closure or attempts to shut down debate on rights concepts or ideas. In contrast, approaching translational activity attentive to futurity provokes constant unsettlement, a sense of never-ending critical engagement with powerful regimes of thinking and living which is not fully possible in the mainstream practice of human rights with its focus on dominant discourses of rights as the frame of reference for translation. The practice of human rights to come as one of futural-focused cultural translation may be thought of as involving activists and other groups making claims to human rights that do not return 'to a wisdom we already have' but that help to provoke 'a set of questions that show how profound our sense of not-knowing must be . . . What, then, is a right? What ought universality to be? How do we understand what it is to be a "human"?' (Butler, Laclau and Žižek 2000: 41). Critical practices of translation in human rights to come must not seek to answer these questions, but rather 'to permit them an opening, to provoke a political discourse that sustains the questions' (Butler, Laclau and Žižek 2000: 41). This political discourse is fundamentally futural in nature, sustaining a critical attention to alterity at the heart of the practice of human rights to come.

So how might activists or groups interested in advancing a practice of human rights to come proceed in this task and use the concept of translation to begin such a practice? What would human rights to come as a disruptive and futural-focused practice of cultural translation look like? Butler's cultural translation can be developed to offer tangible tools for such. These are tools that will indeed be familiar to activists and political groups, but may be taken up slightly differently. First of all, radical thinkers and activists can be encouraged to look at human rights concepts, and human rights as a discourse, in a modified way. Rather than perceiving the current language, concepts and ideas of international human rights law as at the centre of translational activity – standing to be vernacularised or persuaded to incorporate alternative conceptions into its self – such can be repositioned as a competing universal to be engaged in translational dialogue. The dominant universal must be viewed as merely that which currently enjoys dominance, not necessarily holding any privileged position or status. From this new way of looking at human rights, radical activists can move to undertake disruptive political activity to bring to the fore the unfulfilled nature or the alterity of the currently dominant universal and put forward an alternative conception of what it may look like or be capable of meaning. This disruptive work – the work of staging the performative contradiction – may be undertaken in everyday local politics, in politics at the international level or even in legal arenas such as courts or law reform activities.[8] Importantly, however, at this point the practice of human rights to come must foreground the futural. In putting forward an alternative, disruptive competing universal and bringing this into translational dialogue with the dominant, activists must not understand such as the pinnacle of their practice. On the contrary, this must be viewed as just the starting point. To undertake translation conscious of futurity and the 'to come', activists must depart from traditional ways of viewing human rights practice, moving from viewing social transformation as achieved through discrete, individualised activities or key occasions in rights practice – successfully extending rights to new subjects or changing how a right is interpreted – and towards being understood as achieved through ongoing agonistic conversation without end. It is through the work of sustained translational engagements, as opposed to one-off campaigns or achievements, that radical social change may occur through the politics of rights. Through this the practice of human rights to come is perceived as an ongoing disruptive questioning in a range of politico-legal locations that always points towards ineradicable alterity and must be viewed as only effective through its ongoing nature.

To think this through further, let us consider rights practice on the concept of equality. The current understanding of equality in international human rights law is largely read through the assertion that all are equal in dignity and rights and have a right not to be discriminated against. Radical activists may look at the current discourse on this concept and view it as based on limited foundations; that of bounded individualism and sovereignty as opposed to intersubjective vulnerability, for example, or as advancing a complete universal but actually excluding some subjects, so implicitly understanding some as more equal than others. However, viewing this concept through the lens of futural-focused cultural translation would involve understanding the dominant articulation of equality as a competing universal, the one that enjoys dominance at present, which must be reworked based on its alterity to make the value of equality more concrete. Equality is not a rights concept to be 'applied' to advance the aims of those on the margins, but one that must be reworked, debated, opened up again and again in order to do so. Alternative articulations of equality, perhaps that are intersubjective, that work beyond binaries such as male/female, child/adult, ability/disability, can be put forward in political action consciously entering into disruptive, translational dialogue with the dominant to bring forward new understandings that reveal otherwise invisibilised experiences of alterity. In this process, international human rights law and its related norms of equality/non-discrimination must not be viewed as the frame of reference for translational activity, to be appealed to in order to effect change; rather such norms must be brought into translational critique and their authority disrupted. Competing assertions of what the relationship between equality and rights might look like can be advanced by activists and other groups in a range of locations from domestic politics and lawmaking to international forums, and this activity understood as never-ending. To foreground futurity in this activity a more expansive, concrete or intersubjective understanding of equality must not be viewed as achieved via discrete results-based campaigns or action but through ongoing translational work where alternative, disruptive conceptions of equality are put forward again and again and the currently dominant is never final. Translation between competing understandings of equality, and experiences of inequality, is futural in this sense and translational activity is undertaken knowing this is not the end, but only a temporary settlement, another point in an ongoing, conflictual translational conversation. It is in this way that the site of human rights can be understood as human rights to come, a place to engage in never-ending translation responding to alterity and a place to continually reimagine the world anew through such processes.

When those interested in radical politics approach the practice of human rights as one of cultural translation they are engaging in a subtle reiteration of the practice of rights, one that is by its nature more amenable to the ends of radical social transformation and capable of sustaining an ongoing and futural focus on these ends. In beginning to envisage or initiate a practice of human rights to come, Butler's model of cultural translation can be drawn upon to offer a foothold in the transition between theory and practice, characterising translation as disruptive at a foundational level and futural in the sense of involving never-ending agonistic engagement with the ineradicable alterity of universality in the wider context of democratic politics. This latter element is particularly important. To think of the everyday activity of human rights to come as beginning with cultural translation involves explicitly rejecting the possibility of final synthesis from the outset, this very fact being what sustains the ability of human rights to come to continually expose and respond to alterity, and viewing human rights practice not in terms of discrete, compartmentalised activities or engagements but effecting change through ongoing disruptive conversation. While Butler has stressed the element of the futural 'not yet' involved in cultural translation, and has used cultural translation to theorise and advance radical practices of rights such as women's rights and LGBTI rights, she does not explicitly foreground the idea of futurity in relation to such practices. In this respect, thinking the practice of human rights to come as one of futural translation serves to place focus on something not previously at the forefront of engagement with Butlerian cultural translation and human rights. In this analysis, in contrast to mainstream views of human rights which may also accept a form of futurity, the 'to come' of human rights to come is driven by a critical understanding of alterity and power and is used to allow activists and others to carve a useful space for the politics and practice of human rights in radical politics.

For a holistic practice of human rights to come: the role of the translator

Up to this point the practice of human rights to come has been explored as taking up the idea of translation and approaching it in a slightly different way. This involves moving from viewing international human rights as a dominant discourse which requires translation to subordinate levels or a translation of the subordinate into the dominant. Instead, translation must be viewed as an activity which is disruptive – challenging the dominant discourse and its authority at a foundational level – and futural – departing from viewing social transformation as achieved through discrete events, campaigns or applications of rights and towards being achieved through never-ending disruptive translational conversation on alterity. These disruptive and futural translational engagements may be approached as taking place in a variety of locations and contexts where the language of human rights is engaged. As explored above, Butler's conceptualisation of cultural translation offers a starting point for thinking through this practice. However, in envisaging what it might mean to practise human rights to come it is not enough to remain with Butler alone. To envisage and think through a practice that is holistic it is important to extend consideration of cultural translation further. In discussion below I outline what this might involve.

It has been established that human rights to come advances a practice of human rights which is undertaken through translational engagements in diverse locations and contexts. This widespread translation involves radical activists and groups engaging in the everyday politics of rights, but must also involve roles and subjects beyond the activist subject and grassroots politics alone. While grassroots activism may be the primary location where the hard work of disruptive, futural-focused translational activity may take place, an important role can also be envisaged in the practice of human rights to come for others engaging with human rights discourse in wider locations. In particular, it is necessary to consider those interested in advancing the aims of radical politics who are in what could be regarded as 'privileged politico-legal positions'. This could include, for example, those who occupy positions in national and international non-governmental organisations, those involved in formal politics or law, as well as those within academia. Such actors have often been involved in previous work to engage in a more radical practice of human rights, for example, the LGBTI campaign for human rights noted above, and should also be considered as forming an equally important part of the practice of human rights to come. The need to consider such actors and the potential role they may play can also be thought as fitting with the assertion of human rights to come, as a reiterative activity in the sense engaged in Chapter 3, that a radical practice of human rights need not view more institutionalised spaces or discourses as a stumbling block or barrier to radical reiterative activity.

Therefore, in thinking through the practice of human rights to come as one which is multivariate and holistic, consideration cannot remain with grassroots activists and other radical movements or groups alone but needs to be conscious of the role of those in privileged politico-legal positions, also providing these individuals with tools to become engaged in a disruptive and future practice of human rights. It is possible, staying with the concept of translation, that such individuals can be envisaged as having a role as *translators*, encouraging and helping to sustain the translational activity taking place in wider activist practices. These individuals may help bring the competing universals of human rights – the currently dominant and those asserted by radical political groups – into translational dialogue in ways that assist challenge to dominant discourses and regimes of power. Importantly, again distinguishing the activity of human rights to come from that of radical approaches to human rights more broadly, translators may be thought of as having an important role in sustaining attention to futurity and the 'to come' and keeping human rights practice focused on its never-ending nature, keeping the disruptive translational conversation going. In Butler's account of cultural translation, no explicit consideration is given to the role of a translator. Accordingly, in thinking through the place of such individuals and the idea of a translator in the practice of human rights to come and what this may involve it is instructive to return to wider thinking on translation, both already existing practices of translation in human rights, and critical thinking on cultural translation.

The idea of the translator is indeed one that has been considered in approaches to human rights and their practice. For example, in her work Engle Merry considers the way in which 'intermediaries or translators work at various levels to negotiate between local, regional, national and global systems of meaning. Translators refashion global rights agendas for local contexts and reframe local grievances in terms of global human rights principles and ideas' (2006b: 39). These translators can be found, for Engle Merry, in local non-governmental organisations and similar locations and are central to the vernacularisation of human rights, actively encouraging and facilitating engagement between global and local discourses. This role involves both translating from dominant to subordinate, and also between subordinate and dominant, representing the issues of particular cultural contexts in international forums, for example. Thus, the idea and role of the translator is one that is not unfamiliar in the practice of human rights. However, this role, as with this approach to translation more generally, is not fundamentally disruptive. Translators largely work within the power of the dominant to define and legitimise redefinitions of rights as opposed to facilitating a radical challenge to this dominant, its authority and frame of reference. It is possible that in a practice of human rights to come the role of the translator can be considered in a more radical light to assist in facilitating disruptive and futural translation. To come closer to envisaging the kind of role for translators that I am advancing in the practice of human rights to come, it is useful to again return to postcolonial theorisation of cultural translation.

In Bhabha's thinking on cultural translation, the translator occupies a 'third space' of cultural hybridity which he identifies as a space for subversion. For Bhabha (1994), the migrant subject appears as the translator negotiating and transforming the dominant culture. This conceptualisation represented a rejection of the prevalent assimilation approach whereby migrant communities must translate into the dominant culture to allow for a view of how such communities may resist dominant culture. The idea of the translator in cultural translation is also engaged by Spivak who writes from the position of a translator of literary and theoretical works. In 'The Politics of Translation' Spivak draws attention to the role and the task of the linguistic translator, seeking to assert 'that the lessons of translation in the narrow sense can reach much further' (1993: 194). In exploring translation as one way we make sense of the world (1993: 179), and thereby an inherently political activity, Spivak makes clear that translation may be a site for counter-colonialist possibilities where the dominant discourse may be disrupted and challenged. Central to this assertion is the role of the translator whom Spivak urges to take up practices of responsible translation which are attentive to relations of power and dominance/subordination (1993: 179). A number of qualities characterise what Spivak considers as a good translator who can resist the more violent and repressive tendencies of translation. For example, she makes clear that translators 'cannot translate from a position of monolinguistic superiority' (1993: 195). Additionally, for Spivak, the translator is to 'surrender herself to the linguistic rhetoricity of the original text' and, simultaneously, be 'able to discriminate on the terrain of the original' (1993: 189). A translator capable of doing so will require a particular degree of skill and knowledge. The translator must be aware of the meaning-making nature of translation, aware of the subjects, identity creation and audience involved in the translation process and through such an awareness can practise and encourage more responsible and responsive translations.

These thoughts emerging from postcolonial work may be expanded in thinking through the practice of human rights to come and the possibility of those in privileged politico-legal positions interested in advancing the aims of radical politics consciously adopting the role of critical translators who aid challenge to dominant discourses. Such individuals can be considered as occupying a place of hybridity, having a relation to both the currently dominant and competing universal, and so are in an ideal position to encourage and advance translational activity in a way that is conscious of what is at stake and the relations of power involved. This could take the form of drawing attention to radical politics utilising the language of human rights, advancing the competing universal accounts being put forward in grassroots activism in formal legal or political arenas, or potentially even engaging in lawmaking activity which would facilitate translational engagements and effect new, more expansive universal discourses. Through such activities, the reach of the disruptive competing universals advanced by human rights activists may be maximised and brought into translational conversation in locations and forums otherwise difficult for activists and other political groups to reach. In their position, such individuals also have the skills and knowledge reflecting that which Spivak outlines as central for a responsible translator: an understanding of both discourses and their limitations, an awareness of the processes of identity creation central to such discourses, and an understanding of the processes of human rights politics and practice more generally. Rejecting discourses of liberal rationality and sovereignty, such translators cannot be seen as rational and disinterested, and also are not completely free in their activity but also must be considered, within a wider conception of rights as performative, as practising reiterative activities using the tools which are available to them.[9]

In addition, returning to the futural nature of translation characterising human rights to come, translators can be considered as having a particularly important role to play in sustaining a focus on futurity and the 'to come'. It is here that the role of the translator in the practice of human rights to come differs in emphasis from that in traditional approaches to human rights, and indeed from other more general radical approaches. Translators may help to facilitate focus on the futural and thus sustain an ongoing, critical relation to alterity and power. In consciously viewing their role in facilitating translational encounters as contingent, responsive and, indeed, never-ending, translators can help characterise work for social transformation via the practice of rights as beyond discrete, individualised activities but rather as taking the shape of ongoing disruptive conversation and resist the idea of the practice of human rights as ever being closed or finished. This is a particularly important element of the translator's role. When activists may become disheartened by lack of progress or a disappointing outcome of translational politics, the role of the translator appears crucial in foregrounding a conception of human rights practice beyond discrete activities or campaigns, directing back towards the horizon of the 'to come', reminding grassroots politics that the very promise and utility of human rights lies in ongoing disruptive translational conversation. In this way, the translator is central to foregrounding and sustaining the never-ending critical relation to alterity and power that is required in the practice of human rights to come, reassuring that radical change will occur not through 'application' of rights ideas or one-off successes but through never-ending agonistic translation. Those interested in the aims of radical social transformation in privileged politico-legal positions may already be engaging in activities of translation between dominant and subordinate discourses and so, again, the practice of human rights to come may be considered as beginning with this already existing role and thinking it through using slightly different tools which allow for a radical approach to human rights which is specifically 'to come'.

As an example of what it may mean to consciously approach the practice of human rights as a translator, attention can be focused on the critical legal academic interested in using the language of rights to advance enhanced possibilities for living and being. Such a person holds particular knowledge and skills, has an understanding of both the 'languages' of dominant rights discourse and the claims of those on the margins, and so may be in a position to translate between the two in a way that goes beyond 'a position of monolinguistic superiority' (Spivak 1993: 194). Through engaging in academic writing, debate and discussion within and outside the academy, the critical legal academic can translate the claims of those engaging in everyday activism in a way that is sensitive and attentive to the subject identities and processes of subjectification such activity involves and bring such into dialogue with dominant discourses, institutional regimes or ways of thinking which may be difficult, or impossible, for grassroots activists and other political movements or groups to access. This person may be able to encourage translational engagement in spaces such as elite-driven political discussion, academic journals or media outlets, for example, and so expand the reach of radical translational engagement. In addition, the critical legal academic as a translator may consciously adopt a particular role in sustaining focus on alterity and the 'to come' when those engaged in everyday activism may become frustrated with the marginalisation of their voices, or lack of productive results achieving radical social change. Through continuing to advance competing discourses and challenge the dominant in formal and elite locations, the academic translator can continue to encourage the assertion of competing universals, maintaining the momentum of a never-ending radical human rights politics which reflects, but also builds upon, grassroots activity. Following insights such as those of Spivak (1994; 2000), such individuals should be encouraged to think carefully about the way in which they are representing the voices or competing universals of those on the margins but in doing so can potentially, through their unique position, contribute to and sustain the practice of human rights to come as a practice of disruptive and never-ending translation in productive ways.

Conclusion

In this chapter, discussion has begun to envisage what it may mean to practise human rights as human rights to come. This practice has been outlined as beginning with a reiteration of the idea of translation to encourage activists and wider political groups to view the translation of human rights in a more critical and *disruptive* manner, as an activity not using the dominant as a frame of reference but engaging in a more foundational challenge to the dominant, and in a way that is specifically *futural*. The Butlerian model of cultural translation provides activists with a handle to begin practical translational work in this way and in doing so begins to put into practice the theoretical restagings which the concept of human rights to come advances. In stressing the futurity central to this idea of cultural translation a radical practice of human rights can emerge which is distinctive and involves a move from radical social transformation as achieved via discrete activities to being achieved through the work of never-ending disruptive translation. Discussion has also revealed how, following from the way in which this practice is multivariate, involving actors beyond grassroots activists and groups alone, it is also possible to envisage a holistic practice of human rights to come, emphasising the role of the translator. Those in privileged politico-legal positions can be productively encouraged to utilise their skills, knowledge and position of hybridity to encourage and sustain disruptive, futural-focused translational activity and so complement the activity of everyday grassroots politics in a conscious way that fits with the overall underpinnings of the project for human rights to come. This may involve bringing discourses into translational dialogue in elite venues or discussions or carefully representing the voice of those on the margins and the competing universals they advance, mindful of the political nature and colonialising dangers of translation itself.

From this account, as advanced at the outset of discussion, the aim is not, and has not been, to provide a roadmap or blueprint which activists can follow. By its very nature, human rights to come is a contingent practice which must emerge from and in response to particular contexts and demands lest it lose its critical force and become as false and abstract a universal, as the dominant universals it seeks to challenge. While a roadmap cannot, therefore, be provided, it is possible to outline and foreground the key elements which are central to the tangible practice of human rights to come. These are the performative assertion of competing universals which radically disrupt and reveal the alterity of the dominant; the ongoing nature of such activity in pursuit of a universal which must always be considered futural; and the multilayered or holistic nature of the practice of human rights, envisaging cooperation and solidarity across a range of locations and contexts to productively sustain the challenge of the radical and the 'to come'.

Notes

1 For discussion on the diverse practice of human rights, see Goodale and Merry (2007); Goodhart (2013); Pruce (2015).
2 This includes Goodale and Merry (2007); Goldstein (2013); Gal, Kowalski and Moore (2015); Haglund and Aggarwal (2011).
3 See Goldstein (2013).
4 See further Levitt and Merry (2009).
5 For additional critique of this approach to 'vernacularisation', see Reilly (2011: 71).
6 This is explored further in the next chapter, where it is asserted that activity to translate feminist concerns into international human rights law did challenge the content of the dominant norm but did not level a more general foundational challenge to human rights and that which underpins them within the given international law regime – this regime still remained intact and a dominant norm to be appealed to in translational activity.
7 For others who have engaged Butler's translation to consider the practice of human rights, see Lloyd (2007) and Stanton (2016). See also Bhabha who in his work also briefly discusses cultural translation in relation to human rights, stating 'an international community of rights cannot be based on an abstract inherent "value" of humanness; it requires a process of cultural translation that, each time, historically and poetically inquires into the conflictual namings of "humanity"' (2000: 5–6).
8 For further discussion on how Butler's cultural translation may be expanded in the context of contemporary human rights activism, see McNeilly (2016).
9 This is something that Engle Merry gestures towards in her account, stating that 'translators work within established discursive fields that constrain the repertoire of ideas and practices available to them' (2006b: 40). However, unlike the practice of human rights to come, this assertion is not informed by a specifically performative approach to rights.

References

Benjamin, W. (1985) *Illuminations*, H. Arendt (ed.), trans. H. Zohn, New York: Schocken.
Bhabha, H. (1994) *The Location of Culture*, London: Routledge.
Bhabha, H. (2000) 'On Minorities: Cultural Rights', *Radical Philosophy*, 100: 3–6.
Buden, B., Nowotny, S., Simon, S., Bery, A. and Cronin, M. (2009) 'Cultural Translation: An Introduction to the Problem, and Responses', *Translation Studies*, 2(2): 196–219.
Butler, J. (1996) 'Universality in Culture', in M. Nussbaum, with respondents, J. Cohen (ed.), *For Love of Country?: A New Democracy Forum on the Limits of Patriotism*, Boston: Beacon Press, 45–52.
Butler, J. (2004) *Undoing Gender*, New York; London: Routledge.
Butler, J. (2006) *Gender Trouble: Feminism and the Subversion of Identity*, 2nd edn, New York; London: Routledge.
Butler, J., Laclau, E. and Žižek, S. (2000) *Contingency, Hegemony, Universality: Contemporary Dialogues on the Left*, London: Verso.
de Man, P. (1985) '"Conclusions": Walter Benjamin's "The Task of the Translator" Messenger Lecture, Cornell University, 4 March 1983', *Yale French Studies*, 69: 25–46.
Derrida, J. (1985) *The Ear of the Other: Otobiography, Transference, Translation*, C. McDonald (ed.), trans. P. Kamuf, Lincoln; London: University of Nebraska Press.
Engle Merry, S. (2006a) *Human Rights and Gender Violence: Translating International Law into Local Justice*, Oxford: Oxford University Press.
Engle Merry, S. (2006b) 'Transnational Human Rights and Local Activism: Mapping the Middle', *American Anthropologist*, 108(1): 38–51.

Engle Merry, S. (2009) 'Legal Transplants and Cultural Translation: Making Human Rights in the Vernacular', in M. Goodale (ed.), *Human Rights: An Anthropological Reader*, Chichester: Wiley-Blackwell, 265–302.

Gal, S., Kowalski, J. and Moore, E. (2015) 'Rethinking Translation in Feminist NGOs: Rights and Empowerment Across Borders', *Social Politics*, 22(4): 610–635.

Goldstein, D. (2013) 'Whose Vernacular? Translating Human Rights in Local Contexts', in M. Goodale (ed.), *Human Rights at the Crossroads*, Oxford: Oxford University Press, 111–121.

Goodale, M. and Engle Merry, S. (eds) (2007) *The Practice of Human Rights: Tracking Law Between the Global and the Local*, Cambridge: Cambridge University Press.

Goodhart, M. (ed.) (2013) *Human Rights: Politics and Practice*, 2nd edn, Oxford: Oxford University Press.

Haglund, L. and Aggarwal, R. (2011) 'The Test of Our Progress: The Translation of Economic and Social Rights Norms into Practice', *Journal of Human Rights*, 10(4): 494–520.

Levitt, P. and Engle Merry, S. (2009) 'Vernacularization on the Ground: Local Uses of Global Women's Rights in Peru, China, India and the United States', *Global Networks*, 9(4): 441–461.

Lloyd, M. (2007) '(Women's) Human Rights: Paradoxes and Possibilities', *Review of International Studies*, 33(1): 91–103.

McNeilly, K. (2016) 'After the Critique of Rights: For a Radical Democratic Theory and Practice of Human Rights', *Law and Critique*, 27(3): 269–288.

Pruce, J. (ed.) (2015) *The Social Practice of Human Rights*, London; New York: Palgrave Macmillan.

Pym, A. (2010) *Exploring Translation Theories*, London; New York: Routledge.

Reilly, N. (2011), 'Doing Transnational Feminism, Transforming Human Rights: The Emancipatory Possibilities Revisited', *Irish Journal of Sociology*, 19(2): 60–76.

Spivak, G. C. (1993) *Outside in the Teaching Machine*, London; New York: Routledge.

Spivak, G. C. (1994) 'Can the Subaltern Speak?', in P. Williams and L. Chrisman (eds), *Colonial Discourse and Post-Colonial Theory: A Reader*, New York: Harvester/Wheatsheaf, 66–111.

Spivak, G. C. (2000) 'Translation as Culture', *Parallax*, 6(1): 13–24.

Stanton, D. (2016) 'A New Universal for Human Rights? The Particular, the Generalizable, the Political', in S. McClennen and A. Schultheis Moore (eds), *The Routledge Companion to Literature and Human Rights*, London; New York: Routledge, 27–36.

Young, R. (2012) 'Cultural Translation as Hybridisation', *Trans-Humanities*, 15(1): 155–175.

Zigon, J. (2013) 'Rights, Responsibility and Health Services: Human Rights as an Idiomatic Language of Power', in A. Mold and D. Reubi (eds), *Assembling Health Rights in Global Context: Genealogies and Anthropologies*, London; New York: Routledge, 55–70.

Chapter 8

Rereading feminist engagements with rights via human rights to come

Introduction

In the discussion so far, analysis has sought to demonstrate how, via the concept of human rights to come, the theory and practice of human rights may be re-engaged in a way that is more compatible with the political pursuit of radical social transformation and that facilitates a challenge to power regimes which operate in marginalising or restrictive ways. This re-engagement has been presented as offering much potential for radical thinkers, activists and groups and the aims they seek to advance. In this chapter thought remains with the important assertion that it is necessary to envisage human rights to come: as a tangible idea. In order to further reflect on the tangible, this chapter engages with a particular group of thinkers and activists who may usefully approach human rights as human rights to come: feminist thinkers and activists. Through a study of the relationship between feminist work and human rights, the kind of potential that human rights to come may have for the future of human rights in radical politics more generally is brought into view. The purpose of this focus is of course not to assert that the lessons emerging from feminist engagements with human rights can be directly mapped onto any other group or area of radical thought or politics. Such an assertion would not be possible. Rather, the purpose and utility of analysis in this chapter lies in a drawing together of discussion in previous chapters, outlining in a concrete way what one particular group's approach to human rights as human rights to come might look like.

The chapter will proceed through rereading the history of feminist engagements with human rights via what has been advanced as the underlying principles or restagings of human rights to come, considering some key limitations that can be observed within this history from the perspective of analysis in the preceding chapters. Thought will then turn to the future of such engagements, demonstrating how the tools of human rights to come may be employed to address such limitations and usefully move feminist work on rights forward with renewed radical impetus. The concept of human rights to come equips feminist thinkers and activists with a new way of viewing rights and their theoretical underpinnings as well as, drawing from discussion in Chapter 7, a way of practising human rights as a disruptive and futural-focused process of translation. To initiate such a practice, the 'right to gender flourishing' is put forward as a potential competing universal which may be asserted by feminists to initiate such a process and move feminist activity on human rights into a new stage in the contemporary period. The right to gender flourishing is outlined as a concept which may be capable of addressing the limitations identified in previous feminist work and mark a starting point for feminist engagements with human rights as human rights to come.

Rereading the history of feminist engagements with human rights

The discourse of rights, human rights in particular, has had a mixed relationship with feminism. Diverse views have been put forward as to the utility of the language and practice of rights to productively engage gender concerns.[1] Despite the key role that human rights have played in feminist political activity and thinking in recent years, the latter decades of the twentieth century in particular,[2] today feminist work seems to have reached something of a crossroads in relation to rights. While at the formal level of international law and scholarship in this area feminist work is still taking place,[3] it appears that much contemporary feminism perceives opportunities to more fundamentally, or impactfully, challenge problematic gender discourses and regimes via alternative strategies.[4] In this context, the concept of human rights to come may be of use to feminist thinkers, activists and groups. As a way of radically re-engaging rights to become a vehicle of meaningful challenge to dominant power regimes, it can be used to consider the possibility of a return to the language and politics of human rights to advance contemporary aims of radical social transformation in relation to gender. Importantly, this assertion cannot be characterised as advancing a return to the analysis, language and politics of previous decades, simply reapplying these ideas in the current context. In contrast, the discussion below explores how thinking anew about rights via human rights to come may assist in working towards new potential for challenging restrictive gender regimes and advancing wider possibilities for living and being gendered, offering productive tools for a new future for work in this area. This concept may be capable of addressing many of the problems which have characterised past feminist engagement with human rights and led the discourse to be moved away from as a tool in contemporary feminist work.

To consider this further, it is necessary to begin with the history of feminist engagements with human rights. Much has been written on this history.[5] The present analysis does not seek to replicate such writings. Rather, what it does seek to do is to reread the seminal points of this history via the analysis of the previous chapters, and to build on past work using the tools that human rights to come offers. In other words, the theoretical and practical re-engagements that this approach advances can assist in reading the history of feminist engagements with human rights in an alternative way and in signalling towards new productive avenues of thought and action for the future of feminist usages of rights. In considering such, the analysis below breaks feminist theorising and activism on human rights into four broad stages:[6] formal equality (1948–1970s); deconstruction of law (1980s–1990s); reconstruction, reconceptualisation and reinterpretation (1990s–present); and reflection, re-evaluation, and reassessment (2000s–present). While these stages are sequential to a point, it is important to note that a considerable amount of overlap can be found between them (Edwards 2011: 39). In what follows, these stages, and the radical potential contained in each in to use rights to achieve meaningful social change in relation to gender, are considered alongside the problems or limitations which, from analysis in preceding chapters, can be observed before it is proposed that the tools of human rights to come can be of use in moving towards a fifth stage of feminist engagement with human rights in contemporary feminist thought and politics.

Stage one: formal equality (1948–1970s)

Following the first wave of feminist ideas emerging in the late nineteenth and early twentieth centuries demanding equality between the sexes in matters such as voting rights, property rights and marriage, action was taken to ensure feminist views informed the development of the modern international human rights framework (Fraser 1999: 867–889). Work by the Commission on the Status of Women ensured that a right to non-discrimination on the basis of sex was enshrined in the 1948 Universal Declaration of Human Rights. The Commission continued its work after this period which led, during the United Nations Decade on Women 1975–1985, to drafting and subsequent adoption of the Convention on the Elimination of All Forms of Discrimination Against Women (CEDAW). A landmark achievement, CEDAW was perceived as significant in bringing

> into a single international instrument the various international conventions already in existence which define the sphere of womens [*sic*] rights and bring[ing] into the legislative ambit many of the recommendations which have been adopted over the years by the Commission since its inception in 1946.
> (Burrows 1985: 419)

While this initial stage of work was crucial in laying the foundation for further discussion of the experiences of women at the international level, it undoubtedly remained tied to liberalism and its shaping of ideas such as rights and equality. Even CEDAW, which notably recognised both sameness and difference in approaches to equality and went beyond requiring equality of opportunity alone, to equality of result, can be, and has been, critiqued as limited in the scope of its idea of equality – initially omitting issues such as violence against women, abortion and concerns of sexuality – and in its transformative effect – encouraging state-led change, but from the outset being hindered by numerous reservations from states-parties which impeded its implementation (Charlesworth, Chinkin and Wright 1991: 631–634).

Stages two and three: deconstruction of law (1980s–1990s); reconstruction, reconceptualisation and reinterpretation (1990s–present)

From the mid to late 1980s and into the 1990s, feminist theorisation and activism in relation to human rights moved to another stage or, more accurately, stages which took feminist engagements with rights further. These were characterised by deconstruction and subsequent reconstruction, reconceptualisation and reinterpretation. During this period, feminist scholars and activists advanced two criticisms; that issues of concern to women featured very little on the 'mainstream' human rights agenda, and that institutions and procedures focusing on such issues were marginalised (Byrnes 1989: 205). Here writing such as that of Hilary Charlesworth (1995), Christine Chinkin (1994), Charlotte Bunch (1990) and Rebecca Cook (1993a) was central in driving a combined academic and activist campaign united under the now familiar slogan that 'Women's Rights Are Human Rights'. Such work asserted that 'the specific experiences of women must be added to traditional approaches to human rights in order to make women more visible and to transform the concept and practice of human rights . . . so that it takes better account of women's lives' (Bunch 1990: 487). At a number of world conferences held in the 1990s, and through sustained global lobbying, feminist work during this period both interpreted existing human rights provisions as capable of speaking to concerns of women as opposed to men alone,[7] and asserted that key concerns previously invisibilised by the public/private dichotomy of international law,[8] such as violence against women, rape during conflict and reproductive health, were human rights issues.

This deconstruction and subsequent reconstruction of human rights to take better account of the experiences and concerns of women, and to expose the gendered construction, development and interpretation of existing human rights provision, was indeed driven by elements of radical potential, even reflecting some of the ideas explored in previous chapters. For example, at a fundamental level the 'Women's Rights Are Human Rights' campaign recognised that human rights are in excess, capable of alternative articulations to take account of that which is currently excluded within current contexts of power. Writing at the time, Bunch asserted that 'the concept of human rights, like all vibrant visions, is not static or the property of any one group; rather, its meaning expands as people reconceive of their needs and hopes in relation to it' (1990: 487). Following from this perception of human rights as in excess but capable of expansion to meet their current limitations, feminist commentators and activists went about the work of rearticulating human rights through a translational process.[9] Explicitly bringing a feminist-informed reconceptualisation of human rights into translation with current, limited conceptions in international forums and with United Nations bodies, states and international organisations, feminist activists rearticulated human rights with an aim of challenging gendered relations of power. As Andrew Byrnes comments, in this work feminists made 'a concerted effort to expand the range of participants in that dialogue, and to wrest some of the power of defining and speaking from narrow androcentric models to address issues of central concern to women' (1989: 232). In this sense, the feminist work of the 1990s was radical, and to a certain extent gestured towards a translational and reiterative approach to human rights. However, there are also some significant limitations characterising feminist work at this time, indicating that from the perspective of analysis in previous chapters it must be considered as not radical enough.

First, and significantly, the 'Women's Rights Are Human Rights' engagement was based upon an approach to universality which limits the radical potential of such work from the outset. While comments such as that of Bunch above acknowledging that human rights are not a static entity seem to suggest that feminist commentators in the 1980s–1990s understood universal human rights as involving an ongoing process of universalisation, of ongoing development based upon alterity, this understanding was not fully capitalised on to actively depart from traditional approaches to universality. There is an underlying suggestion in the literature of the 1990s that integrating women's concerns into the international human rights framework would make rights 'truly universal' and therefore, by extension, universality is not understood as a process, but reified as an attribute of rights. For example, Charlesworth, Chinkin and Wright characterised their reflections on the gendered nature of *jus cogens* as asserting 'that the concept of the *jus cogens* is not a properly universal one as its development has privileged the experiences of men over those of women' (1993: 67), and that 'fundamental norms designed to protect individuals should be truly universal' (1993: 75).[10] Rebecca Cook demonstrates a similar approach to universality, stating that 'international human rights law has not yet been applied effectively to redress the disadvantages and injustices experienced by women solely because of their gender. In this sense, respect for human rights fails to be "universal"' (1993a: 231). Such assertions, whether conscious or not, imply that if women are 'added to' human rights norms the current problems with their universality will be remedied. This serves to draw attention away from the important focus on alterity which the 1990s campaign initiated, limiting its radical potential by not fully characterising universal human rights as ineradicably constituted by alterity and so requiring never-ending critical reworking. In addition, feminist engagement with human rights at this time can be considered to have further perpetuated traditional approaches to universality by taking part in the debate between universality and cultural relativism. Given that many of the abuses that women face are linked to religious and cultural practices across different regions of the world, feminists were drawn into considerable discussion as to how a balance could be struck between respecting cultural practices and promoting universal human rights which included protection of women from such practices.[11] While this was of course an important discussion, and necessary to the inclusion of women from a wide variety of locations and cultures, approaching universality in such a way as a fixed attribute of rights to be endorsed, rejected or otherwise negotiated in relation to cultural relativism again bolsters traditional understandings of universality and hinders more radical conceptualisation of universality as a process. The politics of the 1980s–1990s feminist human rights movement was, therefore, not one of universality as universalisation, despite the promise contained in observations such as that of Bunch focusing on alterity and the excessive nature of human rights.

The radical potential of the 'Women's Rights Are Human Rights' campaign was also limited by its underlying ontological approach. While feminist work did much to challenge the masculine nature of the subject of human rights, it did not extend to meaningfully challenge the liberal sovereignty characterising that subject. Feminism at this time advanced experiences such as reproductive and maternal health and domestic and sexual violence as injuries or harms the subject of human rights is also open to, but in such work the bounded, sovereign subject remained intact. Women were asserted as born equal in dignity and rights as men, possessing rights as objects to protect them against harm from outside themselves, and from particular kinds of gendered harm which required a legal 'remedy' currently unavailable. In this discourse, a more intersubjective and vulnerable subject was not foregrounded. One area in which this tendency towards sovereignty was particularly clear was that of reproductive rights. Building upon earlier international discussion of reproductive health, including at the 1994 Cairo International Conference on Population and Development, in the 1995 Beijing Platform for Action it was asserted that 'the human rights of women include their right to have control over and decide freely and responsibly on matters related to their sexuality, including sexual and reproductive health' (United Nations 1995: para. 96). Discourses of control and choice underpinned this approach and were central to eschewing the development-based perspective on reproductive health previously dominant.[12] Such an approach continued in subsequent feminist activism seeking to use human rights to achieve access to reproductive health services.[13] While ideas of sovereign choice were central to placing the issue of reproductive health on the human rights agenda, and doing so in a feminist-informed way, they nevertheless further entrenched the sovereign subject of liberalism. As has been explored, this subject is inherently paradoxical and the illusionary advancement of sovereign action invisibilises the inherent vulnerability that the subject is characterised by. Without an embrace of the intersections between living and being gendered and living and being vulnerable, the 1980s–1990s feminist campaign was also limited in its radical potential and bound to remain within the confines of liberalism.

A third limitation of feminist work in stages two and three which stunted its radical potential was that such work was often co-opted into, or succumbed to, an understanding of human rights politics which is outcome-focused and consensus-driven. This understanding detracts attention from the possibilities of the process of politics itself and the important element of dissensus and agonism which may productively characterise human rights politics. This can be detected in particular in relation to the World Conferences on Women which took place from 1975 onwards. Bringing together states, international organisations and women's activists and lobbyists, these conferences were inevitably characterised by dissensus and disagreement, but what was presented as of central importance in conferences was the level of consensus reached. Leslie Obiora outlines that observers of the United Nations World Conferences on Women would attest that building a consensus for resolutions has not come easily at many of these forums. At the First World Conference on Women, held in Mexico City in 1975, the agenda was ensnared in a power struggle regarding who should define its focus and parameters. The second conference in Copenhagen in 1980 and the conference in Nairobi in 1985 were equally mired by controversy . . . The Beijing meetings [at the fourth conference] mirrored the traditional patter of disagreements, gridlocks, dialogues and eventual reconciliation and resolutions.

(1997: 359–360)

Such dissensual dialogue is central to what makes human rights politics a site offering potential for radical political aims, facilitating agonistic debate on alterity and what human rights are capable of meaning, doing and achieving. However, the dissensual nature of the World Conferences on Women and the potential it offered was not the focus of the dominant understanding of human rights politics. As Obiora continues, 'after sustained deliberations, the [Fourth World] Conference culminated in the adoption of a landmark resolution. In and of itself, the achievement of a consensus on the Beijing Platform of Action was an historic accomplishment' (1997: 361). Upon closer inspection, this consensus in Beijing, especially when it came to inclusion of the term 'gender' which was conceived in a way that wholly pleased neither feminists nor religious participants who sought to restrict its definition,[14] was more of a conflictual consensus. Indeed, the outcomes of translational activity such as that of Beijing and the definition of 'gender' in the international human rights system are still subject to ongoing discussion and debate.[15] However, the necessarily temporary nature of consensus emerging from such translational dialogue, and the need to continue to rework the inevitable limits and exclusions of such conflictual consensus in a never-ending manner, was marginalised in the 1980s–1990s. While reaching some form of consensus amongst states on issues of gender at this time was undoubtedly important to place feminist concerns on the international agenda, this period saw feminist activity being drawn into a state-centric politics often characterised to an excessive extent by consensus, not fully directed by a more radical view of politics which seeks to retain focus on agonistic debate and process as opposed to outcome.

Stage four: reflection, re-evaluation and reassessment (2000s–present)

Overall, therefore, while the 'Women's Rights Are Human Rights' campaign of the 1980s–1990s was highly significant in challenging the masculine focus and the public/private dichotomy characterising human rights as articulated in the form of international human rights law, other elements of this campaign limited its radical potential from the perspective of the re-engagements discussed in the preceding chapters. To understand one additional way in which the 1980s–1990s campaign may be thought to demonstrate leanings that are not quite radical enough it is necessary to consider the fourth 'reflection, re-evaluation and reassessment' stage in feminist engagements with human rights, taking place from the mid 2000s until the present day. Much feminist comment in this period has acknowledged the achievements of the 1980s–1990s while simultaneously highlighting a key element underpinning this work which appears problematic for much contemporary feminist thought and politics. The problem identified is that feminist work in stages two and three remained committed to an understanding of sex as a natural biological fact, existing in the binary of male/female and asymmetry of male>female, and gender as an associated social construct of masculinity/femininity.[16]

Summarising the views characterising this fourth stage of feminist engagement, Brenda Cossman asserts that

> in international law, to the extent that feminist scholarship and activism has . . . succeeded in getting gender on the agenda at all, the understanding of gender and its relationship to sex remains fairly traditional. Gender continues to be a category related in some fundamental way to sex. Gender is the social meaning given to the biological differences of sex. In this, sex, then, continues to operate as the biological and natural differences of male and female bodies.
>
> (2002: 281)

Accordingly, for Cossman, the dominant story of sex/gender has not yet been displaced in international law.[17] A commitment to sex and gender as distinct concepts existing in a binary and asymmetrical fashion is indeed evident from a number of elements of the 1990s campaign. For example, the focus on the right to non-discrimination on the basis of sex as a central tool in the recognition of gender-based harms brought to the fore by the 'Women's Rights Are Human Rights' campaign maintained the idea of binary and asymmetrical sex.[18] Writing at the time, Charlesworth, Chinkin and Wright characterised a feminist approach to human rights as based upon such ideas of sex; 'a feminist perspective, with its concern for gender as a category of analysis and its commitment to genuine equality between the sexes [i.e. men and women], could illuminate many areas of international law' (1991: 644). Much discussion was dedicated in this period to debate surrounding sameness/difference approaches to equality, which are underpinned by a commitment to binary and asymmetrical sex, the debate being whether women should be treated the same as or different to men.[19] A similar problematic approach to sex/gender can be detected in the centrality of violence against women to the 1990s campaign. Charlotte Bunch recognises violence against women as 'a touchstone that illustrates the limited capacity of human rights and highlights the political nature of the abuse of women', however, Bunch goes on to discuss such violence within a sex dominance approach: 'victims are chosen because of their gender. The message is domination' (1990: 490). This both characterised gender and women's sexuality as a site of danger rather than freedom (Otto 2014: 624), and maintained a focus on binary and asymmetrical sex.

Work in the fourth reassessment stage of feminist activity on human rights demonstrates why such an approach to sex/gender is problematic. As Otto outlines, 'understanding sex/gender as operating dualistically and asymmetrically prevents an understanding of the diverse ways that sex/gender operates as a technology of power' (2013: 199), and accordingly 'the question that weighs increasingly heavy is whether dualism and asymmetry provide the best way to pursue the emancipatory possibilities for everyone, including ciswomen, that are opened up by recognition that gender is primarily (if not entirely) a social category' (2015: 306). Likewise, following from her observations noted above, Cossman comments that understanding sex/gender beyond binarised and asymmetrical formulations

> introduces a range of marginalized subjects, beyond the subject of woman. It will allow us to tell a story of marginality that has not yet been told . . . the queer subject, the drag queen, the bull dyke, the cross dresser, the transsexual, the transgendered, the sex worker, the S/M dominatrix.
>
> (2002: 289)[20]

The message from such critiques is that in order to effectively respond to and promote the diversity of sexed/gendered identity in the contemporary period it is no longer possible for feminist thinkers and activists to rely on the same understanding of sex and gender that characterised the feminist movement of the 1980s–1990s.

It is at this point that it can be observed that feminist engagements with human rights may have reached somewhat of a crossroads following the momentum of the 1980s–1990s. Traditional feminist work in this area, characterised by activity taking place in stages two and three, has been viewed as incapable of staging the kind of challenge to sex/gender that contemporary feminists may be interested in. In addition to the limitations regarding universality, consensus and ontology, feminist scholarship in the fourth stage reveals an additional limitation regarding approaches to sex/gender in feminist human rights scholarship and politico-legal engagement. Some suggestions have been made from commentators within this period for ways of moving forward; for example, a redeployment of CEDAW in alternative ways to extend its remit to cover more gender identities than women alone,[21] or a revisiting of the already existing mechanisms of gender mainstreaming through adopting an approach which does not rely so heavily on comparisons with men.[22] This work is significant; however, from the perspective of discussion outlined in previous chapters, these suggestions are also not radical enough. To a large extent, they continue to operate within already given structures of human rights, and so implicitly reinforce the power of the dominant international human rights regime to pronounce upon and articulate rights. While these solutions seek to radically break apart gender, they focus less on radically breaking apart the language and politics of rights themselves,[23] and so cannot move contemporary feminist engagement to an approach which addresses all of the limitations of previous feminist work. However, at this crucial juncture I assert that the concept of human rights to come may assist and offer feminist thinkers and activists a way to move to a fifth stage of feminist work on human rights.

A new future for feminist engagements with human rights: human rights to come and the right to gender flourishing

Stage five? Feminist engagements and human rights to come

The question that must be turned to now is how might the concept of human rights to come make a difference or be capable of propelling contemporary feminist activism on rights forward with renewed radical impetus. As explored above, the discussion in previous chapters outlining the manner in which approaching human rights as human rights to come requires a fundamental re-engagement with the underpinnings of rights allows for a critique to be brought to previous scholarly and politico-legal activity in this area; for example, conceptualisations of universality, consensus/conflict and ontology that were not radical enough. More than this, human rights to come offers tools to address these problems or issues anew – moving towards an approach to universality as universalisation, to understanding human rights as a fundamentally agonistic activity and working towards enhanced understanding of vulnerability and a different relationship between sovereignty and vulnerability in the subject of human rights. These re-engagements equip feminist scholars, groups and activists with the means to understand rights differently, and beyond the mainstream. In this respect, human rights to come offers tools to reposition feminist perspectives on rights, what they are and what their politics involves or may be capable of looking like, which departs from what has been thought to date.

In addition, however, and very importantly, human rights to come also offers the potential to reposition feminist activity on rights; to equip feminists engaging in the everyday practice of human rights with the ability to engage in this practice anew. Here, thoughts may return to Chapter 7's discussion on translation. Feminists may engage the tools outlined there to view present human rights concepts or discourse as competing universals to be challenged through agonistic translational activity asserting competing conceptions of rights in a variety of spaces, locations and contexts. In contrast to work undertaken in stages two and three, and the suggestions made in stage four such as to redeploy CEDAW, this translational activity would not reinforce the authority and power of the dominant international human rights regime to articulate and define rights. Rather, the place, power and authority of the dominant universal must be fundamentally disrupted through the work of translation and the assertion of competing universals. Translation must be foregrounded as disruptive of the dominant at a basic level and, as additionally explored in Chapter 7, also futural. To embrace a futural conception of translation in this work, feminist activists and other groups must keep focus on alterity – the fact that human rights, conceptions of gendered life and the relation between the two will always be inadequate in some way – and approach translation as not event-focused, but an ongoing disruptive conversation. This means viewing the 'Women's Rights Are Human Rights' campaign of the 1980s–1990s as not a discrete part of feminist activity on rights, or indeed the end to such through its achievements, but as part of an ongoing, and ever-evolving, disruptive conversation. Feminist thinkers and activists may be encouraged to focus on the futural in order to sustain a place for rights in their work, and to do so in a renewed way informed by the theoretical re-engagements noted above. This allows feminists not to abandon the discourse of rights as of use in working towards social transformation in relation to gender, but to use it to better draw attention to gender marginalisation and oppression.

To demonstrate more concretely what this activity might look like, I assert that contemporary feminist work on human rights can advance via assertion of a competing universal that I am calling a 'right to gender flourishing'. This is a concept which picks up dominant articulations of rights and the relation between rights and gender anew and is also a conception of rights which reflects the theoretical restagings of human rights to come. In this respect, the right to gender flourishing is a competing universal capable of addressing the limitations of previous feminist work in relation to universality, consensus/conflict and ontology, for example. However, the right to gender flourishing is also a competing universal capable of responding to the specific criticism advanced in stage four of feminist activity on rights: that previous feminist engagements were based on an approach to sex/gender that is no longer tenable. Feminist work on human rights may use the right to gender flourishing to move forward with renewed radical impetus in a translational politics of human rights to come. In what follows below this concept is explored, beginning with its potential to address the criticism of stage four of feminist activity in relation to sex/gender before turning to the way in which it can be thought to draw from the key elements of human rights to come and facilitate a re-engagement with the theoretical foundations of rights.

A contemporary competing universal: the right to gender flourishing

First, what does the idea of a right to gender flourishing actually mean? What does it look like as a competing universal that may usefully be advanced by feminist thinkers and activists? Throughout the history of human rights the language and politics of rights has been used by feminists, and other gender activists, to draw attention to and challenge a number of issues pertaining to sex/gender, some already mentioned above. These issues include gender-based violence, sexual violence, reproductive/sexual health, family life, non-discrimination/equality on the basis of sex/gender, sexual orientation and expression, poverty, education, work and their intersection with sex/gender. These issues affect women, but, as the critique in stage four has highlighted, also other gender identities such as gay men, lesbian women, bisexual people, intersex people, those who identify as transgender and others who violate dominant norms of masculinity/femininity more generally. Some may affect one particular group of sexed/gendered subjects more than others, but the majority of these issues intersect in some way with all of the listed forms and varieties of living and being gendered within regimes of heteronormative power, causing diverse injury and harm. While some of these issues have been advanced particularly well in relation to one form of sexed/gendered identity – for example, gender-based violence in relation to women; rights to family life, marriage rights specifically, in relation to LGBTI people – none have been fully understood as affecting multiple gender identities in various ways within the context of gender as a technology of power. Such a joined-up approach has not found much traction. The reason for this stems from the problematic approach to sex/gender identified by the fourth stage of feminist engagement with rights considered above; focus on binary and asymmetrical sex and a reluctance, in the absence of coalitional work, to open up concepts such as gendered violence or reproductive health to consider LGBTI concerns for fear that it would dilute attention to women and their relation to men. In looking towards the future of feminist engagement with human rights, the right to gender flourishing allows us to move beyond this approach.

To do so, it is necessary to look at the issues listed above and consider what they have in common. It is submitted that a useful way of considering the commonality between these issues and their effect on various sexed/gendered identities is that they *all inhibit the ability to flourish as a gendered subject*. When women, gay men or transgender people are subjected to violence, lack of appropriate reproductive/sexual health care or otherwise experience discrimination based on their sex/gender they are prevented from flourishing in their form of living and being gendered. The ability to thrive, to enjoy the widest possible conditions of life and to live unsubordinated as a particular gender is what all sexed/gendered subjects require within the restrictive conditions of heteronormativity. In other words, all have a need for gender flourishing. What limits the ability to flourish as a gendered subject is the operation of heteronormative power. Yet rather than asserting that all gendered subjects require the same conditions to flourish, the concept of gender flourishing seeks to draw attention to the particular form of gender identity in question and its particular experience of harm, linking such experience to the common root of heteronormativity and its limitation of possibilities for living and being sexed/gendered. This idea, when thought in relation to human rights, has the potential to be powerful, to allow for use of the language of rights to assert a right to thrive and flourish as sexed/gendered, and to the conditions or freedoms necessary for this. This would be a right applicable in various contexts, to various issues and capable of assertion by various subjects. Moving from using rights to draw attention to specific issues – violence against women, same-sex marriage equality, for example – towards focusing attention on the common effects of such issues – the negative effects they may have on ability to flourish as a gendered subject, whatever that subject identity may be, within heteronormative conditions – may refocus rights on gender as a technology of power.

The right to gender flourishing, therefore, is a kind of umbrella right, an idea that can be claimed in contingent locations and that is capable of flexible assertion in relation to a myriad of gender issues and sexed/gendered subjects. This right cannot be thought of as having any fixed content in and of itself, but it includes the need to be free from gender-based violence, to reproductive/sexual health, to family life, to non-discrimination/equality on the basis of sex/gender, to sexual orientation and expression, to be free from the negative effects of poverty, lack of education or work because of gender, because all these issues impact on gender flourishing in diverse ways. This list is by no means exhaustive, and it is also important to note the right may be capable of use in more positive ways, for example, to assert a right to sexual freedom and pleasure[24] as a necessary part of being sexed/gendered and flourishing as such. Relying on the right to gender flourishing, making a claim to it in the everyday politics of human rights, allows particular issues affecting particular subjects to be considered and tackled with an eye to the wider context of heteronormative power and its shaping of sex/gender. This serves to approach gendered issues in a way that moves beyond binarised and asymmetrical sex alone and uses rights discourse in a different, more innovative manner which unites the concerns of feminists and LGBTI activists.

It is clear, therefore, that such an approach may be used to facilitate a new perspective on gender and thereby stimulate an alternative, more radical relationship between human rights and sex/gender, responding to the critique of stage four in feminist engagement with rights. However, as asserted above, in moving towards a new, fifth stage what is required is a competing universal which is also capable of addressing the wider limitations of previous feminist work on rights. It is asserted that the right to gender flourishing, as a competing universal stemming from the understanding of rights advanced via human rights to come, may also offer this possibility. This right must be understood as underpinned and driven by the key characteristics of performativity, a critical approach to universality, agonism, a focus on vulnerability and futurity as discussed in previous chapters. Let us explore these in turn and so consider how the right to gender flourishing is a competing universal capable of challenging dominant understandings of sex/gender and rights and, at the same time, the theoretical underpinnings of rights more generally in a way which follows from the idea of human rights to come.

In terms of the first of these elements – performativity – when subjects assert that 'I have a right to flourish as a gendered subject' they can be viewed as going some way towards bringing those conditions for flourishing into existence, challenging restrictive regimes of gendered power through that very utterance and visibilising themselves as subjects in a way that may serve to performatively alter their current position within restrictive heteronormative regimes. This concept may be thought to bring into being alternative social possibilities in relation to living and being gendered through its activity and use in everyday politics and politico-legal engagements. More generally, the right to gender flourishing also capitalises on the performative nature of rights by, as feminist work in stages two and three, rearticulating rights ideas through an attention to their capacity for appropriation in alternative ways to produce new, more expansive conceptions and ideas of rights. Unlike activity in stages two and three, however, the performative rearticulation involved in the right to gender flourishing is more disruptive at a fundamental level. Making a claim to the right to gender flourishing does not depend on use of already existing (state-led and defined) human rights and their politico-legal structures, but involves a deeper rearticulation of the discourse of rights, how it can be perceived and how it can be used which refuses to bolster the authority of the dominant international human rights regime to pronounce on rights.

Important re-engagements also underpin the right to gender flourishing in relation to the universality of human rights. For example, where 1990s feminist work demonstrated a commitment to universality as a static characteristic or attribute of rights, the right to gender flourishing would encourage foregrounding the universality of human rights as an ongoing process of universalisation which is committed to constantly reworking the limits of current ideas and concepts and current relations of power. This is demonstrated in the fact that the idea of a right to gender flourishing is an open concept in itself, not fixed to any particular content and not attached to any particular issue or sexed/gendered subject. This right foregrounds an approach to universality as universalisation in being fundamentally open to further development based on its own alterity, capable of use in a way that is responsive to changing contexts of gender marginalisation and use in relation to emergent gender issues. Use of this right in new or unexpected ways responding to contexts of power is to be welcomed and expected as part of a critical process of universalisation, and the idea is couched in a way that encourages such use, departing from the illusion that adding currently excluded sexed/gendered subjects to existing universal human rights provision will make them 'truly universal'. In this respect, approaching rights using the idea of a right to gender flourishing requires going beyond an approach to universality as an attribute of human rights, and towards a form of rights politics that understands universality as a process offering significant opportunities to sustain an ongoing critical approach to alterity and power. Thinking of the right to gender flourishing via the re-engagement advanced by human rights to come encourages a taking up of these opportunities in a politics of rights which adopts a more critical approach to mainstream discourses of universal human rights and restrictive regimes of power.

Engaging the right to gender flourishing also involves moving beyond the liberal focus on consensus in the politics of rights, foregrounding the site of human rights as one which is of use to the extent that it may facilitate agonistic debate over ideas such as 'gender', 'woman' and 'man', and rejecting any attempt to reach consensus on such terms and their relationship to rights. The term 'gender flourishing', as an open idea capable of flexible appropriation and usage itself, is designed by its nature to stimulate agonistic democratic debate and discussion. Debate on what this term means, in what conditions diverse sexed/gendered identities require to flourish, and how human rights can assist with this is the aim of the right to gender flourishing and the purpose of making a claim to this right. Accordingly, this is not a concept that can readily be engaged in consensus-focused politics, or a pinning down of what rights can do and say in relation to living and being gendered, but is designed to open and sustain ongoing debate on such issues using the language of rights. Through prioritising bottom-up translational activity on, and usages of, the language of human rights, the right to gender flourishing may also offer possibilities to focus to a greater extent on agonism, and the political potential it offers, than approaches which place focus on treaty monitoring bodies or other United Nations forums which are by definition driven by the need to seek consensus and agreed outcomes. While productive opportunities may be found to facilitate translational dialogue and advance the claims of the right to gender flourishing in top-down politics, significant focus, following the impetus of human rights to come, must be on making rights claims at the local level, approaching rights in new ways that do not rely on existing structures but involve a more fundamental break with existing discourses and their underpinnings which is driven by an attention to contingent contexts of alterity. This limits the potential for feminist work to be co-opted into wider state-driven and state-led regimes, and allows for use of the language of rights in a way that may not yet be intelligible at formal levels. Engaging in the politics of the right to gender flourishing, therefore, involves initiating and sustaining agonistic debate regarding gender and its conditions but, in addition, it also involves learning to stay with the unsettled nature of ideas such as sex/gender and, indeed, rights themselves within the wider context of an agonistic politics. This may be in tension with the drive of mainstream international human rights law towards definition, certainty and predictability, but is central in working towards new possibilities for rights and gender.

In addition, the right to gender flourishing may also be utilised to displace the sovereign liberal subject which has remained to a great extent within feminist approaches to human rights up until the present, however unconsciously. In its function of drawing attention to the harm, injury and restricted conditions for flourishing currently experienced within regimes of heteronormative power, it can be thought of as foregrounding a subject who is vulnerable and who exists in an interdependent context, fundamentally impinged upon by others and by discourses of gendered power. This right holds potential to be used to draw attention to the fact that we cannot possess our gender or secure our own flourishing through sovereign action or claiming of juridical remedies but, rather, that we are dispossessed by our gender and this dispossession requires a social response. Thus, the inherent vulnerability of the subject, and its lack of sovereign possession, is indeed at the heart of the right to gender flourishing, is what it seeks to reveal and what it is driven by. Moreover, when a woman, a gay man, a transgendered individual lays bare their experience of gender marginalisation or injury and explicitly asserts 'I have a right to flourish' they can be thought of as using the language of rights to impinge upon those who hear that assertion – communities, family, nation, law and policymakers – reminding these hearers of the social obligations upon him or her, and society more generally, to promote life in its widest sense, including sexed/gendered life. In this respect, a sovereign subject who is asserting a right to flourish as an extension of their agentic choice, their command over themselves and the world around them, is profoundly alien to the right to gender flourishing. In drawing attention to gender as a restrictive technology of power, this concept naturally foregrounds the intersubjective and the demand of the other on the self and so may assist in building of rights discourse on a new ontological foundation beyond the liberal subject.

The final element of human rights to come driving the idea of a right to gender flourishing is futurity. This right can be perceived as an essentially futural concept, and this is central to its radical utility. When approaching making a rights claim to gender flourishing it must be grasped at a fundamental level that it is never possible to fully achieve perfect conditions of gender flourishing for all gender identities; alterity will always constitute dominant ideas of intelligible gender. As such, the concept of gender flourishing and its aim that all sexed/gendered identities may thrive without restriction or marginalisation gestures towards a future that must always remain 'to come', never fully achievable but driving us to strive towards it nevertheless. While perfect conditions of equality between men and women may have been an equally futural element driving earlier feminist work, this work did not necessarily, or fully, focus on the ongoing nature of alterity which ineradicably characterises conceptions of sex/gender. In the right to gender flourishing the futurity of a conception of gender relations that is free from any form of restriction or marginalisation, that has successfully dismantled heteronormative power, works alongside a conception of rights as futural so that the two come into a productive relation to one another. The futurity of both rights and an ideal form of living and being gender must become central to contemporary feminist activists in order to foreground an ongoing attention to alterity. Rights and gender, and the relationship between the two, must be constantly troubled towards a finally complete future that always remains just out of reach.

Accordingly, it is in this sense that the right to gender flourishing seeks to do more than just use existing rights ideas and structures in alternative ways, although a rearticulation of existing discourses of rights is of course part of its work. As a performative rearticulation, the right to gender flourishing holds the potential to challenge the underpinning elements of human rights, facilitating new approaches to universality, consensus and ontology, for example, in a manner previous feminist work did not alongside an alternative approach to sex/gender. Through assertion this right as a competing universal contemporary feminist work may engage in a performative reimagining of rights which is more amenable to the radical social transformation that such work seeks to achieve. However, of course, eschewing an event-focused approach to translation in favour of an ongoing, futural approach means that the competing universal of the right to gender flourishing can only be a starting point, even one of many competing universals to be asserted, not the pinnacle of or all there is to new feminist engagements with rights. At the current cross-roads of feminist thought and activism on human rights the right to gender flourishing is aimed towards initiating a disruptive conversation which then must continue without end. This may be brought into view as a fifth stage of feminist activity on rights. This potential fifth stage involves a continuation of feminist work in this area equipped with a repositioned understanding of what rights are, or what they may be capable of being, and a repositioned approach to their practice, both of which follow from an understanding of human rights as human rights to come.

Conclusion

Discussion above has sought to demonstrate how rereading the history of feminist work on human rights via the lens of human rights to come may help provide a potential way forward into a fifth stage of feminist engagement with rights in the present. This fifth stage, informed by the key tenets of human rights to come explored in the preceding chapters, involves understanding the theoretical foundations of human rights anew and engaging in a disruptive and futural translational practice of human rights via the competing universal of the right to gender flourishing. Through such analysis feminist thinkers and activists may better harness the discourse and site of human rights to facilitate radical social transformation in relation to gender in a way that has not been possible in feminist approaches to rights to date. As asserted at the outset of this chapter, however, this analysis is not designed to be exclusively of use to feminist thinkers and activists alone. The potential that human rights to come offers in beginning to think through contemporary re-engagements with human rights more compatible with facilitating radical social change is not limited to feminist work. A wide range of radical groups, scholars, activists and movements may be able to draw upon the theoretical and practical restagings of human rights to come to better draw attention to experiences of alterity and marginalisation and challenge restrictive regimes of power. The approach of human rights to come holds potential for any radical group seeking to reconsider its past and present engagement with human rights. Naturally, the manner in which the tools this concept offers are deployed will depend on context, location and the aims of the thinkers, activists or groups in question. However, through spending time considering the specific way in which feminist thinkers and activists may engage with the idea of human rights to come the more tangible elements of this concept and its potential come to the fore and it is possible to see how the re-engagements of the underlying principles and concepts of human rights as a discourse, politics and practice can be employed in everyday rights-based activity to offer new directions and productive avenues of thought.

Notes

1 This has included scepticism on the language of rights generally, for example Olsen (1985), MacKinnon and Dworkin (1988) and Schwartzman (1999). It has also,

however, included the advancement of the utility of human rights in feminist work. In this latter category Hilary Charlesworth, for example, has asserted that 'because women in most societies are starting in such a disadvantaged position, rights discourse offers a significant vocabulary to formulate political and social grievances which is recognised by the powerful' (cited in Cook 1993a: 232). Further proponents of the utility of human rights in feminist work are cited in the discussion to follow.
2 For discussion, see, for example, Marx Ferree and Tripp (2006).
3 See Ní Aoláin (2015).
4 For work on contemporary feminist strategies, see, for example Braidotti (2015); Keller (2012); McCaughey and Ayers (2003).
5 See further, for example Fraser (1999); Friedman (1995); Peters and Wolper (1995).
6 This analysis is drawn from Edwards (2011: 38–43).
7 This work included reconceptions of the right to life (Bunch 1990: 489), the right to be free from cruel, inhuman and degrading treatment (Copelon 1994) and the right to health (Cook 1993b), for example.
8 See Romany (1993); Sullivan (1995).
9 For further, see Lloyd (2007). However, as explored below, this translational activity lacked the fundamental disruptive and futural elements of the practice of human rights to come as a practice of translation outlined in Chapter 7.
10 See also Charlesworth, Chinkin and Wright (1991: 644).
11 Rao (1995); Mayer (1995); Brems (1997); Cook (1993a: 235).
12 See, for example, Cook (2006).
13 For further analysis on this approach see McNeilly (2015).
14 See Baden and Goetz (1997); Otto (1996).
15 Molyneux and Razavi (2005); Otto (2013).
16 This assertion stemmed from the insights of queer theory emerging in the 1990s from work such as that of Eve Sedgewick (1990), Judith Butler (2006) and Lauren Berlant (1997).
17 See further Otto (2013), who makes a similar argument.
18 See McNeilly (2014).
19 For discussion, see Cook (1993a: 238); Nash (2002).
20 Wendy O'Brien (2015) also highlights how the sex binary underpinning international human rights fails to account for bodily diversity and so is particularly problematic for intersex and transgender individuals.
21 See Rosenblum (2011); Holtmaat and Post (2015); Otto (2015).
22 See Otto (2015: 304); Charlesworth (2005: 18).
23 For further analysis of this point, see McNeilly (2017).
24 This is an idea advanced by Otto (2014).

References

Baden, S. and Goetz, A. M. (1997) 'Who Needs [Sex] When You Can Have [Gender]? Conflicting Discourses on Gender at Beijing', *Feminist Review*, 56: 3–25.
Berlant, L. (1997) *The Queen of America Goes to Washington City: Essays on Sex and Citizenship*, Durham, NC: Duke University Press.
Braidotti, R. (2015) 'Punk Women and Riot Girls', *Performance Philosophy*, 1: 239–254.
Brems, E. (1997) 'Enemies or Allies? Feminism and Cultural Relativism as Dissident Voices in Human Rights Discourse', *Human Rights Quarterly*, 19(1): 136–164.
Bunch, C. (1990) 'Women's Rights as Human Rights: Toward a Re-vision of Human Rights', *Human Rights Quarterly*, 12(4): 486–498.
Burrows, N. (1985) 'The 1979 Convention on the Elimination of All Forms of Discrimination Against Women', *Netherlands International Law Review*, 32(3): 419–460.

Butler, J. (2006) *Gender Trouble: Feminism and the Subversion of Identity*, 2nd edn, New York; London: Routledge.

Byrnes, A. (1988) 'Women, Feminism and International Law – Methodological Myopia, Fundamental Flaws or Meaningful Marginalisation – Some Current Issues', *Australian Year Book of International Law*, 12: 205–240.

Charlesworth, H. (1995) 'Human Rights as Men's Rights', in J. Peters and A. Wolper (eds), *Women's Rights, Human Rights: International Feminist Perspectives*, New York; London: Routledge, 103–113.

Charlesworth, H. (2005) 'Not Waving But Drowning: Gender Mainstreaming and Human Rights in the United Nations', *Harvard Human Rights Journal*, 18: 1–18.

Charlesworth, H., Chinkin, C. and Wright, S. (1991) 'Feminist Approaches to International Law', *American Journal of International Law*, 85(4): 613–645.

Charlesworth, H., Chinkin, C. and Wright, S. (1993) 'The Gender of *jus cogens*', *Human Rights Quarterly*, 15(1): 63–76.

Chinkin, C. (1994) 'Rape and Sexual Abuse of Women in International Law', *European Journal of International Law*, 5(3): 326–341.

Copelon, R. (1994) 'Recognizing the Egregious in the Everyday: Domestic Violence as Torture', *Columbia Human Rights Law Review*, 25(2): 291–368.

Cook, R. (1993a) 'Women's International Human Rights Law: The Way Forward', *Human Rights Quarterly*, 15(2): 230–261.

Cook, R. (1993b) 'International Human Rights and Women's Reproductive Health', *Studies in Family Planning*, 24(2): 73–86.

Cook, R. (2006) 'Abortion, Human Rights and the International Conference on Population and Development', in I. Warriner and I. Shah (eds), *Preventing Unsafe Abortion and its Consequences: Priorities for Research and Action*, New York: Guttmacher Institute, 15–34.

Cossman, B. (2002) 'Gender Performance, Sexual Subjects and International Law', *Canadian Journal of Law and Jurisprudence*, 15(2): 281–296.

Edwards, A. (2011) *Violence Against Women under International Human Rights Law*, Cambridge: Cambridge University Press.

Fraser, A. (1999) 'Becoming Human: The Origins and Development of Women's Human Rights', *Human Rights Quarterly*, 21(4): 853–906.

Friedman, E. (1995) 'Women's Human Rights: The Emergence of a Movement' in J. Peters and A. Wolper (eds), *Women's Rights, Human Rights: International Feminist Perspectives*, New York; London: Routledge, 18–35.

Holtmaat, R. and Post, P. (2015) 'Enhancing LGBTI Rights by Changing the Interpretation of the Convention on the Elimination of All Forms of Discrimination Against Women?', *Nordic Journal of Human Rights*, 33(4): 319–336.

Keller, J. M. (2012) 'Girls' Blogging Communities, Feminist Activism, and Participatory Politics', *Information, Communication & Society*, 15(3): 429–447.

Lloyd, M. (2007) '(Women's) Human Rights: Paradoxes and Possibilities', *Review of International Studies*, 33(1): 91–103.

McCaughey, M. and Ayers, M. (2003) *Cyberactivism: Online Activism in Theory and Practice*, New York; London: Routledge.

MacKinnon, C. and Dworkin, A. (1988) *Pornography and Civil Rights: A New Day for Women's Equality*, Minneapolis: Organising Against Pornography.

McNeilly, K. (2014) 'Gendered Violence and International Human Rights: Thinking Non-Discrimination Beyond the Sex Binary', *Feminist Legal Studies*, 22: 263–283.

McNeilly, K. (2015) 'From the Right to Life to the Right to Livability: Radically Reapproaching "Life" in Human Rights Politics', *Australian Feminist Law Journal*, 41(1): 141–159.

McNeilly, K. forthcoming (2018) 'Sex/Gender is Fluid, What Now for Feminism and International Human Rights Law: A Call to Queer the Foundations', in S. Harris-Rimmer and K. Ogg (eds), *Research Handbook on the Future of Women's Engagement with International Law*, Cheltenham: Edward Elgar.

Marx Ferree, M. and Tripp, A. M. (eds) (2006) *Global Feminism: Transnational Women's Activism, Organizing, and Human Rights*, New York: New York University Press.

Mayer, A. E. (1995) 'Cultural Particularism as a Bar to Women's Rights: Reflections on the Middle Eastern Experience', in J. Peters and A. Wolper (eds), *Women's Rights, Human Rights: International Feminist Perspectives*, New York; London: Routledge, 176–188.

Molyneux, M. and Razavi, S. (2005) 'Beijing Plus Ten: An Ambivalent Record on Gender Justice', *Development and Change*, 36(6): 983–1010.

Nash, K. (2002) 'Human Rights for Women: An Argument for "Deconstructive Equality"', *Economy and Society*, 31(2): 414–433.

Ní Aoláin, F. (2015) 'Feminism Facing International Law', *European Journal of Women's Studies*, 22(4): 457–462.

Obiora, L. A. (1997) 'Feminism, Globalization, and Culture: After Beijing', *Indiana Journal of Global Legal Studies*, 4(1): 355–406.

O'Brien, W. (2015) 'Can International Human Rights Law Accommodate Bodily Diversity?', *Human Rights Law Review*, 15(1): 1–20.

Olsen, F. (1985) 'Statutory Rape: A Feminist Critique of Rights Analysis', *Texas Law Review*, 63(3): 387–432.

Otto, D. (1996) 'Holding up Half the Sky, But for Whose Benefit? A Critical Analysis of the Fourth World Conference on Women', *Australian Feminist Law Journal*, 6(1): 7–28.

Otto, D. (2013) 'International Human Rights Law: Towards Rethinking Sex/Gender Dualism and Asymmetry', in M. Davies and V. Munro (eds), *The Ashgate Companion to Feminist Legal Theory*, Aldershot: Ashgate, 197–216.

Otto, D. (2014) 'Between Pleasure and Danger: Lesbian Human Rights', *European Human Rights Law Review*, 6: 618–628.

Otto, D. (2015) 'Queering Gender [Identity] in International Law', *Nordic Journal of Human Rights*, 33(4): 299–318.

Peters, J. and Wolper, A. (eds) (1995) *Women's Rights, Human Rights: International Feminist Perspectives*, London; New York: Routledge.

Rao, A. (1995) 'The Politics of Gender and Culture in International Human Rights Discourse', in J. Peters and A. Wolper (eds), *Women's Rights, Human Rights: International Feminist Perspectives*, New York; London: Routledge, 167–175.

Romany, C. (1993) 'Women as Aliens: A Feminist Critique of the Public/Private Distinction in International Human Rights Law', *Harvard Human Rights Journal*, 6: 87–126.

Rosenblum, D. (2011) 'Unisex CEDAW, or What's Wrong with Women's Human Rights', *Columbia Journal of Women and Law*, 20(2): 98–194.

Schwartzman, L. (1999) 'Liberal Rights Theory and Social Inequality: A Feminist Critique', *Hypatia*, 14(2): 26–47.

Sedgwick, E. K. (1990) *Epistemology of the Closet*, Berkeley: University of California Press.

Sullivan, D. (1995) 'The Public/Private Distinction in International Human Rights Law', in J. Peters and A. Wolper (eds), *Women's Rights, Human Rights: International Feminist Perspectives*, New York; London: Routledge, 126–135.

United Nations (1995) Beijing Declaration and Platform for Action, Adopted at the Fourth World Conference on Women, 15 September 1995, UN Doc. A/CONF. 177/20 (1995) and A/CONF. 177/20/Add. 1(1995).

Chapter 9

Conclusion as non-conclusion

> To assume responsibility for a future, however, is not to know its direction fully in advance, since the future, especially the future with and for others, requires a certain openness and unknowingness; it implies becoming part of a process the outcome of which no one subject can surely predict.
>
> Judith Butler (2004: 39)

What can be concluded from the re-engagement with human rights in the foregoing chapters seeking to imagine rights as a vehicle of use for radical ends, a tool to meaningfully challenge problematic regimes of power? To reflect on the link between human rights and radical social transformation going forward it is useful, at least briefly, to go back. Immediately prior to the finalisation and official delivery of the Universal Declaration of Human Rights (UDHR) in 1948, Eleanor Roosevelt penned an article entitled 'The Promise of Human Rights' which was published in *Foreign Affairs*. Acting at the time in her role as the first chairperson of the newly established United Nations Commission on Human Rights, Roosevelt opened the article by stating that 'the real importance of the Human Rights Commission . . . lies in the fact that throughout the world there are many people who do not enjoy the basic rights which have come to be accepted in many other parts of the world as inherent rights of all individuals' (1948: 470). Although Roosevelt did not actually explicitly articulate her view of the promise of human rights in the article, we can gather from this opening statement that what she saw as the promise of rights was the achievement of a future where oppression and marginalisation were eradicated, where all enjoy adequate provision to allow them to live what may be termed a livable life (Butler 2004; 2006). The UDHR and its provisions are in turn implicitly presented as capable of achieving this future, or at the very least substantially working towards bringing it into being. Accordingly, Roosevelt appears to confirm what has been identified as central to human rights in their modern form; that they have from the outset been driven by a utopian promise and such has been fundamental to their utility.[1]

While Roosevelt clearly places faith in the UDHR and its possibility to advance these utopian ends, if asked she, as others committed to or invested in the mainstream approach to human rights driven by the United Nations and international law over recent decades, may have agreed that a global situation in which even the basic rights provisions for all are adequately fulfilled and no one lives in marginalisation or oppression is ultimately unachievable. This fact, however, is not openly engaged in reflection on the promise of human rights. Indeed, on the contrary, it remains a spectre holding possibility to weaken, as opposed to strengthen, the discourse of human rights and what it can offer. Therefore, while mainstream ideas of human rights from 1948 onwards have been underpinned by a utopian promise, they have not fully embraced or foregrounded the 'not yet' and self-refuting nature of this promise. It is this foreclosed element that I have asserted as in fact containing the promise of human rights – standing in contrast to the false promise that any human rights provision, even as seminal as the UDHR, can grant adequate conditions of living and being for all – and have outlined as that which gives rights their radical utility. By foregrounding the fact underplayed by Roosevelt and others that the promise of human rights remains self-refuting, it is possible to engage in a never-ending critical investigation of exclusion and alterity in and through the politics of human rights which is of use in radical politics aiming to challenge dominant power regimes and radical social transformation.

Following on from previous critical engagements highlighting towards the futural nature and the 'not yet' of human rights,[2] I have sought to take up the challenge of this 'not yet', to explore what foregrounding this element of human rights may mean, and how it can be utilised as a starting point for a holistic re-engagement with rights in contemporary radical politics. Returning to the 'not yet' and fully understanding this as the promise of human rights requires approaching the theoretical underpinnings and the practice of rights in an alternative way, as has been explored in the preceding chapters, all of which works together to allow opportunities to arise to think and use human rights to advance the claims of those on the margins and critique, as opposed to reify, restrictive regimes of power. In this respect, it is possible to remain committed to the utopian promise of rights which has defined modern human rights from the outset but, modifying the view of Roosevelt and others working within mainstream conceptions of rights, the self-refuting nature of this promise must come to the fore in conversation with a critical relation to power. Those whose needs remain unmet by human rights do not represent the failure of this discourse, but its ineradicable alterity which forms the starting point for more radical possibilities for human rights to be used to achieve more than a mere reshuffle of existing relations of power (Wall 2014: 108).

In terms of what conclusions may be drawn from this study of the futural nature of human rights, it is imperative to note that, naturally, any conclusion must be a non-conclusion, must highlight the impossibility of conclusion for human rights, their politics and how such may be reapproached for the ends of radical social transformation. A futural conception of human rights cannot be neatly tied up, contained, understood or approached in a way that lends itself to final conclusion. Indeed, in this respect a conclusion must remain as 'to come' as human rights themselves. While this may be a finishing point which is satisfactory for some, it may be less satisfactory for others. For example, what does this mean for radical groups and activists interested in understanding human rights as human rights to come? How can radical politics progress in pursuing the promise of human rights within the context of non-conclusion? In what follows in these closing remarks I want to consider some of the consequences of a futural approach to rights for radical thinkers, groups and activists; the possibilities as well as the challenges that conclusion on human rights and radical social transformation as non-conclusion offers or poses.

The possibilities of non-conclusion

To begin with, let us consider some of the possibilities that may be opened by the lack of conclusion which follows an understanding of human rights as human rights to come. The first, and most valuable, possibility offered by the assertion that human rights must remain unsettled and in a state of non-conclusion is the possibility to sustain ongoing critique. This can be thought on a number of different levels. Because a final conclusion can never be reached on understandings of human rights, because their alterity is ineradicable, thinkers and activists can, and must, engage in an ongoing politics of human rights which does not use rights to advance the claims of those on the margins merely once, but in a continual and never-ending way, always attentive to the limits of current articulations of rights. Accordingly, a never-ending critical scrutiny of human rights is sustained by their inevitable 'not yet'. However, this ongoing critical relation to alterity can be considered in another way; in this process, human rights may emerge as a productive site for radical politics to retain focus on critique and the critical more generally, encouraging and facilitating ongoing scrutiny of and critical challenge to restrictive regimes of power. The non-conclusion of human rights and the ongoing critical relation to alterity it requires allows human rights to become a key space or resource for critical work to take place and to be sustained. In this sense, the non-conclusion of human rights to come holds possibility to bolster and spur on the ongoing critical relation to power which is central to radical political work, retaining critical focus on the 'not yet' of a perfected future free from domination and exclusion which must be strived towards.

In addition to sustaining outward-looking critique of human rights as a concept and of restrictive regimes of power more generally, the lack of conclusion which is central to a futural approach to human rights also facilitates a more inward-looking ongoing critique of the *way in which* human rights are re-engaged in radical politics. Because a final conclusion can never be reached on rights and their politics, the re-engagements which have been advanced as part of the concept of human rights to come must be viewed as contingent and responsive. By its nature this concept, and the restagings of the theoretical underpinnings and practice of human rights it has been outlined as involving, cannot be final or definitive. The form of critical engagement with human rights in radical politics is itself unsettled and open to development, open to alteration or rethinking to respond to the needs or demands of changing times or contexts. The concept of human rights to come, therefore, is not a conclusion or a solution, but just a starting point which requires further tuning in line with ongoing critical scrutiny of what works and what does not in radical re-engagements with rights. Resultantly, the element of non-conclusion following from a futural conception of human rights promotes an ongoing retention of the critical in relation to human rights as concepts and to related restrictive regimes of power, as well as to the specific form or manner of the concept of human rights to come. Rather than weakening this concept's value and utility, this retention of inward-looking critique is a key possibility offered by the non-conclusion of human rights to come.

Approaching human rights as futural, unsettled and always resisting conclusion additionally offers important possibilities to move human rights and their politics away from the structures and thinkabilities of law. As has been recognised by many, including Costas Douzinas, 'the juridification and internationalisation of human rights has led to attempts to impose a logic of closure and planned extension which invalidates the messy and open practice of human rights' (2000: 175). Embracing the non-conclusion of human rights involves radical politics being opened up to unpredictable new possibilities for rights which exceed their current order and articulation within law and legal structures. We do not, and cannot, know how human rights may be used in the future and this includes the fact that human rights may be thought and used beyond their current form, remit or understandings after we have placed them into crisis. Here it is possible to return to Butler's comments where, reflecting on her thinking on universality explored in this work as central to re-engaging with the idea of universal human rights, she states that 'what comes of certain dialectical crises is "the new", a field of possibility which is not the same as an order of possibility' (Butler and Connolly 2000: n.p.). This insight appears salient for radical politics in the context of human rights to come. The non-conclusion of this approach to human rights, which places their presently dominant form into crisis, offers expansive possibilities for rights to move beyond the way in which they are currently understood, approached or discussed which has been characterised by ever-increasing legal codification. The futural promise and non-conclusion of human rights belongs to the people, to the grassroots and bottom-up politics, not to law and state, their order and their interests. This view of human rights cannot tie radical politics to the same order as before, but by its nature opens up a new field of possibilities to move beyond the current order towards something new in a fundamental way.

Thus, the non-conclusion which must necessarily follow from a futural conception of human rights does provide significant and interesting possibilities for radical thought and politics, allowing for a continually developing and responsive critical approach to power and rights to emerge which cannot be predicted in advance or neatly contained in existing politico-legal structures. However, it is also important to note that the lack of conclusion on, and in, human rights and their politics can simultaneously pose a number of challenges which thinkers, groups and activists must face alongside these possibilities. While these challenges need not be thought of as reason to abandon the pursuit of human rights in the sense of human rights to come, they must be taken into account and carefully addressed.

The challenges of non-conclusion

The first challenge posed by non-conclusion relates to the practical burden of political engagement and work which it necessarily places on radical activists and groups. Given the constant articulation and rearticulation and never-ending critical relation to alterity and power which is central to the lack of conclusion characterising human rights to come, activists seeking to engage human rights in such a way should be aware of the significant commitment to ongoing political struggle that this requires. Viewing human rights as unfinished concepts and their promise as futural involves an ongoing working and reworking of human rights concepts through futural-focused translational engagements across a range of places, contexts and times. In addition to radical activists and groups being required to view these engagements as never-ending, the engagements characterising a futural approach to human rights must also be understood as not guaranteed to succeed. Returning to the performative nature of human rights politics, there is no way to ensure that any rearticulation of human rights will take hold or will have the desired effect. When taken together with the need to continually engage in political dialogue to rearticulate human rights, this poses both a long-term and potentially exhausting challenge. Thus, embracing non-conclusion has significant practical effects in that it demands much of activists and groups, requiring them to engage in an uncertain and unpredictable critical politics with no end. While this challenge is significant, it is only through such ongoing struggle that human rights may be of use and their 'not yet' effectively exploited; no short-term or less demanding solution can be substituted for the hard, political work that human rights to come demands.

A second, and interrelated, challenge emerging for radical thinkers, activists and groups from the non-conclusion of human rights is that of uncertainty and risk. While this has been outlined above as one of the possibilities for radical politics – opening rights to new and unpredictable usages – this also poses a significant challenge. Because human rights must remain open to futural and unpredictable reiterations, radical political thinkers or activists cannot approach the politics of human rights with any degree of certainty. The agonistic contest which characterises rights politics is an uncontrollable process, and engaging in such contest requires an abandonment of any attempt to control political engagement or outcomes. This reflects the wider uncontrollable nature of democracy itself which 'is not a predictable process; it must be undergone, like a passion must be undergone' (Butler 2004: 39). This uncertainty may quite naturally involve an element of anxiety or discomfort. The uncertainty posed by the futural and its non-conclusion involves a significant risk for radical groups and activists. There is a risk that in engaging in the translational politics of articulation and rearticulation the new articulation of human rights will not be satisfactory or less restrictive than the last, a risk that the result of engaging in the politics of human rights will not be positive for radical politics.[3] Radical thinkers, activists and groups can only approach such risks in an open and responsive way, prepared to let go of any element of control or expectation in political processes and must do so again and again.

In this sense, the possibilities offered by non-conclusion are not without difficulty or demand. Indeed, returning to Butler's comments on placing current universal discourses into crisis to allow for new fields of possibility to emerge, she continues that

> many people will recoil from this possibility, fearing that the new which is not predictable will lead to a full-scale nihilism. And it is, in a way, a risky moment in politics. What the new form of universal brings will not be necessarily good or desirable.
>
> (Butler and Connolly 2000: n.p.)

This statement has much resonance for a contemporary project to re-engage human rights. However, it is important in considering the challenges of non-conclusion for radical political engagement with human rights to echo Butler's ultimate conclusion that 'it is equally true that nothing good or desirable will arrive without the new' (Butler and Connolly 2000: n.p.). It is not possible to engage in a fundamental challenge to dominant conceptions of human rights without hard political work and some degree of risk and uncertainty, especially so when the conclusion of such challenge must inevitably be non-conclusion. Yet without encountering such difficulties there is no chance of moving towards something new, or towards radical social transformation.

A future in the futural

It is impossible, therefore, to reach a conclusion on human rights, and while this lack of conclusion offers important possibilities, it also poses a number of challenges which must be faced. The final question remaining is how can this be done? How may radical politics encounter and process the risk and uncertainty of a critical and futural perspective on human rights, and do so productively? This is an important question which does not emerge from Roosevelt's brief consideration of the promise of human rights, nor from what has been perceived as the mainstream perception of the promise of human rights more broadly. It is one that emerges only when the promise of human rights is fully grasped as contained in the 'not yet' and a never-ending critical relation to power, and the demands this makes are fully considered. I cannot provide a precise answer to this question and this itself is unsurprising, for this is only the beginning of taking up the challenge of the 'not yet' in human rights. Much ground remains to be explored. The question of how to productively encounter and process the risk, uncertainty and broader challenges of human rights to come must be worked through together in an ongoing way in radical politics. This process itself holds productive possibilities for how to do and think such politics. It is this working together that must come next in understanding and pursuing a future in the futural and the radical promise of human rights. In this respect, the non-conclusion of human rights to come must be grasped as not an ending, but just another beginning.

Notes

1 For further discussion on thinking through the relationship between human rights and utopia, as noted in previous chapters, Moyn (2010) and Goodale (2009) are instructive.
2 See in particular Douzinas (2000), but also more widely Golder (2010); Fitzpatrick (2007); Baxi (2012: 157).
3 Indeed, in Derrida's thinking the promise of the 'to come' must be haunted by the possibility of its own perversion (Bennington 2000).

References

Baxi, U. (2012) 'Reinventing Human Rights in an Era of Hyper-Globalisation: A Few Wayside Remarks', in C. Gearty and C. Douzinas (eds), *The Cambridge Companion to Human Rights Law*, Cambridge: Cambridge University Press, 150–170.
Bennington, G. (2000) 'Double Tonguing: Derrida's Monolingualism', *Tympanum*, 4: 1–12.
Butler, J. (2004) *Undoing Gender*, New York; London: Routledge.
Butler, J. (2006) *Precarious Life: The Powers of Mourning and Violence*, 2nd edn, London: Verso.
Butler, J. and Connolly, C. (2000) 'Politics, Power and Ethics: A Discussion Between Judith Butler and William Connolly', *Theory & Event*, 4(2): n.p.
Douzinas, C. (2000) *The End of Human Rights: Critical Legal Thought at the Turn of the Century*, Oxford: Hart.
Fitzpatrick, P. (2007) 'Is Humanity Enough? The Secular Theology of Human Rights Law', *Social Justice & Global Development Journal*, (1): 1–14.
Golder, B. (2010) 'Foucault and the Unfinished Human of Rights', *Law, Culture and the Humanities*, 6(3): 354–374.
Goodale, M. (2009) *Surrendering to Utopia: An Anthropology of Human Rights*, Stanford, CA: Stanford University Press.
Roosevelt, E. (1948) 'The Promise of Human Rights', *Foreign Affairs*, 26(3): 470–477.
Moyn, S. (2010) *The Last Utopia: Human Rights in History*, Cambridge, MA: Harvard University Press.
Wall, I. (2014) 'On a Radical Politics for Human Rights', in C. Douzinas and C. Gearty (eds), *The Meanings of Rights: The Philosophy and Social Theory of Human Rights*, Cambridge: Cambridge University Press, 106–120.

Index

activists/activism 1–4, 7, 10–11, 42–3, 47–51, 105, 111, 116–18, 121–8, 158, 160–1; LGBTI 7, 19, 69, 121–2, 147; feminist 21, 69, 135–8, 140, 142–5, 147, 150–1; migrant rights 22; grassroots activism 4, 10, 18–19, 26, 57, 117, 128, 130–2, 159
agonism 9, 76–7, 81–92, 140, 147–9
Albertson Fineman, M. 10, 96, 101–2, 104
alterity 7–10, 116, 157–8, 160; and excess 16, 24–9; and performativity 38–9, 41, 43, 45; and universality 55, 60–5, 67, 70, 72; and consensus/conflict 76, 80–1, 84–5, 89; and vulnerability 96, 100–2, 104–5, 107, 109, 112; and translation 116–17, 119–27, 130–2; and feminist engagements with rights 139–41, 144, 148–51
American Revolution, the 17
antagonism 82–4, 86–8, 90–1, 124
articulation/rearticulation 7, 9, 116, 160–1; and excess 15–16, 20–1, 23–6, 28–9; and performativity 34–5, 38–9, 42, 44, 48–51; and universality 60–3, 65–8, 70; and consensus/conflict 79, 81, 84–5, 87–8; and vulnerability 97, 105–6, 109–12; and translation 116–17, 119, 121, 124, 126; and 'Women's Rights are Human Rights' 138; and the right to gender flourishing 147–8, 150
Austin, J.L. 8, 36–7, 40

Benhabib, S. 147–8
binaries 45, 55–6, 58–9, 126, 142–3, 146–7
Bhabha, H. 10, 117, 120–1, 129
Bloch, E. 27
Brown, W. 2

Butler, J. 1–2, 7–10, 159–61; performativity 35–7, 40–1, 45–9, 51, 109–110 ; universality 9, 61–3, 71–2, 121, 123–4, 159; vulnerability 96, 101–2, 104, 109–110; cultural translation 10, 117, 121–5, 127–8, 132; livable life 156

capitalism 2, 15–19, 21–2, 46, 48, 98
colonialism 57–8, 120; and translation 132 *see also* postcolonialism
conflict: in human rights politics 9, 28, 76–86, 88–92, 124, 144–5; conflictual consensus 76, 83, 85–6, 141
content of human rights 9, 18, 25, 29, 34, 42, 56–7, 85, 119; and universalisation 63–8, 72
contingency 3, 29, 36, 62, 65, 67, 105, 117, 130, 132, 158
consensus 9, 28, 76–89, 124, 140–1, 143–5, 148–50
Convention on the Elimination of All Forms of Discrimination Against Women 137, 143–4
crisis 2–3, 5–6, 159, 161: of capitalism 2, 19
cultural relativism 55–6, 58, 103, 139
cultural translation 10, 117, 120–9, 132 *see also* Butler, J.

Declaration of the Rights of Man and the Citizen 17–18, 21, 99
Declaration of the Rights of Women and the Female Citizen 21
democracy: agonistic democracy 5, 76–7, 82, 84, 86, 89–91; democratic politics 9, 80, 82, 89–91, 127; democratic politics and human rights 85–6, 90–1, 121; liberal democracy 4, 17, 82–3, 87–8;

democracy to come 9, 76–7, 89–90; 'post-democratic' 80–1
Derrida, J. 26, 37, 45, 90, 120
dispossession 17, 149
disruption: and politics 80; and human rights 24, 26, 39, 44, 125–8, 135–6, 150–1; disruptive translation 10–11, 117, 119, 121–2, 125–32, 144–5, 151
dissensus 80–1, 140
doing in futurity 9, 34, 39, 41–4, 51
Donnelly, J. 66–7
Douzinas, C. 1–3, 19–20, 22, 27–8, 41, 58–60, 69–70, 100, 159

equality 2, 4, 21–3, 44, 68, 82, 87, 91, 101, 126: and feminism 137, 142, 145, 147, 150
excess 7–8, 15–16, 20–6, 28–9, 70, 138, 140–1; and consensus 83

feminism: feminist thinking 7, 28, 101; and human rights 11, 38, 69, 135–51 *see also* activism
floating signifier 69–70
Foucault, M. 46
French Revolution, the 17, 22, 69,
futurity 6–11, 16, 25–9, 157–61; and performativity 39–44; and universality 55–6, 59–61, 63–8, 70–2; and consensus/conflict 76–7, 79–81, 84–5, 89–92; and vulnerability 97, 104–5, 111–12; and translation 117, 119, 120–30, 132; and feminist engagements with human rights 136; and the right to gender flourishing 144–5, 147, 150–1

gender 36, 98; and human rights 21, 24, 11, 136–45 *see also* sex/gender
gender flourishing, the right to 11, 136, 145–51
Global South, the 57
global politics 1–2, 4, 6, 58; and human rights 18, 77, 87, 129, 157; globalisation 56, 87, 120; global and local 118, 129
Gouges, O. de 21–2, 24
grassroots politics *see* activism

Habermas, J. 87, 90
Harvey, D. 3

heteronormativity *see* power
history of rights 15, 28: mainstream 8, 16–19; parallel 20–3; and universality 56; and vulnerability 99–100
Hobbes, T. 17, 21, 99
Holocaust, the 6
human of human rights, the 5, 44, 69–71, 121, 123

Ignatieff, M. 78, 85
inequality 102, 107, 126
impossibility 1, 8, 26–7, 43, 68–9, 72, 88–91, 124, 157
international law: and human rights 5–6, 18, 20, 35, 57, 65, 79, 121; and public/private dichotomy 138; and sex/gender 142
internationalism 15–16, 18–20, 46, 48
iterability 45–6; and human rights 46–7; democratic iterations 48–9

Kennedy, D. 3

Laclau, E. 59
Laclau, E. and Mouffe, M. 82, 90
Lefort, C. 2, 5
LGBTI 71, 145 *see also* activism
liberalism 15–16, 34, 59–60, 68, 78–9, 82–3, 87, 98, 130, 137; and human rights 15–25, 28–9, 46–8, 50, 71, 78–9, 81, 87, 89, 102; and consensus 84, 148; classical liberalism 16–17, 21, 24, 78, 97, 99; and the sovereign subject 97, 108, 123, 140, 149–50
life, the right to 38, 97
Locke, J. 17, 21, 97

MacPherson, C. 17, 97
mainstream conceptions of human rights 3n6
market economy 17, 79, 98
Marxism 19, 28; post-Marxism 2, 19
migrant rights 22, 24, 70 *see also* activism
Mouffe, C. 5, 9, 76–7, 82–90

Nancy, J. L. 5
natural law 16–17, 21, 27, 57, 97, 99
neoliberalism 2, 5, 6
'not yet' 1, 27–8, 62, 72, 124, 127, 157–8, 160–1
non-discrimination 126, 137, 142, 145, 147

ontology 9–10, 28, 83, 96–113, 123–4, 140, 143, 144–5, 150
other, the 83, 99–106, 110, 112, 123, 150

paradox 10, 96–101, 107–13
performativity 36, 109–11; and human rights 9–10, 34–51, 59, 62–63, 68, 79, 106, 109, 111, 122–3, 132, 147–8, 160; performative gender 36, 40–1, 45–8; performative contradiction 62–3, 121, 125 *see also* Butler, J.
political, the 5, 77, 83–4, 86–7, 100
possessive individualism 17–18, 21, 24
postcolonialism 57, 69, 79, 120, 129–30 *see also* colonialism
'post-democratic' *see* democracy
power: restrictive operation of 2–10, 15–16, 18–29, 38–9, 41–4, 65–6, 82, 89–90, 110–11, 135–6, 157–9; subjectifying operation of 46, 71; state power 3, 18–19, 49; speaking back to power 3, 119; and human rights 5, 7, 8–10, 15–16, 18–29, 38–9, 46, 49–51, 59, 61, 64, 66–7, 71–2, 76, 78–81, 84–92, 96–8, 104–7, 109–12, 116–17, 120–1, 125, 127, 136, 138, 143, 151, 156–60; colonial power 57–8; and vulnerability 101–4, 108; and translation 118–20, 128–31, 144; and gender 138, 143, 146–7, 149–50; heteronormative power 4, 38, 41, 146–7, 149–50; and the right to gender flourishing 148
practice of rights, the 2, 4–5, 7–8, 10–11, 116–19; practice of human rights to come, the 7–11, 29, 38–39, 43, 48, 80–6, 88–9, 105–8, 110–13, 116–17, 121–32, 158
present, the: connection to the future 6, 26–7, 34, 39, 40–1, 42, 43, 51
Property: protection of 17–18, 21, 97; rights to 24, 137

queer 109, 143

radical democracy: radical democratic thought 7, 28, 82–3, 86, 90; radical democratic politics 88
radical politics: definition of 2n3; and human rights 2–4, 6–8, 11, 47–49, 80–1; and human rights to come 26–9, 50–1, 63–4, 81, 107–8, 110–11, 127–8, 157–62

radical social transformation 1; definition of 2n4; and human rights 2–8, 61, 98, 111–12, 150–1, 156–8, 161; and ontology 102, 111; and translation 131–132
Rancière, J. 2, 5, 80–1
rationality 78–80, 82–4, 87, 97–98, 130
*Re*doing (of rights) 9, 34–5, 39, 44–8, 50–1
reproduction 98; and rights 38, 138, 140, 145–7
resistance 10, 20, 72, 97, 100, 107–12, 120, 124, 129–30
revolution/revolt 2, 17, 69
risk 62, 110, 160–1
rights revisionism 2–3, 5, 7, 19
Roosevelt, E. 156–7, 161

Second World War 6, 18, 57
Schmitt, C. 83, 85
sex/gender 142–3, 145–7, 149–50 *see also* gender
socio-economic rights 22
sovereign individual 10, 97, 99, 105; and Judith Butler 40, 45
Spivak, G. 10, 117, 120–1, 129–31
statism 15–16, 18–20, 22–3, 46, 50
subjectivity 37, 98, 106, 111; subject of human rights, the 1, 9, 56–7, 64–65, 68–71, 96–100, 107–10, 140, 144; sovereign subject 9, 48, 96–100, 101–4, 106–8, 110, 112, 140, 150

temporality: of rights 26; and performativity 40
terror/War on Terror 2, 19
'to come' 7, 27, 80, 157; Derrida 26; and performativity 41–3; and universality 9, 55, 60–64, 70–2; and consensus/conflict 76–77, 89–91; and vulnerability 104, 112; and translation 116, 119, 122–5, 127–8, 130–2; and the right to gender flourishing 150
translator 10, 117, 127–32
twentieth century 1, 16, 22, 49, 57, 59, 136–7
twenty-first century 2, 3, 16

United Nations 4, 20, 137, 138, 141, 149, 156
Universal Declaration of Human Rights 57, 65, 77, 97, 137, 156

universality: of human rights 9, 28, 55–60, 64–72, 123–5, 139–40, 143–4, 147–8, 150; as universalisation 9, 55–6, 60–72, 123–4, 127, 139–40, 144, 148; in poststructuralist thought 59 *see also* Butler, J.
unpredictability: of human rights 27, 48, 79, 159–60; and performativity 40–2; and translation 124
utopia: and human rights 6, 27, 156–7; and performativity 41

vernacularisation 118, 125, 129
violence 102; against women 137–8, 140, 142, 145–6, 147

vulnerability 10, 96–97, 123–4, 126, 140, 144, 147, 149; and performativity 46–51, 109–10; and sovereignty 98–100, 112–13; and a critical approach to power 101–7; and resistant action 107–11; feminist perspectives on 101–2

Western/the West 3, 18–19, 22, 24, 57–58, 87, 119
Winstanley, G. 21, 24
'Women's Rights Are Human Rights' 138–42, 145

Žižek, S. 1